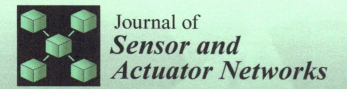

Wireless Sensor and Actuator Networks for Smart Cities

Edited by
Burak Kantarci and Sema Oktug

Printed Edition of the Special Issue Published in
Journal of Sensor and Actuator Networks

www.mdpi.com/journal/jsan

Wireless Sensor and Actuator Networks for Smart Cities

Wireless Sensor and Actuator Networks for Smart Cities

Special Issue Editors

Burak Kantarci
Sema Oktug

MDPI • Basel • Beijing • Wuhan • Barcelona • Belgrade

Special Issue Editors
Burak Kantarci
University of Ottawa
Canada

Sema Oktug
Istanbul Technical University
Turkey

Editorial Office
MDPI
St. Alban-Anlage 66
4052 Basel, Switzerland

This is a reprint of articles from the Special Issue published online in the open access journal *Journal of Sensor and Actuator Networks* (ISSN 2224-2708) in 2018 (available at: https://www.mdpi.com/journal/jsan/special_issues/wireless_smart_cities)

For citation purposes, cite each article independently as indicated on the article page online and as indicated below:

LastName, A.A.; LastName, B.B.; LastName, C.C. Article Title. *Journal Name* **Year**, *Article Number, Page Range.*

ISBN 978-3-03897-423-9 (Pbk)
ISBN 978-3-03897-424-6 (PDF)

Contents

About the Special Issue Editors

Burak Kantarci, Dr., Asst. Professor: Burak Kantarci is an Assistant Professor with the School of Electrical Engineering and Computer Science at the University of Ottawa. From 2014 to 2016, he was an assistant professor at the ECE Department at Clarkson University, where he currently holds a courtesy appointment. Dr. Kantarci received his M.Sc. and Ph.D. degrees in computer engineering from Istanbul Technical University, in 2005 and 2009, respectively. During his Ph.D. study, he studied as a Visiting Scholar at the University of Ottawa. He has co-authored over 150 papers in established journals and conferences and contributed to 12 book chapters. He is the Co-Editor of the book Communication Infrastructures for Cloud Computing. He has served as the Technical Program Co-Chair of ten international conferences/symposia/workshops. He has been the PI/co-PI of several federally/provincially funded research projects supported by Natural Sciences and Engineering Research Council of Canada (NSERC), U.S. National Science Foundation (NSF), and Ontario Centres of Excellence (OCE). He is an Associate/Area Editor of IEEE Communications Surveys and Tutorials, IEEE Access, IEEE Transactions on Green Communications and Networking. He also serves as the Chair of the IEEE ComSoc Communication Systems Integration and Modeling Technical Committee. He is a senior member of the IEEE and a member of the ACM.

Sema Oktug, Dr., Professor: Sema Oktug is a Professor with the Department of Computer Engineering, Istanbul Technical University. She also serves as the Dean of the Faculty of Computer and Informatics Engineering, Istanbul Technical University. She received her B.Sc., M.Sc., and Ph.D. degrees in computer engineering from Bogazici University, Istanbul, Turkey, in 1987, 1989, and 1996, respectively. She was a postdoc researcher in the Department of Electrical Engineering at New York Poly (currently, Polytechnic Institute of NYU) in 1996. Her research interests are in modeling and analysis of communication networks, wireless networks, low power WANs, and smart city applications. She is the author of more than 100 journal and conference papers. She is also the partner/leader/coordinator/researcher of the international and national research projects funded by EU, CNRS, TUBITAK, Istanbul Technical University, and other distinguished organizations. She is a member of the IEEE Communications Society.

Editorial

Special Issue: Wireless Sensor and Actuator Networks for Smart Cities

Burak Kantarci [1],[*],[†] and Sema F. Oktug [2],[*],[†]

1   School of Electrical Engineering and Computer Science, University Ottawa, Ottawa, ON K1N 6N5, Canada
2   Department of Computer Engineering, Faculty of Computer and Informatics Engineering, Istanbul Technical University, 34469 Istanbul, Turkey
*   Correspondence: burak.kantarci@uottawa.ca (B.K.); oktug@itu.edu.tr (S.F.O.);
     Tel.: +1-613-562-5800 (ext. 6955) (B.K.); +90-212-285-3584 (S.F.O.)
†   All authors contributed equally to this work.

Received: 14 November 2018; Accepted: 15 November 2018; Published: 17 November 2018

1. Introduction

Our lives are being transformed by the interplay between mobile networks, wireless communications, and artificial intelligence. This transformation is an outcome of the emerging Internet of Things (IoT) concept, and the advancements in computer architectures that translate into high computing power, high-performance processing, and huge memory capacities. In addition to the IoT, as a very close concept, cyber–physical systems target seamless integration of physical systems with computing and communication resources. Furthermore, in urban areas, the integration of the "software-defined sensor networks" and "sensing as a service" concepts with legacy Wireless Sensor Network (WSN)-based systems is leading to the transformation of conventional city services towards smart cities.

Smart energy, smart driving, smart homes, smart living, smart governance, and smart health are just a few services that can be offered by smart cities. Furthermore, while these concepts are major application areas, smart citizens close the loop by participating in sensing, actuating, and decision-making processes. In smart cities, legacy WSN-based services are extended by having citizens that act as sensors. Opportunistic or participatory sensing models enable groups of individuals to collaboratively work toward the same goal with strong interaction links, even though this does not always require strong social links between them. Thus, dedicated and nondedicated wireless sensors form communities, and collaborating communities form social networks where interaction can occur in the form of software-defined sensing. This transformation in WSNs introduces unique solutions for the communication plane of smart cities.

In addition to communication-plane challenges, smart environments require IoT and WSN sensors to report massive amounts of unstructured data in a heterogeneous format, which, in turn, leads to the big sensed data phenomenon. Additionally, addressing the high volume by effective machine-learning or data-mining techniques, novel data-acquisition and -processing methodologies for big sensed data are emergent in order to address the high-velocity, -variety, and -veracity aspects. Moreover, in order to effectively offer smart-city services, it is viable to envision a massive amount of connected wireless/wired sensors/IoT devices. Thus, scalability remains an open issue when integrating the components of a smart city that are mentioned above. While ensuring the scalability and connectivity of this infrastructure remains an open issue, the battery limitation of wireless sensors is a great challenge, especially in time-sensitive services in smart cities.

In this Special Issue, we sought contributions that focus on novel solutions for Wireless Sensor and Actuator Networks (WSANs) in smart cities. The Special Issue has had contributions from academic and industry researchers in computer science and engineering, electrical engineering and communication engineering, as well as ICT industry engineers and practitioners. The contributions were original articles in all aspects of wireless sensor networks and actuator systems for smart cities. Particular topics of interest were as follows:

- Physical layer challenges in WSNs in smart-city applications.
- Cross-layer solutions for WSNs and IoT to support smart-city services.
- WSN and IoT architectures, protocols, platforms, and algorithms.
- Device-to-device networks for smart cities.
- Application-layer protocols for WSNs to enable efficient smart-city applications.
- Planning of sensor networks in smart cities,
- The interplay between dedicated and nondedicated sensing.
- Opportunistic and participatory sensing in smart cities.
- Design and Management of Mobile Crowd-Sensing Systems in smart cities.
- Energy-harvesting solutions for WSNs in smart cities.
- Vehicular sensing solutions for smart-city applications.
- Novel sensory data-acquisition techniques.
- Real-time and near-real-time data analytics on sensory data,
- Software-defined sensor networks and sensing as a service in smart cities.
- Security, privacy, and trust in smart-city sensing.
- Smart-city big data and open data.
- Standards for IoT and WSNs in smart-city applications.
- Application, deployment, testbed, experimental experiences, and innovative applications for WSN-enabled smart cities.
- IoT-driven smart governance, smart economy, and smart environments.

The Special Issue has covered most of these research topics by an outstanding collection of featured articles that have been selected through a rigorous peer-review process. The accepted articles have introduced further investigations beyond the listed topics under the smart-cities context. The contributions of the articles in this Special Issue are summarized in the following section.

2. Summary of Contributions

This special issue is a collection of unique contributions that address various issues in WSANs and smart cities by providing useful insights for future research in this field. After a rigorous and iterative peer-review process, eight papers have been selected by considering recommendations and feedbacks of at least three independent reviewers per paper in at least two rounds of review. The papers in this Special Issue have been contributed by 27 authors from academia and industries spanning various regions in the world, particularly North America, Europe, Asia, and North Africa. Each paper cites high-impact and scholarly references in the literature that make up a pool of 251 state-of-the-art references in total for further investigation in the research topics.

The articles that appear in this Special Issue form a diverse collection of topics studied under the scope of WSANs for smart cities. These include low-cost IoT implementation for smart-village settings [1], smart parking systems exploiting WSNs [2], Machine-To-Machine (M2M) Networking over LTE for smart-city services [3], WSN-driven smart waste-management systems for sustainable cities [4], user-support systems with wearable sensors and cameras [5], a SmartInsoles Cyber–Physical System (CPS) for mobile gait analysis [6], energy-harvesting systems for WSNs [7], and IoT for WSNs in smart cities [8].

Smart villages are promising infrastructures under the smart-cities concept. The selection of proper wireless access technologies for smart villages is of paramount importance. The author of Reference [1] presents a smart-village setting and proposes a conceptual framework to evaluate the cost of IoT deployment. The author presents the viability of launching an IoT project in a smart village with limited upfront investment and minimum external funding. The author considered WiFi for the networking infrastructure as opposed to LPWAN technologies including LoRaWan. To this end, with a single gateway's capability to serve the whole smart village, replacing the WiFi APs with a single LoRa gateway could reduce the number of cellular data subscriptions would increase the cost of hardware equipment. On the other hand, the author acknowledges the popularity, shareability, and stability of WiFi as its strengths for being preferred today. However, as those aspects are forecast to possibly change in the upcoming years, the paper recommends to set a solid ground for the deployment of LPWan technologies to realize IoT support for smart villages.

Smart parking is an important application in urban smart-city services. The authors of Reference [2] present a smart parking system by exploiting the benefits of WSNs. The WSN-based smart parking system calls an adaptable and hybrid self-organization algorithm for the WSN so that it runs under both linear and mass parking cases while providing a better energy-management service for sensors so that the battery lifetime of every sensor can be prolonged, which would consequently prolong the lifetime of the entire WSN. Furthermore, besides the communication- and energy-related issues, the system also facilitates driver assistance through an effective search mechanism for available parking spots in the vicinity.

M2M networks are inseparable components of smart-city communication ecosystems. The authors in Reference [3] present a priority-based M2M overlay network over LTE for smart-city services. Thus, the overlay network is designed to allow the coexistence of a massive number of M2M devices with Human-to-Human (H2H) traffic, and further access the network bypassing the full LTE handshake procedure. In order to support multiple priority classes in the M2M network traffic, the IEEE 802.15.6 standard is adopted. Performance analysis of the M2M system combined with the H2H traffic reveals the trade-offs required to meet the targets for sufficient performance and reliability for M2M traffic when the H2H traffic intensity is known upfront. The authors show that their performance results are promising to support this approach in various applications including crowd sensing, smart-city monitoring, and beyond.

Smart cities also involve the introduction of policies for sustainability and community health at the municipal and governmental levels. The authors of Reference [4] present a smart waste-management system that uses WSNs to monitor accumulated waste levels in garbage bins within the borders of a municipal region. The data collected from the WSN are aggregated in a Cloud platform and are fed into a fast heuristic algorithm to determine the number of trucks, route per truck, and the order of collection per bin in order to minimize the delay for the citizens, and/or minimize the cost of garbage collection (in terms of mileage cost and pollution penalties) from the municipality's standpoint. The authors also present optimization models to verify the effectiveness of their proposed heuristic approaches.

Activity recognition aims at effective user-support systems in smart environments. The authors of Reference [5] present a user-support system for fine-grained activity recognition by using two main sources: wearables and cameras. The proposed system aims to identify the text at which a user is gazing. This is based on the assumption that the text content is related to the user activity at that time. The authors point out the fact that the text meaning depends on the location. Thus, they use wearable sensors and a fixed camera so that the global location of the text is acquired via image matching by using the local features of the images captured by these devices. Then, the feature vector is coupled with the content of the text. The authors present experimental results with real participants in a lab environment.

Smart health is an important application area in smart cities, and gait monitoring is one of the fundamental well-being aspects. With this in mind, the authors of Reference [6] present a SmartInsoles Cyber–Physical System (CPS) to measure gait parameters of multiple users in a restriction-free setting. Participants involved in the experimental study performed 10 walks on the Tekscan Strideway gait-mat system, while the SmartInsoles CPS system was worn at the same time. Analysis of spatiotemporal data reveals useful information about seven parameters, namely, stride time, stance time, swing time, double support time, step time, cadence, and gait time. The authors conclude that the outputs of the two systems highly coincide, and the presented CPS system offers high accuracy as a multidevice multisensory system for gait monitoring and analysis.

Battery lifetime of wireless sensor nodes has been a challenge since the very first days of WSNs. The ubiquity of smart-city services can only be ensured with the significantly increased lifetime of sensors and WSNs. The authors of Reference [7] propose an efficient solar-energy-harvesting system with pulse-width modulation (PWM) and maximum power-point tracking (MPPT) to sustain the batteries of WSN nodes. Following the design of several models for a solar-energy harvester system, the authors run a series of simulations for solar powered DC-DC converters with PWM and MPPT to obtain optimum results. The simulation study showed that the ambient solar-energy harvesting system could ensure 87% and 96% efficiency by using PWM control and MPPT control techniques, respectively. In order to validate their simulations, the authors also present an experimental study for the PWM-controlled solar-energy-harvesting WSN.

In accordance with energy efficiency of WSNs, energy harvesting solutions should also be complemented with smart network protocols. As a protocol-level solution to sustain WSNs in smart cities, the authors of Reference [8] present a new routing WSN scheme in a context where IoT is used in an opportunistic manner with the motivation of reducing the communication overhead in WSN nodes. In the proposed scheme, a WSN is deployed in a smart-city setting, and it forwards the data toward the sink node by interacting with IoT devices. To enable WSN–IoT interaction in an opportunistic manner so as to significantly reduce the energy consumption of the WSN nodes, the authors presented a prototype integration platform. The authors evaluated their proposal in a simulation environment and presented interesting results that support the viability of opportunistic IoT usage in WSN routing.

3. Conclusions

The Special Issue on Wireless Sensor and Actuator Networks for Smart Cities features eight high-quality articles, each of which addresses a different aspect of the subject. The contributions to this Special Issue can be classified under two categories: application-driven/application-specific studies and infrastructure/communication-driven studies. The former presents a selection of high-quality works that tackle the effective use of WSANs on smart parking, user-support systems, smart health, and smart waste management from the standpoint of application layer. The latter includes a pool of high-quality studies that aim to address the communication challenges in the deployment of WSANs, their coexistence with other wireless-networking technologies in smart cities, and overcoming battery limitations through the lens of power and communications engineering.

In spite of the variety of their research foci under the scope of this Special Issue, all of the featured articles in this issue are in agreement that research on WSANs for smart cities will continue to uncover many outstanding issues and challenges for researchers and professionals in the sectors that are involved with projects for realizing smart cities and communities.

Acknowledgments: We would like to thank Dharma P. Agrawal (Editor-in-Chief) for his support in guest-editing this Special Issue. We also greatly appreciate the assistance of everyone in the editorial office, and particularly the managing editor, Louise Liu. Furthermore, the anonymous reviewers of this Special Issue have helped us significantly, and they all deserve very special thanks. Last but not least, we would like to thank all authors who have contributed to this Special Issue. Without their contributions, this Special Issue would not have been made possible.

Conflicts of Interest: The authors declare no conflict of interest.

References

1. Ciuffoletti, A. Low-Cost IoT: A Holistic Approach. *J. Sens. Actuator Netw.* **2018**, *7*. [CrossRef]
2. Hilmani, A.; Maizate, A.; Hassouni, L. Designing and Managing a Smart Parking System Using Wireless Sensor Networks. *J. Sens. Actuator Netw.* **2018**, *7*. [CrossRef]
3. Khan, N.; Mišić, J.; Mišić, V.B. Priority-Based Machine-To-Machine Overlay Network over LTE for a Smart City. *J. Sens. Actuator Netw.* **2018**, *7*. [CrossRef]

4. Omara, A.; Gulen, D.; Kantarci, B.; Oktug, S.F. Trajectory-Assisted Municipal Agent Mobility: A Sensor-Driven Smart Waste Management System. *J. Sens. Actuator Netw.* **2018**, *7*. [CrossRef]

5. Chiba, S.; Miyazaki, T.; Sugaya, Y.; Omachi, S. Activity Recognition Using Gazed Text and Viewpoint Information for User Support Systems. *J. Sens. Actuator Netw.* **2018**, *7*. [CrossRef]

6. Arafsha, F.; Hanna, C.; Aboualmagd, A.; Fraser, S.; El Saddik, A. Instrumented Wireless SmartInsole System for Mobile Gait Analysis: A Validation Pilot Study with Tekscan Strideway. *J. Sens. Actuator Netw.* **2018**, *7*. [CrossRef]

7. Sharma, H.; Haque, A.; Jaffery, Z.A. Modeling and Optimisation of a Solar Energy Harvesting System for Wireless Sensor Network Nodes. *J. Sens. Actuator Netw.* **2018**, *7*. [CrossRef]

8. Hanif, S.; Khedr, A.M.; Al Aghbari, Z.; Agrawal, D.P. Opportunistically Exploiting Internet of Things for Wireless Sensor Network Routing in Smart Cities. *J. Sens. Actuator Netw.* **2018**, *7*. [CrossRef]

Article

Low-Cost IoT: A Holistic Approach

Augusto Ciuffoletti

Department of Computer Science, University of Pisa, 56127 Pisa, Italy; augusto@di.unipi.it

Received: 5 April 2018; Accepted: 4 May 2018; Published: 8 May 2018

Abstract: The key factors for a successful smart-city project are its initial cost and its scalability. The initial cost depends on several inter-related aspects that cannot be designed and optimized separately. After the pilot deployment, scaling-up takes place only if the cost remains affordable: an initial financial support may induce dependencies from technologies that become unsustainable in the long period. In addition, the initial adoption of an emerging technology that fails to affirm may jeopardize investment return. This paper investigates a smart-village use case, the success of which strongly depends on the initial cost and scalability, exploring a low-cost way for Internet of Things (IoT). We propose a simple conceptual framework for cost evaluation, and we verify its effectiveness with an exhaustive use case: a prototype sensor designed and tested with its surrounding eco-system. Using experimental results, we can estimate both performance and cost for a pilot system made of fifty sensors deployed in an urban area. We show that such cost grows linearly with system size, taking advantage of widely adopted technologies. The code and the design of the prototype are available, so that all steps are reproducible.

Keywords: Internet of Things (IoT); smart village; low-cost; REST/HTTP; WiFi; virtual clock

1. Introduction

While several metropolitan cities have already successfully launched experiments for environmental monitoring (like Barcelona [1] or Amsterdam [2] in Europe), there is a declared interest to extend the experience to small towns, in the framework of wider projects [3–6]. A challenging aspect of such initiatives is their long-term sustainability, especially in the transient from a pilot phase to large scale deployment, as pointed out in [2]. This condition, per se critical, is definitely compromised if external funding is suspended, and, unfortunately, sometimes a pilot project happens to lose interest when its success is demonstrated.

Therefore sustainability has to be evaluated in the early stages of long-term perspective projects: designers and administrators should bear in mind that a small community is unwilling to support an expensive service, once the cost of success falls on its shoulders. Low cost, so long as system performance is adequate for the task, allows taking full advantage of the efforts needed to launch the project. This is why the low-cost keyword is relevant, and its importance is in fact demonstrated by the frequency with which this feature appears in Internet of Things (IoT) literature.

Despite being so crucial, this concept is often left implicit, or imprecisely defined, considering only a few components in the overall financial impact. Consequently, it may happen that an unexpensive sensor depends on an expensive infrastructure, or that low costs are actually reached, but only in the large scale.

In this paper, we consider the most restrictive situation, that of a small size project without perspectives of economies of scale, and we define all the costs entailed in its realization. We keep into account and exploit the presence of a collaborative social community, which significantly contributes to lowering the project cost: this happens when users actively participate in its implementation and support. The community expects from project realization a better quality of life, but gains also the ability to share experiences and data with others, possibly with a financial return.

We will use the term smart village, mediated from [3], to indicate the framework hosting the project. In short, the smart village is a small community, with limited resources, but the solid intent to improve its control on environmental resources, including air, water, energy, roads, parking lots, etc. From such experiences, more than from generously financed pilot projects, others may obtain useful hints, thus making the IoT really improve our lives.

The Cost of an IoT Project

The financial investment needed to implement an IoT project is split into several components; each of them must be evaluated in order to pursue an overall low-cost strategy. Let us indicate five relevant items:

- several sensors/actuators, that collect data, pre-process them, and implement the requested actions,
- a network that connects the sensors to data aggregators,
- a service infrastructure that aggregates and renders the information,
- salary for the developers and maintainers,
- energy requirements.

The task of minimizing the cost of a single component is not challenging, since prices are steadily decreasing in this sector: it is more complicated to find a compromise that makes the whole project affordable, which is the aim of this paper. Let us explore the dependencies among these components, summarized in Figure 1.

The first two items in the above list are strongly related, since the sensor needs to interface with the network infrastructure. At this moment, two Low Power Wide Area (LPWA) technologies are in the process of reaching the market: the Long Range technology (LoRa), which operates on unlicensed frequencies with a proprietary scheme, and the Narrow Band IoT, integrated in the Long Term Evolution (4G-LTE) standard, which operates on licensed frequencies. Both of them promise to become low-cost carriers for IoT data, but, at this moment in time, they are quite expensive in terms of equipment and deployment or licenses, and introduce a further risk related with their success and diffusion. Looking at more established technologies, we find the WiFi, with a solid experience in the creation of urban networks, and the 3G cellular network, which entails relevant per-unit costs.

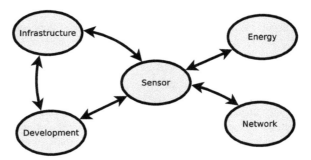

Figure 1. Cost components and their relationships.

Considering the processing infrastructure, the diffusion of specific IoT cloud services simplifies the task of deploying the infrastructure, and delegates maintenance, power, and logistics to the provider under a pay-per-use policy. A cloud deployment is elastic by nature, the initial cost being possibly null, smoothly increasing with the size of the project. There is currently a number of providers that offer attractive user interfaces, one of them being the popular ThingSpeak, but it is also possible to take advantage and compose raw cloud resources, like data storage and web servers, that are available at lower prices.

The utilization of cloud services implies a connection from the network of things to the Internet, and we find several infrastructures whose business model encapsulates cloud components, like SigFox.

Concerning development costs, we argue that they are tightly related with the quality of higher education: they are lower when the project is based on popular technologies, which new generations learn in Information and Communication Technology (ICT) courses. On the contrary, cutting edge technologies have high costs. Using a popular technology, a collaborative community can contribute to further lower the development costs: consider the case of a sensor implemented as a high school course competition, or as the result of a crowd-sourcing initiative.

Energy consumption is the last component in the list, and the less relevant. Although our target community does not ignore green precepts, it also does not want to incur relevant costs in order to have devices that consume 0.5 mW instead of 50 mW. Nonetheless, it is relevant to evaluate this aspect, in order to understand whether the device depends on the electrical grid, or may operate for months on batteries (which, by the way, have a carbon footprint), or gathers energy from the environment (solar, wind, bumps etc.), thus incurring a significant initial cost.

Finally, although costs are an issue, system performance needs to be adequate for the purpose. The design may trade-off certain features, but there is a kernel of functions that needs to be present. In other words, it is important to minimize the cost, but keeping the service useful.

This paper focuses on IoT affordability, trying to define a viable entry point for a small community with a limited budget. For each of the components listed above, we are going to indicate the tools that help to start an IoT project with limited resources.

It is a valuable and original contribution, since most papers address one aspect of the design, disregarding the others. Instead, we want to undertake a holistic approach for the definition of a viable strategy for smart villages.

2. Low-Cost Internet of Things

Let's start our discussion from the networking infrastructure, which is the cornerstone of an IoT system; the current trend is to deploy a dedicated infrastructure for IoT data, using Low Power Wide Area Network (LPWAN) technologies, in addition to the ones already existing for voice and human oriented Internet. Although LPWANs are rather stable from the technical point of view, on the commercial side, strong contrasts are arising between hardware and service providers. Therefore, our target community is not willing to take part in this game, in the fear of losing investments in a technology that soon becomes outdated and unsupported.

The alternative is to use established technologies, like WiFi or 3G. From the technical point of view, they have very little in common, but both exhibit the basic capability to send or receive small pieces of data, being powered only when needed.

The advantage of 3G is that it does not need the deployment of an infrastructure to connect a device to the Internet, since the local telecom provider is in charge of it. Although such service comes at a cost, many 3G plans are emerging that prepare the market for the advent of LTE-IoT products, with a cost of a few dimes per month. The cost of a 3G interface is in the range of $20, and Single Board Computers (SBC), with integrated 3G capabilities are available for around $60.

In contrast, a WiFi deployment needs a network of access points (AP), a complex and expensive operation. However, WiFi is a serious competitor of 3G in a smart village perspective, since the same infrastructure is reusable for other services, like an urban WiFi service for shops, schools, and libraries. In some cases, then, the service is already in place, and the IoT network can simply take advantage of it. Another point in favor of WiFi is that interfaces are currently sold for a few dollars. Although we may expect that, in the near future, LTE-IoT interfaces will reach similar costs; as a matter of fact, the same budget can buy ten 3G interfaces or two WiFi hotspots with fifty interfaces. Depending on whether the target application is sparse or dense, today either one of them is the best choice.

Among LPWan technologies, LoRaWan offers an attractive trade-off between WiFi and 3G, coupling a wide range reach, with a non-proprietary infrastructure. A comparison between LoRaWan and other LPWan technologies is found in [7], cost analysis included, and a critical view of LoRaWan is in [8]. There are three reasons that suggest to defer the adoption of such technology:

- popularity: the development is more expensive, since there is less experience and support for this sophisticated technology;
- shareability: the LoRaWan, as any LPWan infrastructure, is dedicated to IoT, while WiFi provides other services;
- stability: LoRaWan technology is rapidly evolving and has strong competitors [9]. It is therefore exposed to improvements that are going to make existing equipment obsolete.

The price of LoRaWan devices is still slightly higher than that of WiFi: in the conclusive section, we sketch a comparison between LoRaWan and WiFi, and discover that the difference of hardware costs is an extra 50% for LoRaWan. Since popularity, stability and price are all exposed to change, in the future, a LPWAN approach may become attractive for low-cost IoT systems.

To understand the advantages of a popular, shareable, and stable technology, consider the case of a deployment in a supportive community, where families and shops with a public or private Access Point are happy to adopt a mote, at the cost of a weekly battery recharge, or with a negligible contribution in power and bandwidth. Although this opportunity depends on the connectivity of the surroundings, there is no doubt that adopting a popular technology has social aspects that increase the level of participation and contribution.

Sensor technology is tightly related to software production costs: if a popular development tool is available for the sensor device, standard skills are sufficient to write the driving code. This is favorable on the side of salary and development time. If the devices exhibit a common structure, we obtain a similar advantage since designers accumulate experience, and one design is readily reused in others.

Two low-cost candidates with popular coding tools are the boards based on AVR chips (Atmel, San Jose, CA, USA) (including the Arduino), and on the ESP8266 (Espressif Systems, Shangai, China). Both are programmable using the Arduino Integrated Design Environment (IDE), which is successfully used in schools of any degree (and even in a CoderDojo Kata). Other popular candidates are not equally appropriate for the task, for reasons related with costs or development tools. For instance, the Raspberry Pi, as well as other similar Single Board Computers (SBC), has a cost, power consumption, and management complexity that dis-encourage its adoption as a low-cost sensor device; another example is Particle Photon, which is not as popular as the Arduino family, and is currently more expensive. STM32 based boards are a concrete alternative, but not as popular as the Arduinos.

While choosing an IoT-specific cloud service, one needs to take into account the risks of lock-in and price escalation. A user can be locked in an IoT service in various ways that extend those found in cloud computing. Here are listed four commercial policies that tend to lock-in an IoT business:

- data lock-in: when data can't be easily ported to other providers and technologies, as with any other cloud provision,
- technology lock-in: when the data repository is immersed in an ecosystem of smart services that permeate the application,
- device binding: when the IoT device is bound to use only a given data repository,
- code binding: when the code for the IoT device is bound to use a given code repository.

Every cloud provider uses a different mix of the above commercial strategies, and it is difficult to foresee which is more dangerous for a smart village. In order to protect the investment, probably device and code binding should be avoided at all costs. Technology lock-in may be attractive, since it helps to simplify the application, thus reducing development costs. Data lock-in is not relevant if the application does not make use of historical data, like in a simple sensor/actuator loop control; otherwise, the designer should check that periodic data download is feasible.

Price escalation occurs when the implemented project becomes popular and needs more resources to grow: this may jeopardize scaling. In some cases, the price curve may be more than linear as the project leaves the small scale of a pilot deployment: cloud services are often provided for free in early stages. Even in the favorable hypotheses of a linear price growth, the community should be prepared to an increment of service cost, after it becomes really useful.

To cut the costs, it is possible to create an infrastructure using general purpose cloud services, which are usually less expensive than specialized ones: for example, a PaaS web server as user interface and data upload end-point, and a cloud storage as data container. The infrastructure costs are lower than those of an IoT specific service, but development costs rise.

A further alternative consists of the creation of a server, either in the cloud or not, running one of the available open-source IoT servers: ThingSpeak is one of them. In this case, the community needs to pay for the server (either on premises or in the cloud) and for its maintenance.

The server should also provide data access not limited to raw measurements, but encapsulated in web applications and services. Although it is possible to commission this task to external developers, it is preferable that data are left open to those that contribute to the project, so that apps emerge directly from the users. This option is viable only if the competence to create such applications is present in the community: the adoption of cloud services with well known, standard interfaces helps.

The rest of this paper is organized as follows: after a survey of works that directly address low-cost IoT systems, we introduce a case study that exemplifies and gives concreteness to the design principles defined above. A fundamental step on this way is the definition of a benchmark, a set of features that we want to be present in our system: such step states the rationale for the technical options that are finally introduced in the prototype, and allows future comparisons with other solutions that aim to reach the common goal of an affordable IoT architecture.

3. Brief Survey of Research Papers on Low-Cost IoT

This section is dedicated to a brief survey of recent IoT papers that have been selected because they mention low-cost as one of the requirements. As we will see, this attribute is usually applied only to one aspect of the problem, disregarding the overall cost, and frequently not fully justified.

Most of them come from developing countries, which demonstrates that IoT is considered as a way to improve their quality of life, filling the gap with developed countries.

The applications considered in the selected papers may be divided into two families: urban mobility, and management of primary resources, like water or energy.

The first family may be further divided into two sub-streams: traffic monitoring, and public transportation management.

In the first sub-stream, Ref. [10] investigates traffic and road surface control using a compact device that embeds a number of sensors, including a GPS receiver and an accelerometer. The paper does not mention experimental results or implementation details to produce the device. Its cost is estimated of $30, and the study comes from the USA.

With a similar target, Ref. [11] uses branded devices to fetch traffic characteristics, which are made available to drivers. They expect a favorable impact on air pollution and economy. There is no explicit statement about cost, though the authors claim to pursue a low one. The study comes from India.

In Ref. [12], the authors design a system that helps drivers find a free parking lot. Low-cost is not addressed in this paper, but the design actually adopts low-cost technologies for hardware and networking that are complementary to those explored in this paper: namely, an STM32 (STMicroelectronics, Geneva, Switzerland) for the SBC, and Narrowband IoT (NB-IoT) for networking. The study comes from China.

The public transportation sub-stream is represented by [13], which uses WiFi sniffing techniques to count people at bus stops and thus make a more effective use of coaches. The authors claim a low-cost result, but the sensor device is a Raspberry Pi, a rather expensive, though powerful, SBC, with a relevant power consumption. On the topic of power consumption, Ref. [14] quantifies the difference between the Raspberry and Arduino-like boards. The authors do not evaluate the cost of the device, but illustrate experimental results of an on-field experiment. The paper comes from the USA.

There is another family of IoT applications where low-cost requirements are frequently found: it aims to improve primary resources management.

The quality of the air is fundamental for an urban environment, and we have found three papers on the subject:

- Ref. [15] uses a BeagleBone SBC (similar in concept and cost to a Rasperry Pi) equipped with sensors and a GPS receiver. Low-cost, mentioned in the abstract, is not quantified. The work comes from India.
- Ref. [16] is the paper that, in this survey, is most aware of aspects related to the cost. The authors describe the prototype design and evaluate energy consumption, showing its dependency from the target application. The Web infrastructure is based on an on-premises server, while sensor networking uses WiFi. The work comes from Chile.
- Ref. [17] uses the GPRS infrastructure to deliver data obtained by low-cost sensors. The authors tackle the goal of using low-cost sensors, which dominate other costs in these kinds of applications. The paper marginally describes the infrastructure needed to collect, process, and present the data. The work comes from Serbia.

Low-cost IoT solutions are also proposed for the management of supply networks.

The authors of [18] design a device for billing water consumption and to detect leakage and losses: they do not introduce a new service, but aim at reducing the cost of an existing one. Several ways to deliver data collected by sensors are explored, including handheld devices, GPRS and wireless Local Area Networks (LAN). The design is from an Indian institution.

The electric grid is considered, with a similar purpose, in [19]. Energy consumption is measured by an Arduino-like SBC and forwarded to a nearby Bluetooth device, where data are collected and possibly uploaded to a database. The intent is to reduce costs and improve accuracy of conventional devices. The authors are from Egypt.

In [20], the authors want to improve the management of electrical energy coming from several renewable sources by controlling dynamic parameters of distribution lines and accumulators. The paper gives little detail of the infrastructure used, and concentrates on end user applications and sensors. The authors are from an Indian institution.

The reliability of the power supply grid is the target of [21]. An Arduino SBC is used to capture signs of overload from electrical transformers using low cost sensors. Data are uploaded to a cloud database using a wireless LAN, and records are kept for analysis. Also this work comes from India.

An application that is receiving increasing attention consists of a dense deployment of low-cost, non-intrusive devices to monitor the safety of resorts areas, like parks and historical sites. Video capture and WiFi sniffing allow a fine grain analysis of people around, but are not respectful of privacy. Instead, coarse grain devices, like sound monitors and infrared sensors, gather relevant information without compromising privacy and at a lower cost. In [22], the authors give the details of an IoT system based on such kinds of sensors. The paper describes how data is gathered and filtered to obtain significant data, and analyze the aspects of energy harvesting to power sensor devices. The authors are from Singapore.

In summary, none of the papers gives sufficient details of all the aspects that contribute to the cost. Likewise, none of them gives enough information to reproduce the solution. An analytic cost evaluation and design reproducibility are the focus of this paper.

4. A Case Study: Arduino, WiFi, and ThingSpeak

Our case study is based on three cornerstones: Arduino, WiFi, and ThingSpeak. Around them, we have implemented a complete solution, and we want to evaluate its limits and strengths: in this section, we explain why we consider them as low-cost; in the next section, the solution is matched against a benchmark application.

We start considering the sensor/actuator, which is the heart of an IoT solution. This component is replicated, and the number of replicas is a measure of the size of the system; thus, the impact of its design is also multiplied. A flexible design may bring an economy of scale in the development, since software components are reused.

Our choice for this component is Arduino, which is indeed the name of a family of development SBCs (Single Board Computer) built around an Atmel AVR. We discard Arduino boards that have an integrated WiFi interface: in fact, a survey reveals that such boards have a cost that is considerably higher than the sum of the parts. In addition, the adoption of an integrated architecture restricts design options, and often binds to external libraries and firmware. We conclude that the adoption of two distinct boards, one for the SBC, another for the network interface, has a favorable impact on costs, while keeping the design open and flexible.

For our purpose we need a board in the Arduino family that is suitable for deployment, not markedly oriented to development. The Arduino Mini-pro board meets such requirements, and costs a few dollars: it hosts a Atmel Mega328p MCU, the same as the popular Arduino Uno, and program development can be carried out with the same Integrated Design Environment (IDE). The cost of a Mini Pro is lower than that of an Arduino Uno: on eBay, $2 and $4, respectively. Power consumption is also lower, since the $16U2$ ISP programmer is not included in the board (the schematics are available on [23,24] respectively). Pinning is standard Dual In Line (DIP), which is compatible with all sorts of prototype boards and printed circuit design tools. It can be programmed using specific pins that allow the connection of the external ISP programmer. Its size is six times smaller than that of the Arduino Uno: 6.5 cm^2, instead of 35 cm^2, allowing a reasonably compact device.

Considering development costs, the Arduino IDE is extremely popular, which makes its utilization easy and supported by a huge number of know-how sources and projects. The development process with the Mini-pro is not distinguishable from that of the Uno, so that an Arduino-grown developer feels at ease.

Another viable alternative, offering higher performance at a lower cost, are STM32 based boards ([25]). However, their IDE is far less popular, and the learning curve is steep. Here, we need to trade-off development costs for processing power, and we want to privilege the former.

The WiFi technology has the advantage of a ubiquitous distribution, with low-cost devices for the infrastructure, and affordable network interfaces. In the introduction, we discussed the possibility of engaging the community itself in the provisioning of the WiFi infrastructure, using the connectivity provided by shops and homes, when they have sufficient coverage. This option makes it expensive to extend the reach of the IoT beyond city limits, since reaching the Internet from the sensor device may require a dedicated Access Point, or a broadband device. Therefore, the use case is applicable only within city limits, excluding the countryside.

The interface between the sensor and the WiFi network is implemented using an ESP-01 device, a 4 cm^2 board based on the ESP8266 processor.

The ESP-01 exposes a serial interface, controlled by a hardware UART, from which it receives commands that control the embedded WiFi interface. They are encapsulated in an AT syntax, that mimics the one of old telephone modems: for instance, the command `AT+CWJAP="mywifi","friend"` is used to join the WiFi network the Extended Service Set Identification (ESSID) of which is `mywifi`, using the password `friend`. In case of success, the response is an `OK`, with an additional content depending on the invoked command.

Data transport is performed with a sequence of two or more commands: the first one specifies length and target of the operation, and is followed by a sequence of frames containing the data. The initial command prepares the buffers and arranges the transport level connection, while the following send or receive data.

Notably, the standard socket abstraction is not present, and the coordination between SBC and WiFi interface is not straightforward: a library is needed to simplify the task of application developers. The alternative consists of using another library that provides the standard socket interface (like [26]). However, we observed that such library uses most of the available memory resources, thus requiring a more powerful SBC: in the trade-off between development and device costs, we opted again for the latter. The penalties are that coding a library is more expensive, since it requires deeper professional skills, and that using a non-standard tool-set also complicates the application developer task.

To attenuate the latter aspect, the library provides a simplified application level interface: the transport layer is still accessible, but application layer short-cuts are also available. To select the concepts to implement in the library, we observe that a number of application protocols are emerging that explicitly address IoT—for instance, the Message Queue Telemetry Transport (MQTT) protocol (see [27]). We prefer to adopt HTTP: although less powerful, it is more stable, known, and adopted than any other application level protocol. Security measures are easy to implement in an HTTP infrastructure, since a proxy server can secure IoT data exchange between the encrypted WiFi network, and a remote HTTPS server, without implementing the Secure Socket Layer (SSL) protocol on the sensor. In addition, IoT cloud servers frequently adopt an HTTP interface conforming to the Representational State Transfer (REST) paradigm.

Our case study uses the ThingSpeak service. Its offer includes, besides the REST interface for data upload, a rich set of satellite services that simplify the application design, but expose to technology lock-in. The designer should be aware of that, since the service is rather expensive, and costs grow linearly after a generous initial free plan. To contain the costs, the ThingSpeak server may be moved on premises, since its source code is available: this may attenuate the impact of technology lock-in, but has a cost related with equipment and maintenance.

Figure 2 illustrates the architecture for our case study: hardware components are vertical stacks, and horizontal layers correspond to the Internet ones, from network to application. The leftmost hardware component is the Arduino, with library and application code discussed above. The former uses a serial interface with the ESP-01 to perform operations at transport level. The shortcuts provided by the library enable a direct interface from the application sketch to the ThingSpeak channel implemented on the server. No intermediate components are interposed along the data path, in contrast to edge computing or fog approaches. As discussed in [28], such concepts are quite popular in IoT literature, and are introduced to allow integration of components with limited computing and communication capabilities, which becomes mandatory in the presence of networking infrastructures with an extremely low bandwidth, as in the case of LPWAN. However, they have a significant impact on hardware costs, and in design complexity. In this paper, we show how to avoid edge computing in a smart village application, despite the limited computing capabilities available on sensor nodes.

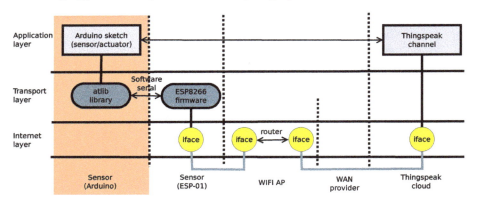

Figure 2. The proposed architecture envisions application level communication between the sensor and the service provider, thus reducing development costs.

Now that the architecture has been defined, we proceed to define a benchmark, a kernel of capabilities that characterize our application, before checking them in a prototype implementation.

5. A Benchmark for Prototype Evaluation

The definition of a benchmark allows understanding the limits of an implementation, and gives the basis for comparison. In our case, the benchmark consists of relevant features that are implemented on the sensor, but that depend on the overall architecture. We found a number of such features during the design of the prototype in [29], and the benchmark we propose focuses on three of them: clock synchronization, upstream/downstream communication, and power saving.

Clock synchronization is mandatory to coordinate the operation of several components, for instance to control traffic lights in a street. We may want that traffic light B becomes green ten seconds after light A: in that case, an accurate time reference is needed, but its resolution is coarse, in the order of a second. The benchmark requires the availability of a time reference, and measures its accuracy.

Communication consists of two sensor-centered activities: posting new values (upstream), and downloading commands (downstream). The sensor controls update operations, and can implement resource saving policies, for instance powering the network interface only when needed. Communication in the other direction is controlled by the upstream device, and a protocol is needed to preserve sensor resources. A solution is based on a polling mechanism controlled by the sensor, which periodically queries for the presence of pending commands. Another consists of turning on sensor receivers at predictable times, thus avoiding expensive transmissions, but requires synchronization. The simplest alternative consists of coupling upload and download operations. All the above alternatives share a drawback: the sensor-actuator loop has a long time constant. This prevents real-time reactions, unless power saving requirements are significantly relaxed.

Here, we prefer to consider power as a valuable, and possibly scarce, resource. Thus, the benchmark requires the implementation of power saving policies, especially in the WiFi interface management for communication and clock synchronization, but regards a timely reaction from the system as not relevant. An evaluation of power consumption is also needed to adopt a cost-effective power supply.

The implementation of the above core functions hits against Arduino limits, since clock drift is significant, the available memory is limited, and sleeping degrades response. Regarding memory, it is split into two parts: program memory (30K bytes), and data memory (2K bytes). Real limits are even lower, to take into account that memory requirements change at runtime, in response to dynamic memory allocation events. As a matter of fact, the Arduino IDE rejects programs that exceed 60% of the available memory.

To determine the feasibility of the core functions, we evaluate the storage footprint of the benchmark application that implements them. The energy footprint is measured using as a reference the capacity of a pack of three rechargeable AAA batteries, 800 mAh nominal. Given a voltage supply of 3.6 V, the available energy is 2.9 Wh. Dividing this figure by the measured autonomy of the device in hours, we obtain an easily reproducible approximation of power consumption.

Program development complexity is difficult to evaluate, but such figure is important to understand the effort needed to solve a specific use case. The count of statements is used for this purpose, but we know that the library has development costs higher than applications.

In summary, the benchmark requires implementing three relevant features on the sensor/actuator:

- a clock with a bound accuracy with respect to a standard reference,
- an HTTP/REST client with GET/POST capabilities,
- functions to switch to low power mode the WiFi interface.

The evaluation of their implementation is split into four metrics: clock accuracy, storage footprint, program complexity, and power consumption. Regarding the storage footprint, we need to take into account that data acquisition and command actuation, i.e., the business code of the sensor, are not included in the benchmark.

5.1. A Prototype and Its Evaluation

The prototype system [30] is composed of the architectural components in Figure 2: a sensor/actuator, a communication network, and a cloud service infrastructure. The development process targets the sensor: such component has a high impact on project sustainability since it is replicated, and therefore exposed to scale-up issues. This component also determines energy consumption.

The sensor/actuator is implemented by assembling an Arduino Pro Mini and an ESP-01 on a 5×7 cm prototype board: the two components are mounted on a socket to be easily replaced and reused, but a more compact assembly is easily done. Figure 3 is the electronic layout, and in Figure 4 a breadboard prototype.

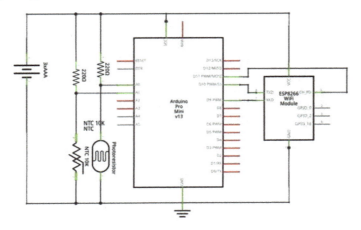

Figure 3. Schema of the sensor used in the evaluation prototype.

Figure 4. An early prototype of the sensor, mounted on a breadboard.

The two components have the advantage to be available as Commercial Off-The-Shelf (COTS) devices, but still have the limits of development boards: in order to be user friendly, they carry hardware, like power LEDs and stabilizers, that is useless when the device is in operation. This aspect leaves some space for an economy of scale, once the experimental phase is complete.

Power supply is from three AAA rechargeable batteries, the nominal capacity of which (800 mAh) is used to quantify power consumption. Given that battery voltage is compatible with the requirements of both boards (3.3 V), there is no power adapter between them.

The Pro-mini has an 8 Mhz clock, and is connected to the ESP-01 through a serial interface with a baudrate of 57,600. On the Arduino side, the interface is implemented in software, while the ESP-01 uses its own hardware UART (see Figure 3).

The Arduino library that simplifies the utilization of the serial WiFi interface [31] implements a class that encapsulates the ESP-01 device. It offers two distinct kinds of methods: a wrapper for AT commands, and application utilities.

The application utilities provide:

- a REST interface to interact with a ThingSpeak server,
- the capability to enable or disable the operation of the ESP-01 device,
- an accurate virtual clock.

Note that Arduino libraries already exist for the three tasks (the mentioned WiFiEsp [26], the ThingSpeak library, and the NTP library). However, the Arduino can't support the three of them together. Instead the ad hoc library provides the desired functions, and leaves enough resources for business code.

Communication with the ThingSpeak server follows the HTTP, and is therefore split into a Request and a Response. The Request is implemented using a raw AT command to establish a TCP connection, and one or more calls to send the fragmented HTTP Request to the server. The Response is processed by another library function that parses the input from the server, and reports about the success of the operation, returning the Response message body when present. Such functions make a greedy usage of buffers, and 250 bytes are sufficient for the task.

Two methods are devoted to switch on or off the ESP-01 device. The function that implements the switch-on, besides raising the enable pin of the ESP-01 board, also takes care to process the output from the ESP-01, since the device automatically joins the AP using the credentials stored in the flash memory. This latter feature of the ESP8266 helps to limit the size of the sketch, which does not implement the WiFi join procedure.

Clock synchronization capabilities are split into two library functions: one that periodically gets in touch with an NTP server and computes the current drift and offset of the hardware clock, another that returns the UTC time by correcting the local clock value using such drift and offset. The function does not use the NTP protocol itself, but the time service available on port 37. The primary advantage is a very compact code on the sensor. In addition, it is easy to implement the time service on an on premises server equipped with a GPS receiver.

The sensor is connected to the Internet using a commercial WiFi ADSL router as Access Point (AP). The association of a sensor with the AP occurs every time the ESP-01 on the sensor wakes up to perform network operations, like delivering data or synchronizing the virtual clock.

The IoT infrastructure is provided by ThingSpeak: using that service the sensor is able to upload measurements, download commands and configuration parameters, send and receive tweets, trigger actions based on time and data. All such services are reached through the REST API provided by ThingSpeak.

5.2. Measurements and Results

The Arduino Mini-Pro runs a benchmark application [32] that verifies and stresses the three features anticipated in Section 5: clock synchronization, REST interface, and power saving. As business code, every two seconds, it samples the value of two sensors, an NTC and a photo-resistor that are visible in Figure 4.

Every fifteen minutes (or 900 s) the sensor connects to the WiFi AP and performs the following tasks:

- it updates the virtual clock parameters with a TCP connection to an accurate time server,
- it uploads eight measurements, included the average temperature and lighting during the period, to a ThingSpeak channel with an HTTP POST,
- it downloads a command from a ThingSpeak TalkBack resource with an HTTP GET.

When the three operations are complete, the WiFI interface is switched-off until the next communication round.

The first result we obtain is that hardware is sufficient for the task: the application uses 42% of the 30 KBytes available for programs, and another 42% of the 2 KBytes available for the memory. As a reference, the official ThingSpeak library requires 99% of the program memory to implement a single feed (using an Arduino Ethernet shield), while the WiFiEsp library uses 43 percent of the available memory for a single GET, leaving little space for further functions.

The complexity of the development task is condensed in the number of lines required by the library, which is 300 lines long, and of the program, which is 200 lines long. The library is an expensive but reusable part of the project, which is split into nine methods that contribute to the definition of a class. Each method is typically twenty lines long, except for the HTTP response parsing method that is 100 lines long with a complex structure.

The main program has a straightforward loop structure that runs the sampling task and the periodic connection. This latter is implemented by another function, which performs a sequence of three connections, respectively for clock synchronization, data upload and command download.

We consider that development is split into subtasks—the library and the applications—each of them manageable by a single moderately trained C++ programmer with Arduino experience.

To evaluate the performance of the prototype, we run the benchmark described in the previous section, measuring:

- the time spent performing the communication tasks,
- the roundtrip time with the NTP server,
- the measured drift,
- the time error measured at each re-synchronization,
- the power supply.

The benchmark application stops when batteries run lower the brown out threshold, which is 2.9 V: this allows estimating power consumption.

Drift measurement is a critical task that encompasses sensor and network functions: its success proves, alone, that system performance is stable in time.

The drift is computed using the formula below:

$$drift = \frac{utc_1 - utc_0}{ck_1 - ck_0}, \tag{1}$$

where utc_1 and ck_1 represent the current UTC time and the current clock, and utc_0 and ck_0 represent the same figure at system startup. Since all figures have a one second resolution, the resolution of the time service, a drift estimate is computed using an Exponentially Weighted Moving Average (EWMA) with gain 4. The result is shown in Figure 5.

The EWMA has a significant effect only during the initial transient, when the two terms of the ratio in Equation (1) are very close.

The drift stabilizes around 3000 ppm, corresponding to approximately 2.7 s every fifteen minutes. We note that, unless compensated, such a drift prevents the utilization of the internal clock for synchronizing distributed activities within the desired one second window. Using the drift estimate, it is possible to implement a virtual clock [33] with the required precision. The effectiveness (and correctness) of drift compensation is shown in Figure 6, which represents the difference between the value of the compensated virtual clock, and the time value received from the NTP reference.

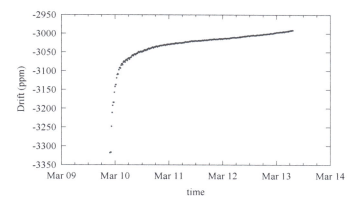

Figure 5. Drift estimate during the experiment.

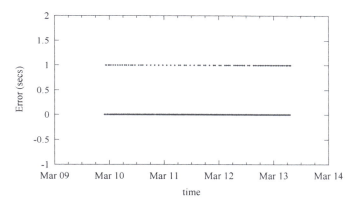

Figure 6. Time offset between the internal virtual clock and the reference time server, as measured during clock synchronization.

The first value of the series exceeds the requirement of a one second precision, since drift estimates requires at least two clock readings to work. However, after the first value, the error remains confined in the [0, 1] range.

The roundtrip measurement refers to a Stratum 0 Network Time Protocol (NTP) server at the USA National Institute of Standards and Technology (NIST), and shows that network communication is stable. It successfully recovers after an apparent network problem (see Figure 7): in that case, the roundtrip time jumps to 5 s, without compromising the application. The average roundtrip is 419 ms, and the standard deviation is 290 ms, as shown in the frequency distribution in Figure 8, with an intriguing bi-modal pattern. The average roundtrip time dis-encourages an effort towards accuracies significantly lower than one second. With the provision of a local time server, the roundtrip time could be reduced of one or two orders, allowing an accuracy in the range of tens of milliseconds.

The real-time capabilities of the prototype are limited in the tens of seconds, since the update of the Thingspeak channel on the public cloud requires a time narrowly centered around 15 s (see Figure 9). The presence of an on premises Thingspeak server, or a multi-tier architecture [34], would certainly improve the real-time capabilities, at a cost.

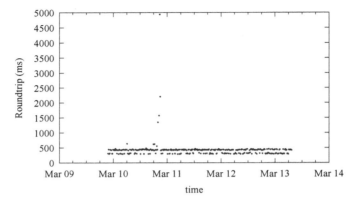

Figure 7. Round-trip time with the reference time server, as measured during clock synchronization.

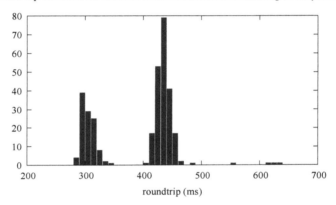

Figure 8. Frequency distribution of round-trip times in Figure 7.

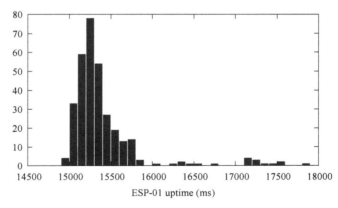

Figure 9. Frequency distribution of the time spent with the WiFi interface switched on during each round.

We infer power consumption from the capacity of the batteries, nominal 800 mAh, and the duration of the experiment, that lasted 327 rounds of 15' each, corresponding to 81.75 h (more than three days). The rate between battery capacity and experiment duration returns an estimate of the average current, 9.8 mA, and of the average power consumption, that, assuming an average 3.5 V supply (see Figure 10), is 35 mW. Gathering such power from the environment is not difficult: for instance, a postcard sized solar panel (2 W/6 V) might be sufficient for the task.

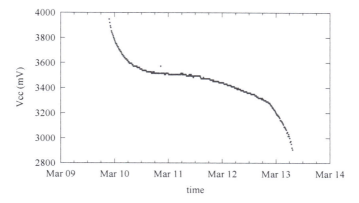

Figure 10. Variation of the power supply (Vcc) during the experiment.

Understanding the distribution of power consumption between the two devices, the Arduino Mini-Pro and the ESP-01, helps to devise a power-saving strategy. To this purpose, we run a further experiment, reducing the period between successive communication sessions from 15 to 5 min. Since the overall power consumption can be split into two components, one with the network device in sleep mode, the other with the same device awaken, we can write:

$$C_{acc} = t_{sleep} \times I_{sleep} + t_{wake} \times I_{wake}, \tag{2}$$

where C_{acc} is the accumulator capacity, t_{sleep} is the time spent with the WiFi device off, t_{wake} the time spent with the WiFi device on, I_{sleep} and I_{wake} the supply currents in the two cases.

The linear system obtained using the values from the two experiments is the following:

$$80.33\,\text{h} \times I_{sleep} + 1.42\,\text{h} \times I_{wake} = 800\,\text{mAh},$$
$$56.84\,\text{h} \times I_{sleep} + 3.25\,\text{h} \times I_{wake} = 800\,\text{mAh},$$

which is solved with

$$I_{sleep} = 8.1\,\text{mA},$$
$$I_{wake} = 104.3\,\text{mA},$$

which are reasonably consistent with datasheets.

Considering the benchmark execution—with a period of 15′—the average supply current of the whole device is 9.8 mA, with a constant contribution of 8.1 mA from the Mini-pro, corresponding to 83%. This candidates the Mini-pro as a target for the application energy saving policies.

There are plenty of ways to reduce power consumption of an Arduino [35]. One way is to enter the *powerDown* state for a definite amount of time. In our use case, the sampling period is two seconds long and the sampling operation is rather fast. It is a favorable situation, and power saving is in fact significant, but the solution can not be generalized.

To quantify the power consumption when the Arduino is in the PowerDown state, we run another experiment with the same period, but entering the PowerDown state during the time between sampling operations. The 800 mAh accumulator lasted 165.5 h (nearly one week), with an average power consumption of 17 mW. To compute the power consumption shares, we write the following equation:

$$C_{acc} = t_{powerdown} \times I_{powerdown} + t_{sleep} \times I_{sleep} + t_{wake} \times I_{wake}, \quad (3)$$

where we have added a new term for the time when both units are in the power saving state. Using the results of the previous step, and the data from the new experiment, we obtain:

$$800 \text{ mAh}/ = 159.79 \times I_{powerdown} + 2.91 \text{ h} \times 8.1 \text{ mA} + 2.80 \text{ h} \times 104.3 \text{ mA}, \quad (4)$$

and we obtain a value for $I_{powerdown}$:

$$I_{powerdown} = 3.0 \text{ mA}.$$

Since the average current during the experiment is now 4.8 mA, $I_{powerdown}$ corresponds to 60% of the overall power consumption. Both boards are in power saving mode, and datasheets claim that their power consumption should now be far less than 1 mA , while we estimate 3 mA. We conclude that parasite components significantly contribute to $I_{powerdown}$: in fact, we have two power LEDs and one unused stabilizer on the boards. We conclude that producing an ad hoc board without development-oriented components would further reduce power consumption.

6. Conclusions

We have shown how a smart village can launch an IoT project with a limited initial investment and little or no external funding.

To reach this conclusion, we have considered the whole project as split in tightly interdependent components. We have found a consistent set of low-cost solutions, one for each project component, and we have verified that the overall system is able to support a benchmark application. We do not claim it to be the optimal solution, but one ensuring low cost and the presence of a defined set of features. The approach is driven by the holistic principle that the presence of one single low-cost component does not ensure that the same property holds for the whole project.

In Table 1, we give cost details for a pilot deployment according to the prototype design: we envision five WiFi Access Points (AP), 50 sensors, and three different applications. Sensors have individual 6 V 2 W solar panels, a step-down board recharging a 3.7 V 4.2 Ah Li-Ion battery, with an estimated autonomy of 20 days. Prices are found on eBay, considering bulk sales.

Table 1. Price details.

Resource	# Pieces	Cost	Unit
Arduino Mini-Pro	50	2	dollars
ESP-01	50	1	dollars
Printed circuit board	50	2	dollars
Solar panel	50	5	dollars
Battery	50	2	dollars
WiFi AP	5	50	dollars
Total hardware	-	**850**	dollars
Library	1	200	lines
Applications	3	200	lines
Total software	-	**800**	lines
ThingSpeak	1	750	dollars/year
3G subscriptions	5	24	dollars/year
Total services	-	**870**	dollars/year

The most expensive resource is the ThingSpeak subscription, which may be regarded as not strictly needed, since the operation of the pilot system fits the ThingSpeak free plan, which is reserved to non-profit experiments, as a matter of fact, with the intentions of the service provider.

We have chosen WiFi for the networking infrastructure, disregarding the highly dynamic family of LPWAN technologies, the promising LoRaWan included. To have an idea of its cost, we consider that a single gateway is sufficient for the whole smart village deployment, replacing the WiFi APs with a single LoRa gateway and reducing also the number of 3G subscriptions. Despite that, the cost for hardware equipment (considering 200 dollars for a concentrator and 15 dollars for each sensor) rises from $850 to $1400 (+65%). However, stronger reasons that make WiFi preferable today, as illustrated in the Introduction are: popularity, shareability and stability. Since such aspects are going to change in the near future, in favor of the upcoming LPWan technologies, a wise administration should prepare the ground for the change.

The sum of $2500 is comparable to a limited street maintenance task: an affordable investment even for a rural community. It may be acceptable also in developing countries, in case it helps to satisfy primary needs. The community incurs yearly expenses to sustain the system, which amount to $1000; they consist of the ThingSpeak subscription, and of the telephone company charges.

Project costs scale less than linearly with system size. The only component with linear scale-up is related to hardware: sensors and the infrastructure. The ThingSpeak fee remains unchanged until project size scales up 10 times, i.e., from 50 to 500 components, while telephone charges increase linearly. Software remains unchanged, although further revisions are needed. Yearly costs grow less than linearly, until the 500 components threshold is reached.

Under such assumption, if the project scales up ten times after the initial pilot phase, without adding new applications, we have the costs outlined in Table 2. In the scenario of an exponential growth, a successive jump, from ×10 to ×100, incurs a nearly linear growth of yearly expenses.

Table 2. Scale-up with scale factors ×1 (pilot), ×10 and ×100.

Kind	pilot (×1)	×10	×100	Unit
Hardware	850	8500 (×10)	85,000 (×100)	dollars
Software	800	800 (×1)	800 (×1)	lines
Services	870	1950 (×2)	13,500 (×15)	dollars/year

The sensor design presented in this paper has been successfully applied to the development of a sound-monitor for traffic analysis [36]: an amplified microphone analyses street noise using a Fourier Transform, and detects traffic jam, or passing vehicles. The results are uploaded to a ThingSpeak channel, where data can be used for statistics or real-time alerts.

There are limits in the kind of applications that are compatible with our benchmark, and they should be understood from the beginning. For instance, air pollution sensors are expensive, the management of short events is power consuming, and video processing is precluded. However, the door is open to test the ground with small scale, sustainable deployments.

Conflicts of Interest: The author declares no conflict of interest.

References

1. Gascó, M. What Makes a City Smart? Lessons from Barcelona. In Proceedings of the 2016 49th Hawaii International Conference on System Sciences (HICSS), Koloa, HI, USA, 5–8 January 2016; pp. 2983–2989. [CrossRef]
2. Van Winden, W.; van den Buuse, D. Smart City Pilot Projects: Exploring the Dimensions and Conditions of Scaling Up. *J. Urban Technol.* **2017**. [CrossRef]
3. Hogan, P.; Cretu, C.; Bulc, V. *EU Action for SMART VILLAGES*; Technical Report; European Commission: Brussels, Belgium, 2017.

4. European Union. CORK 2.0 Declaration—"A better life in rural areas". In *Cork 2.0: European Conference on Rural Development*; European Union: Brussels, Belgium, 2016. [CrossRef]
5. United States Environmental Protection Agency. *Smart Growth in Small Towns and Rural Communities*; United States Environmental Protection Agency: Chicago, IL, USA, 2002.
6. Tragos, E.Z.; Angelakis, V.; Fragkiadakis, A.; Gundlegard, D.; Nechifor, C.S.; Oikonomou, G.; Pöhls, H.C.; Gavras, A. Enabling reliable and secure IoT-based smart city applications. In Proceedings of the 2014 IEEE International Conference on Pervasive Computing and Communication Workshops (PERCOM WORKSHOPS), Budapest, Hungary, 24–28 March 2014; pp. 111–116. [CrossRef]
7. Mekki, K.; Bajic, E.; Chaxel, F.; Meyer, F. A comparative study of LPWAN technologies for large-scale IoT deployment. *ICT Express* **2018**. [CrossRef]
8. Adelantado, F.; Vilajosana, X.; Tuset-Peiro, P.; Martinez, B.; Melia-Segui, J.; Watteyne, T. Understanding the Limits of LoRaWAN. *IEEE Commun. Mag.* **2017**, *55*, 34–40. [CrossRef]
9. Raza, U.; Kulkarni, P.; Sooriyabandara, M. Low Power Wide Area Networks: An Overview. *IEEE Commun. Surv. Tutor.* **2017**, *19*, 855–873. [CrossRef]
10. Balid, W.; Refai, H.H. On the development of self-powered IoT sensor for real-time traffic monitoring in smart cities. In Proceedings of the 2017 IEEE SENSORS, Glasgow, UK, 29 October–1 November 2017; pp. 1–3. [CrossRef]
11. Rizwan, P.; Suresh, K.; Babu, M.R. Real-time smart traffic management system for smart cities by using Internet of Things and Big Data. In Proceedings of the 2016 International Conference on Emerging Technological Trends (ICETT), Kollam, India, 21–22 October 2016; pp. 1–7. [CrossRef]
12. Shi, J.; Jin, L.; Li, J.; Fang, Z. A smart parking system based on NB-IoT and third-party payment platform. In Proceedings of the 2017 17th International Symposium on Communications and Information Technologies (ISCIT), Cairns, Australia, 25–27 September 2017; pp. 1–5. [CrossRef]
13. El-Tawab, S.; Oram, R.; Garcia, M.; Johns, C.; Park, B.B. Data analysis of transit systems using low-cost IoT technology. In Proceedings of the 2017 IEEE International Conference on Pervasive Computing and Communications Workshops (PerCom Workshops), Big Island, HI, USA, 13–17 March 2017; pp. 497–502. [CrossRef]
14. Spachos, P.; Song, L.; Gregori, S. Power consumption of prototyping boards for smart room temperature monitoring. In Proceedings of the 2017 IEEE 22nd International Workshop on Computer Aided Modeling and Design of Communication Links and Networks (CAMAD), Lund, Sweden, 19–21 June 2017; pp. 1–6. [CrossRef]
15. Desai, N.S.; Alex, J.S.R. IoT based air pollution monitoring and predictor system on Beagle Bone Black. In Proceedings of the 2017 International Conference on Nextgen Electronic Technologies: Silicon to Software (ICNETS2), Chennai, India, 23–25 March 2017; pp. 367–370. [CrossRef]
16. Velásquez, P.; Vásquez, L.; Correa, C.; Rivera, D. A low-cost IoT based environmental monitoring system. A citizen approach to pollution awareness. In Proceedings of the 2017 CHILEAN Conference on Electrical, Electronics Engineering, Information and Communication Technologies (CHILECON), Pucon, Chile, 18–20 October 2017; pp. 1–6. [CrossRef]
17. Verma, P.; Kumar, A.; Rathod, N.; Jain, P.; Mallikarjun, S.; Subramanian, R.; Amrutur, B.; Kumar, M.S.M.; Sundaresan, R. Towards an IoT based water management system for a campus. In Proceedings of the 2015 IEEE First International Smart Cities Conference (ISC2), Guadalajara, Mexico, 25–28 October 2015; pp. 1–6. [CrossRef]
18. Suresh, M.; Muthukumar, U.; Chandapillai, J. A novel smart water-meter based on IoT and smartphone app for city distribution management. In Proceedings of the 2017 IEEE Region 10 Symposium (TENSYMP), Cochin, India, 14–16 July 2017; pp. 1–5. [CrossRef]
19. Aboelmaged, M.; Abdelghani, Y.; Ghany, M.A.A.E. Wireless IoT based metering system for energy efficient smart cites. In Proceedings of the 2017 29th International Conference on Microelectronics (ICM), Beirut, Lebanon, 10–13 December 2017; pp. 1–4. [CrossRef]
20. Singh, A.; Kumar, A.; Kumar, A. Network controlled distributed energy management system for smart cities. In Proceedings of the 2016 2nd International Conference on Communication Control and Intelligent Systems (CCIS), Mathura, India, 18–20 November 2016; pp. 235–238. [CrossRef]

21. Kamlaesan, B.; Kumar, K.A.; David, S.A. Analysis of transformer faults using IoT. In Proceedings of the 2017 IEEE International Conference on Smart Technologies and Management for Computing, Communication, Controls, Energy and Materials (ICSTM), Chennai, India, 2–4 August 2017; pp. 239–241. [CrossRef]

22. Billy, L.P.L.; Wijerathne, N.; Ng, B.K.K.; Yuen, C. Sensor Fusion for Public Space Utilization Monitoring in a Smart City. *IEEE Internet Things J.* **2017**, *5*, 473–481. [CrossRef]

23. Arduino Mini Pro Schematics. Available online: https://www.arduino.cc/en/uploads/Main/Arduino-Pro-Mini-schematic.pdf (accessed on 30 April 2018).

24. Arduino UNO Schematics. Available online: https://www.arduino.cc/en/uploads/Main/Arduino-uno-schematic.pdf (accessed on 7 May 2018).

25. STMicroelectronics. STM32 32-Bit ARM Cortex MCUs. Available online: http://www.st.com/en/microcontrollers/stm32-32-bit-arm-cortex-mcus.html (accessed on 29 March 2018).

26. Portaluri, B. Arduino WiFi Library for ESP8266 Modules. Available online: https://github.com/bportaluri/WiFiEsp (accessed on 29 March 2018).

27. Kodali, R.K.; Mahesh, K.S. A low cost implementation of MQTT using ESP8266. In Proceedings of the 2016 2nd International Conference on Contemporary Computing and Informatics (IC3I), Greater Noida, India, 14–17 December 2016; pp. 404–408. [CrossRef]

28. Baccarelli, E.; Naranjo, P.G.V.; Scarpiniti, M.; Shojafar, M.; Abawajy, J.H. Fog of Everything: Energy-Efficient Networked Computing Architectures, Research Challenges, and a Case Study. *IEEE Access* **2017**, *5*, 9882–9910. [CrossRef]

29. Ciuffoletti, A. Design and implementation of a low-cost modular sensor. In Proceedings of the 13th IEEE International conference on Wireless and Mobile Computing (WiMob), Rome, Italy, 9–11 October 2017.

30. Ciuffoletti, A. A Low-Cost WiFi Sensor/actuator. 2018. Available online: http://fritzing.org/projects/a-low-cost-wifi-sensoractuator (accessed on 30 April 2018).

31. Ciuffoletti, A. A Wrapper for the AT Interface of the ESP8266. 2017. Available online: https://bitbucket.org/augusto_ciuffoletti/atlib (accessed on 30 April 2018).

32. Ciuffoletti, A. Implementation of a Benchmark for a Low-Cost Sensor/Actuator. 2018. Available online: https://bitbucket.org/augusto_ciuffoletti/benchmark_155 (accessed on 30 April 2018).

33. Ciuffoletti, A. Sharing a common time reference in a heterogeneous distributed system. In Proceedings of the 7th EUROMICRO Workshop on Parallel and Distributed Processing, Funchal, Portugal, 3–5 February 1999; pp. 359–366.

34. Naranjo, P.G.V.; Pooranian, Z.; Shojafar, M.; Conti, M.; Buyya, R. FOCAN: A Fog-supported Smart City Network Architecture for Management of Applications in the Internet of Everything Environments. *arXiv* **2017**, arXiv:1710.01801.

35. Gammon, N. Power Saving Techniques for Microprocessors. 2015. Available online: http://www.gammon.com.au/power (accessed on 29 March 2018).

36. De Filicaia, J. Un prototipo IoT: Dall'ideazione alla Promozione. Master Thesis, Università di Pisa, Pisa, Italy, 2018. (In Italian) [CrossRef]

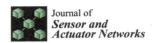

Article

Designing and Managing a Smart Parking System Using Wireless Sensor Networks

Adil Hilmani * , **Abderrahim Maizate and Larbi Hassouni**

RITM-ESTC/CED-ENSEM, University Hassan II, Km7, El jadida Street, B.P. 8012, Oasis, Casablanca 8118, Morocco; maizate@hotmail.com (A.M.); lhassouni@hotmail.com (L.H.)
* Correspondence: adil.hilmani@ofppt.ma; Tel.: +212-633-33-22-12

Received: 10 April 2018; Accepted: 31 May 2018; Published: 6 June 2018

Abstract: For several years, the population of cities has continued to multiply at a rapid pace. The main cause of this phenomenon in developing countries like Morocco is the rural exodus. In fact, rural youth are increasingly attracted by the modern way of life and the opportunities of employment offered by cities. This increase in population density has a large number of negative effects on the quality of life in the city. The most obvious is the intensity of the traffic, which has become an almost insurmountable problem and which causes a great deal of damage, such as the increase in the number of accidents that cause serious bodily harm to the road users, the pollution caused by the large amount of CO_2 released by the vehicles, and the continuous stress of drivers who must drive in often narrow and very busy roads and who must look for a long time to find a space to park. Thus, to solve the parking problem, several modern technologies have been created to equip car parks with smart devices that help road users identify the nearest car park that has a free space. These technologies most often use wireless sensor networks and Internet of Things (IoT) technology. In this paper, we present the design and development of a smart parking system using the latest technologies based on wireless sensor networks (WSN). Our system uses an adaptable and hybrid self-organization algorithm for wireless sensor networks that adapts to all types of car parks existing in the city (linear and mass parking), and offers a better management of the energy consumption during the wireless communication to increase the lifetime of the sensor nodes and the longevity of the WSN. This system also offers innovative services which facilitate the task to the drivers when looking for an available parking space in the city near their destination, in a fast and efficient manner.

Keywords: parking system; smart parking; wireless sensor networks; RFID (radio-frequency identification)

1. Introduction

With the change of the global economy and modern life, the Information and Communication Technologies (ICT) sector has experienced a vital acceleration in its process, to adapt at such change. Today, people spend most of their time outside of their home environments, they travel daily to work, and they frequently go shopping centres and attractions, without forgetting the displacements to the centre of the city. This certainly caused an imbalance in the daily mobility that led to the development of parking services to avoid unnecessary driving around the city centre to simply search for a parking space. This, on the one hand, causes additional carbon dioxide emissions and damages the environment of the city's ecosystem. On the other hand, it increases drivers' frustration and traffic congestion in the city, which will certainly cause traffic accidents. All of this degrades the experience of the modern city's ecosystem and has become a major challenge in the development of future smart parking systems.

Smart parking systems are systems that manage the difficulty of parking in the city in public or private areas, using several recent technologies, including WSNs (wireless sensor networks) and

RFID (radio frequency identification) [1–4]. These systems obtain information on the available parking spaces in a parking area using real-time data collection by the sensor nodes scattered in the parking area, which allows users to use the additional services implemented by these systems, such as the automated payment service compatible with mobile phones, so that people can reserve their parking space in advance. Figure 1 illustrates the general architecture of a smart parking system.

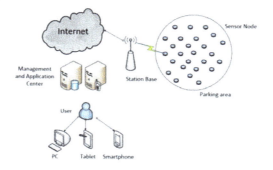

Figure 1. Smart parking system.

The system we propose in this article offers a solution based on an adaptable and hybrid self-organization algorithm for WSN networks, which allows to find a parking space in the two types of outdoor parking in a city. The first one is the "linear outdoor parking area" (Figure 2) which is a parking area located mainly on the main streets, alleys, and the centre of the city, where all parking spaces of the parking area form a single line. There are currently three types of linear outdoor parking areas (Figure 3). Slash-type parking is the easiest to park while the horizontal is the most difficult, followed by the vertical one. The second type is "Mass outdoor parking" which has a larger parking space than the linear car parks and are in the peripherals of the city and in larger areas like a technological park, shopping centre, etc. (Figure 4).

Figure 2. Linear outdoor parking.

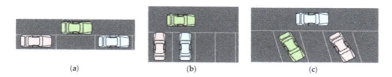

Figure 3. The types of linear outdoor parking (**a**) Horizontal type; (**b**) Vertical type; (**c**) Slash-type.

Figure 4. Mass outdoor parking.

Many smart parking management systems use self-organization algorithms for wireless sensor networks that are efficient and effective for a single type of parking (linear parking or mass parking), but they do not have the same performances for another type of parking. For example, for linear car parks, most of the self-organization algorithms used are based on chain formation, knowing that there are few sensors in the parking area, which allows minimizing the energy consumption between the different nodes and improving the energy efficiency in the network. However, this type of algorithm is not efficient and effective for mass parking knowing that there are many sensors in the car parking that introduce delays in the delivery of data to the gateway and that will create a load unbalance between the different nodes of the chain. For this reason, the self-organization algorithm for wireless sensor networks adopted by our system is adaptable for both types of parking (linear and mass) by forming chains or clusters according to the type, and which considers the limits of these networks in terms of energy consumption during the wireless communication process in order to increase the lifetime of the sensors and the longevity of the WSN network, by creating a powerful and sustainable system.

Our system also offers other very useful features, such as the management of parking spaces by identifying and checking vehicles parked in appropriate locations, the improvement of security against theft, the identification of available parking spaces near the destination of the drivers, and the control of the payment according to the duration of parking. The proposed system uses RFID technology (RFID readers and tags) to accomplish these tasks.

This system implements a web application and a mobile application to facilitate the task for drivers to quickly find a parking space at their destination on the one hand, and, on the other hand, for realize the payment of the duration of parking and effect online reservations in the case of private parking to make the system convenient for users.

The rest of the document is organized as follows: Section 2 provides an overview of the different types of WSN self-organization protocols used to manage the different types of car parks. In Section 3, we will propose the architecture of our car park management system based on WSN. Then, in Section 4, we will give a new contribution based on a proposed new smart parking management system using a hybrid self-organization protocol that can be adapted to any type of parking. After, in the Section 5, a comparison is presented to show advantages and disadvantages of each different smart parking systems and a comparison of technologies used in every system. Finally, we conclude with a perspective and a conclusion in Section 6.

2. Existing Smart Systems for Parking Management

To manage and administer the various existing car parks in the city, there are two types of self-organization protocols for WSN: linear and mass.

2.1. Linear Protocols

Linear protocols are self-organization protocols used by wireless sensor nodes that are dispersed in an area of interest (in this case: parking areas) to form and construct a chain topology for collecting all the data detected and transfer them to the base station (Sink). Car park management systems that use these linear protocols include the following:

In [5], the proposed system is a system that uses two modules: a monitoring module and a reservation and security module. The surveillance module employs the network of wireless sensors to detect available spaces in a parking area, these sensor nodes are installed in each location forming a chain to collect information related to the states of the parking spaces. This information is sent to the car park management centre for efficient use towards the drivers (display of spaces, etc.). The reservation and security module uses the global system for mobile communication (GSM) system whose drivers must send an SMS to reserve their space in the parking. In return, the drivers receive a password with the number of the space in the parking area, so that they can enter and exit with all normality and with all security.

In [6], this article is based on the use of networks of wireless sensors whose nodes are infrared sensors that help to detect the presence of cars in parking spaces. The system consists of two modules: a monitoring module and a master module. The monitoring module consists of a ZigBee transmission and reception unit, a liquid-crystal display (LCD), and a peripheral interface controller (PIC) microcontroller which controls the data detected by the infrared sensor. Once the sensor detects the presence of a car, it informs the microcontroller, to display the status of this parking space on the LCD and, afterwards, it sends this data through the ZigBee transmission interface to the master module using a chain topology. The ZigBee technology used in data transmission shows a high performance in terms of energy consumption during wireless communication and is inexpensive to implement.

In [7], the system is based on the use of infrared sensors to detect the existence of cars in parking spaces. This system consists of three modules: the first module is the monitoring module which is responsible for the detection of parking spaces by the infrared sensors, and these sensors contain a PIC controller for data processing and a ZigBee system for data transmission using chain topology. The second module is the reservation module composed by a GSM module for the transmission and reception of data via SMS, allowing the reservation of parking spaces. The third module is the security module which uses the password already provided by the system allowing entry and exit only to authorized persons and who have an a priori reservation. The system of reservation based on GSM technology can be saturated with a high solicitation of the spaces of parking by the users, which can negatively affect the proper functioning of the parking system.

The proposed system CPF (Car Parking Framework) [8] manages a smart parking system that combines sensors (detection of parking spaces), RFID tags, and readers (parking access authorization, car's location, and prevention against thefts). This system uses a communication model based on the master/slave model between the sensor nodes in the bus mode with a serial cable communication. All nodes send their data to the master via cable, and afterwards it sends the detected data to the sink via a wireless communication. The installation of the serial cable for the communication between the nodes is expensive to implement and it limits the system for a future extension of the parking, which will cause complications in the development of the system.

In [9], the proposed system introduces a new smart parking system (SPS) based on the use of the latest technologies, such as WSNs, ZigBee, RFID, and NFC. The WSN constructs a topology in the form of a chain to collect information about available spaces in the parking area. This array of sensors consists of three types of sensors that communicate with the ZigBee technology. Sensor R detects the presence of a car in an available parking space, then it sends these data through various sensors R until it reaches sensor C (the smart gateway). Sensor C collects all the information and sends it to the central server. The RR sensors detect the RFID tags installed on cars authorized to park in special parking spaces. Once the label has been detected, this information is sent via multiple hops by nodes R, until reaching node C, which passes it to the central server. The SPS uses two applications to better manage the parking system, one for drivers, which helps them find parking spaces quickly and easily using the Google Maps navigation system with an online payment system (NFC). Another application, for authorities, allows them to receive alerts from the central server via GCM (Google Cloud Messaging) on unauthorized cars that have parked in the special spaces.

These linear protocols are not useful for the mass parking areas because these protocols will form longer chains which will create on the one hand delays in the delivery of data to the base station, and on the other hand, immense energy consumption during the transmission of the data. For this reason, mass protocols have been developed to deal with these problems in the efficient management of parking spaces in this type of parking area.

2.2. Mass Protocols

Mass protocols are self-organization protocols based on the deployment of WSNs in car parks allowing the creation of clusters or tree structures. The following systems use these protocols in car park management:

In [10], a new smart parking system (PGIS) is proposed, based on the use of networks of wireless sensors to control and manage parking by implementing a guidance system using LED screens. This system is based on a WSN which consists of three types of sensor nodes: a monitoring node (for detecting the presence of vehicles in parking spaces), a routing node (for routing and to route the detected information to the sink node), and the sink node (which gathers all information from the network to transfer it to the information and management centre). These nodes are installed in the car park and they form a tree topology. The PGIS uses a guidance system using LED screens that are installed at the entrance and in the corners of the car park so that drivers can orient themselves and find the assigned parking space efficiently and effectively. The PGIS information and management centre supports the management and maintenance of the entire system, processes the data collected by the monitoring nodes, calculates the optimal parking space for the new car, manages the parking costs of each parked car and controls all parking screens.

In [11], the author proposes a smart parking system that is based on the implementation of networks of wireless sensors for the management of vacant parking spaces for drivers who are looking for empty spaces. This system uses less expensive sensors (light sensors) to collect information on the status of parking spaces in order to send them to a central server through an aggregated server. The central server is installed and connected via the Wi-Fi network, and it receives all the information of all integrated web servers of each parking available in the city. This system uses a mobile application so that drivers can get information on vacant parking spaces. The light sensors used are influenced in most cases by ambient light and are sensitive to pollution, which can affect the quality and on the reliability of vehicle detection in parking spaces.

In [12], the author proposes a new smart parking system based on the implementation of various technologies, such as WSNs, RFID, and ZigBee. The network of wireless sensors is used to detect the presence of vehicles in the parking spaces with ultrasonic sensors installed in these spaces, and which inform the base station on the states of these locations (empty or full). These sensors are composed of two types of nodes: monitoring nodes that are installed in the parking locations, and the routing nodes that are responsible for transferring the information collected by the monitoring nodes to the base station by creating a tree topology. The communication between the various sensors and the base station is based on ZigBee technology which allows short distance communication and with reduced energy consumption. This parking system offers a new RFID technology that has a very important role in identifying vehicles which have just parked in an empty space and has a crucial role in pricing by controlling the time between check-in and check-out.

In [13], the author has developed s smart parking system based on the use of hybrid wireless sensors (infrared sensors + RFID), which form a cluster-tree structure. Each of them is equipped with three LEDs (red, green, blue) to control and manage the availability of parking spaces. This proposed system consists of four essential modules that are the online booking module, the input module, the output module, and the parking management module.

In [14], the author created a new smart parking system (SIMERT) based on the installation of two wireless sensors in each parking space to detect the presence of vehicles and to control the good parking of vehicles in the parking spaces. This system uses WSN technology composed of three types of sensors (surveillance sensor nodes, routing nodes, and a sink node) that form a cluster topology. The parking space is divided into areas (clusters) where each agent is responsible for each area. This system implements two Android applications, one for drivers to see the available parking spaces, and the other for agents, whose system sends alerts on any event that occurs in the parking area of each agent.

In [15], the author implemented wireless network sensors to monitor and manage parking spaces in a parking lot. To detect the presence of vehicles, the author used proximity sensors consisting of an Arduino Uno which sends the data to a Raspberry Pi which is configured as a client (Sink) and which, in turn, sends the data received to the back-end server via Wi-Fi by creating a tree topology. This system uses a mobile application based on the data stored in this server to inform and locate the available parking areas closest to the destination of the drivers. The author has improved the system by adding a payment system using RFID tags that will be checked at the entrance of the car parks to realize the correspondence between RFID ID and the reserved space, and in the output, to realize the payment efficiently and quickly on the one hand, and on the other hand, to control the flight of cars in this parking area.

The Smart Parking Management System proposed in [16] is based on the implementation of three types of technologies used in the IoT domain, radio frequency identification (RFID), automatic license plate recognition (ALPR), and a wireless sensor network (WSN). The wireless sensor network executes a mass algorithm that allows the creation of a cluster topology between the different nodes, these sensor nodes are divided into three types. The SN nodes are in each space in a parking area to detect the availability of this space. The GN nodes are strategically located in the parking area to collect occupancy states transmitted by a defined number of SN nodes for transfer them to the CN node. The CN node is responsible to manage all information of the entire parking lot area and communicate it to a database server. This system uses additional services such as a mobile application to receive real-time updates and NFC (near-field communication) for the reservation of parking space and the online payment.

In [17], the author has developed a smart parking system based on the use of the wireless sensor network and IoT to manage the parking problem in outdoor car parks in the city. These nodes are installed in each parking space, and they are composed of an ultrasound sensor to detect the presence of a vehicle in the parking space and a Wi-Fi communication module to send the state of occupation to a server Cloud that manages all the parking spaces in the city. This WSN network implemented in this system does not form any network topology between the different sensor nodes to transfer the detected data to the cloud server. The stored data in the cloud server is exploited using an Android application (ParkX) so that users can consult and navigate to available parking spaces near their destinations. Wi-Fi wireless communication consumes a great deal of energy during data transmission, which will negatively affect the battery lifetime of the nodes and on the longevity of the network. However, this technology shows excellent performance in terms of obstacle penetration compared to ZigBee.

The author of [18] proposes a smart parking management system to manage the parking problem in mass parking in areas like an airport or a campus using RFID. The RFID readers are installed in each parking space and at the entrance and exit to secure the parking area and manage the availability states of parking spaces. The RFID readers activate the passive RFID tag on the card of the driver entering or exiting or parking the car in the area and read the information of the tag, which contains a unique identification number, to transfer them to the database of the system via a multi-hop communication using Wi-Fi technology, to update the occupation states of the parking spaces in real-time.

These mass protocols have improved delays in the delivery of the data to the base station and they downplayed the enormous energy consumption when transmitting this data compared to the linear protocols. However, these protocols are only applicable for car parks with a group or mass structure, which makes it possible to create clusters that are not useful for linear car parks of which they will create, on the one hand, a load imbalance between the sensor nodes and, on the other hand, minimize the lifetime of the entire network.

3. Architecture of the Smart Parking System

The proposed system contains three essential parts: parking detection centre, parking monitoring centre, and global information management centre.

- The parking detection centre is composed mainly of hybrid sensor nodes (sensors + RFID readers) that are installed in each parking space in each area, these sensor nodes form a wireless sensor network (WSN) allowing to collect the states of all the parking spaces (available or occupied) to send them to the gateway (Sink) of this area, this information will be sent afterwards to the central server to store them in the global database.
- The parking monitoring centre is responsible for identifying and checking the cars that have just parked in a reserved or available space. This centre uses the RFID technology to control and monitor the one hand the parked cars, and the other hand, for identify and manage the payment of parking time.
- The global information management centre is a database where all information detected and collected from all car parks in the city is recorded and exploited in real-time by web or mobile applications. In this way, drivers will have all the information on the available spaces in all the car parks of the city, to consult these spaces according to their destination, and to pay the parking fees.

Figure 5 shows the architecture of the proposed smart parking system:

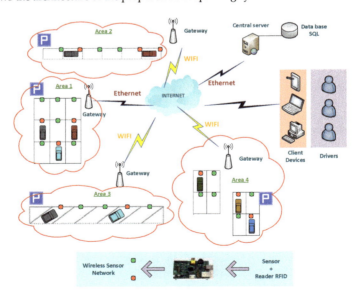

Figure 5. The proposed architecture of smart parking systems based on a WSN.

4. Proposed Smart System for Parking Management

4.1. Parking Detection Centre

The parking detection centre uses two very recent technologies, wireless sensor networks (WSN) and RFID technology. The formation of the sensor network changes according to the type of parking in the area. For linear car parks, a chain topology will be formed in the network and, on the other side, a network topology in cluster form will be created in mass car parks. The formation of different topologies is based on the execution of a hybrid self-organization algorithm that is adaptable to the type and structure of parking that allows to form either a chain (Figure 6) or clusters (Figure 7), according to the distribution of the nodes and how they are scattered in the parking area.

Figure 6. Formation of the chain topology in the linear parking.

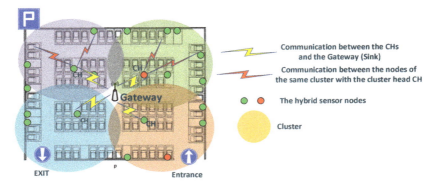

Figure 7. Formation of cluster topology in the mass parking area.

To form a network topology by the sensor nodes in an outdoor parking, all the nodes send their coordinates to the gateway which executes Algorithm 1 making it possible to calculate and detect the type of topology to be formed. In the case of linear parking, the gateway detects that all the nodes have the same X coordinate or the same Y coordinate as a function of the distribution of the nodes in the parking area. In this case, the gateway requests the nodes to create a chain topology in the network to minimize power consumption between the nodes using the multi-hop communication to the gateway (Figure 8).

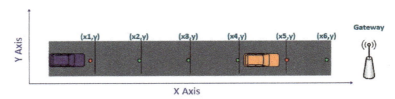

Figure 8. Example of a distribution of the sensor nodes in a linear parking area.

Algorithm 1. Topology detection algorithm.

1:    For i = 1 to N do   //   N: Number of nodes in the WSN network

2:           Send coordinates (X_i, Y_i) from Node (i) to the gateway

3:    End for

4:    C1 ← 1

5:    C2 ← 1

6:    For i = 2 to N do

7:        If $(X_i == X_{i-1})$ then

8:           C1 ++

9:        Else if $(Y_i == Y_{i-1})$ then

10:          C2++

11:       End if

12:   End for

13:   If (C1 == N || C2 == N) then   // Chain topology

14:      Return 1

15:   Else   // Cluster topology

16:      Return 0

17:   End if

In the contrary case (mass parking), the gateway detects that all the nodes do not have similitude in one of the coordinate parameters (X or Y), so it will order the nodes to form a cluster topology to increase the longevity of the network knowing that, in this case, there are a large number of nodes scattered in the parking area (Figure 9).

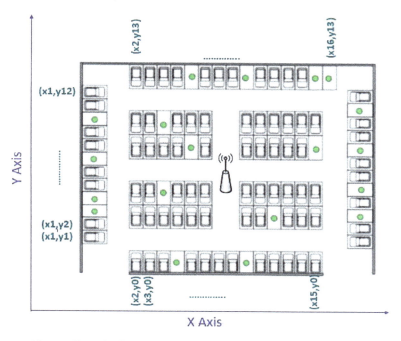

Figure 9. Example of a distribution of the sensor nodes in a mass parking area.

After the execution of the adaptable self-organization algorithm (Algorithm 2), a chain of the sensor nodes will be formed in the city's linear car parks, where all the nodes dispersed in each parking area will send their detected data via multiple hops to the node leader, who will gather and transfer all data from the parking to the gateway of each parking area. In the case of mass car parks, a cluster topology will be created in each parking area in the city where all sensor nodes will form clusters and in each cluster a CH will be elected to receive the detected data from all nodes in its cluster, and transfer them via a single hop to the Gateway (sink).

The formation of the chain or the formation of clusters will be based on the residual energy of the nodes and the overall energy of the network to maximize the lifetime of the nodes and increase the longevity of the network WSN.

Algorithm 2. The adaptive self-organization algorithm.

1:	Use Algorithm 1 to detect the type of topology to be formed (Chain or Cluster)
2:	T ← Algorithm 1
3:	If (T == 1) then
4:	Formation of the chain topology by the sensor nodes
5:	Selection of the leader node
6:	Each node sends data to one of the closest nodes via a single hop until arriving at the leader node who sends all the data to the Gateway
7:	Else
8:	Formation of the cluster topology by the sensor nodes
9:	Selection of the CHs
10:	Each CH receives data from all nodes in its cluster
11:	All CHs send the data from their cluster to the Gateway
12:	End if

The sensor nodes are installed in each parking space and in each of the parking areas, which makes it possible to detect the presence or the absence of the vehicles in the latter. Each parking area (parking) is identified by an IDzi, and each parking space in a parking area is identified by IDpj, so each sensor node is identified by two pairs of the identifiers {IDzi, IDpj}. Once a car has just parked, the sensor node detects the presence of the latter and sends the occupied state of this space with both identifiers to the gateway. Afterwards, this information will be sent and saved in the central server.

To better illustrate the process of managing parking spaces in different parking areas, Algorithm 3 shows the operations performed by the sensor nodes in each parking area.

Algorithm 3. Algorithm surveillance parking spaces in different parking areas by sensor nodes.

1:	For i = 1 to N do // N: Number of parking areas in the city
2:	For j = 1 to M do // M: Number of parking spaces in each parking. M change according to the parking area
3:	If (Sensor node in {IDzi,IDpj} detects the presence of a vehicle) then
4:	send occupied state of the parking space to the gateway to update it in the central server
5:	Else
6:	send available state of the parking space to the gateway to update it in the central server
7:	End if
8:	End for
9:	End for

The wireless communication between the different sensor nodes and the gateway acts a crucial role in the deployment of the WSN network in the outdoor car parks, where much of the energy consumed by the nodes is highly dependent on the energy consumed during wireless communication:

$$E_{Sensor} = E_{Sens} + E_{Proc} + E_{Comm}$$

$$E_{Sensor} \approx E_{Comm}$$

where E_{Sens} is the energy consumed during the detection process, E_{Proc} is the energy consumed during the treatment process, and E_{Comm} is the energy consumed during the communication process.

To detect the availability of parking spaces in an outdoor parking lot in an efficient and reliable manner, the system must deploy one of the most used wireless communications technologies (Wi-Fi, Bluetooth, ZigBee, etc.), so to minimize the energy consumption of the nodes and to increase the longevity of the WSN network. The networks based on ZigBee technology generally consume less energy compared to Wi-Fi and Bluetooth networks.

The following table (Table 1) shows the advantages of ZigBee over other wireless communications technologies.

Table 1. The advantages of ZigBee over other wireless communications technologies.

Wireless Parameter	Bluetooth	IEEE 802.11 b	IEEE 802.11 ah	ZigBee
Frequency band	2.4 GHz	2.4 GHz	Sub-1 GHz	2.4 GHz
Range	9 m	75 to 90 m	1000 m (without repeaters)	100 m (without repeaters)
Current Consumption	60 mA (Tx mode)	400 mA (Tx mode) 20 mA (Standby mode)	90–140 mA (Tx mode) 5 µA (Standby mode)	25–35 mA (Tx mode) 3 µA (Standby mode)

On the other hand, the deployment of the WSN sensor network in outdoor car parks obliges sensor nodes to be installed in the ground, where the signal propagation is obstructed by cars and is affected by their noises. For this type of application, many previous works have shown that conventional wireless standards, such as Bluetooth or Wi-Fi, are not suitable for this type of network in terms of quality and performance compared to the ZigBee standard based on some parameters such BER (bit error rate) and SNR (signal-to-noise ratio) [19–21]. The following figure demonstrates the performance of ZigBee compared to other types of networks (Figure 10).

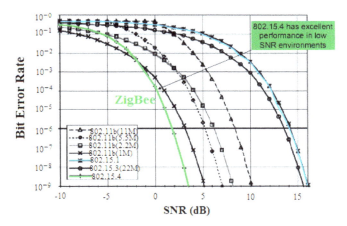

Figure 10. 802.15.4 ZigBee performance based on BER-SNR.

For this reason, we will use ZigBee wireless communication technology, adopted by the proposed self-organization protocol, to extend the battery lifetime of the sensor nodes and to increase the longevity, efficiency, and performances of the WSN network in the outdoor car parks.

4.2. Parking Monotoring Center

The parking monitoring centre uses wireless sensor networks (WSN) and integrated RFID technology in these sensor nodes installed in each parking space. RFID technology is a technology based on radio frequency identification that helps to check and identify objects by radio waves. Thus, vehicles will be identified and parking fees will be collected via this system, to manage and monitor the parking area in an efficient and convenient manner.

Once a car has just parked in a space i in a parking area j, the appropriate sensor detects the presence of the vehicle and it sends the two identifiers {IDzi, IDpj} with the occupied state of that space to the gateway, to transfer them to the central server in order to store them in the database. The RFID reader, integrated in each sensor node, reads the driver's data using the RFID tag installed in the vehicle (name, first name, vehicle number, telephone number, etc.) and transfers them by merging them with the state of the space towards the central server. This server will be used to calculate the duration of parking and to control the detected incidents during the parking of a vehicle. In the case of cars without any RFID tag, a message is sent to the parking officers with the two parking identifiers {IDzi, IDpj}, to register the vehicle registration number into the system to guarantee the payment of parking fees. Algorithm 4 illustrates the process of managing the parking space in each area by the central server, when a vehicle arrives at the parking area.

Algorithm 4. Algorithm of managing the parking space in each area, when a vehicle arrives in the parking area.

1:	Do
2:	While (Reception the occupied state of a parking space {IDzi, IDpj})
3:	Update the information received in the database
4:	Increment the number of occupied spaces
5:	Decrease the number of available spaces
6:	If (The RFID tag is detected) then
7:	Update occupied space with RFID data received in the database
8:	Else
9:	Send a message to the parking agents with {IDzi, IDpj} of the parking space that has just been occupied
10:	The agent of the area IDzj introduces the registration number of the car parked in IDpj in the database
11:	End if
12:	Start counting the parking time: Tparkij //j = the parking area i = the parking space in the area j
13:	Goto 1

Once the car leaves the parking space, the sensor concerned detects the availability of the space by sending the two identifiers {IDzi, IDpj} to the central server through the gateway so that it updates the state of the space in the database. After release of the space in the database the system checks whether the driver has made the payment for the duration of parking, otherwise a notice of infraction and a fine will be sent to the authorities after one hour so that the parking fees will be paid by the drivers.

The payment of the parking time is made online using the mobile application or manually in the automated teller machine in each area. In both cases, only the registration number of the parked vehicle must be entered so that the system can detect it in the database and make the payment. The algorithm below (Algorithm 5) shows the operations performed for the management of the parking spaces in each area when a car leaves the parking area.

Algorithm 5. Algorithm of managing the parking space in each area, when a vehicle leaves the parking area.

1:	Do
2:	While (Reception the availability state of a parking space {IDzi, IDpj})
3:	Update the information received in the database
4:	Decrease the number of occupied spaces
5:	Increment the number of available spaces
6:	Save the time when the car left the parking space: Tout
7:	Stop parking time Tparkij
8:	While (The parking payment is not performed) do
9:	If (The current time < Tout + 1H) then
10:	Wait 15 min
11:	Else
12:	Send a notification to the authorities with the registration number of the car for a fine
13:	Goto 16
14:	End if
15:	End
16:	Update the database with the available state of the space {IDzi, IDpi}

4.3. Global Information Management Centre

The global information management centre relies on the data stored in the database to develop extra services to the users and drivers by facilitating the task of searching for an available space in their destination, such as the consultation of the available parking spaces, the navigation to these spaces, and also the online payment of parking fees. A mobile application is developed that allows drivers to take advantage of these services in a practical and simple manner.

- Consultation of parking areas: Drivers use the mobile application which allows them to consult and find open parking spaces near their destination, before moving to avoid unnecessary travel and also not to create congestion of traffic. This application uses the information that is stored in the database to make available to drivers, the open parking areas closest their destination with the number of available and busy spaces in real-time, by indicating the parking price (Figure 11).
- Navigation to parking areas: This service is based on the use of Google MAP to orient and guide drivers towards the desired parking areas. The driver opens the mobile application to look for an open parking near his destination. Then, depending on the results displayed by the application, the driver selects a parking area and the app opens Google MAP to guide the driver to the selected area. Once arriving in the area, the application displays the available spaces and busy squares in this parking area. Figure 12 illustrates the operation of navigation to the parking areas.
- Payment of parking fees: Before leaving the parking space, the driver must pay the parking fees, this payment is made either manually by moving to the automated teller machine of the parking lot by entering the number of vehicle registration. Either online, the driver uses the same mobile application with the same manipulations of the automatic teller machine to realize the payment of the parking fees in this parking area.

Figure 11. The consultation of the areas and the prices of parking.

Figure 12. Navigation to a parking area.

Algorithms 6 and 7 shows the operation of the global information management centre of our smart parking system.

Algorithm 6. Navigation to the parking area.

1:	Open the mobile application
2:	Introduce destination
3:	Do
4:	Display the closest parking areas with their prices
5:	The user selects the desired parking area
6:	While (No available space in the selected area)
7:	do
8:	Navigation to the area
9:	While (The driver did not arrive at the area)
10:	Display available and occupied spaces

Algorithm 7. Payment of parking fees via a mobile application.

1:	Open the mobile application
2:	Realize the payment
3:	Insert the registration number of your car
4:	If (The registration number of the car exists in the database) then
5:	Display parking fees with information of the parking space in the area
6:	Pay
7:	Else
8:	The registration number of the car does not exist
9:	You have a fine has paid
10:	Contact the authorities
11:	End if

---

5. Discussion

According to the different architectures of smart parking system studied in this article, Tables 2 and 3 summarize the advantages, disadvantages, technologies, and services used by these architectures. There is no system that adapts to the different types of architectures and structures of parking (linear and mass). There are parking systems that only work for linear car parks and do not have the same impact at the deployment level of sensor networks in mass parking, and vice versa.

The complexity of the algorithms used in the management of parking spaces plays an important and crucial role in the development and design of a robust and efficient smart parking system. The majority of the algorithms proposed by our system are not complex, they are easy to be implemented, and they are executed at the server level, which minimizes the exhaustion of the sensors and does not overload them, so that they do not consume a large amount of energy in order to increase the duration of the lifetime of their batteries.

Energy efficiency is one of the important parameters for many self-organization algorithms that allows the creation of a solid network topology in order to optimize the energy consumption between the different sensor nodes and to increase the longevity of the WSN network. The self-organization algorithm adopted by our system is a flexible and unique algorithm, compared to the algorithms implemented by the smart parking systems studied in this article, which allows the creation of a chain topology for linear parking areas and a cluster topology for mass parking areas, in order to balance the load between the different sensors and minimize the energy consumption during the transmission of data to obtain a better energy efficiency management and increased the lifetime of the nodes.

For this reason, we will offer an adaptable smart parking system that allows for the creation of flexible WSN network topologies for any type of existing parking in the city, based on many services and technologies offering convenience to the driver. Systems technology with an adaptable wireless sensor network (WSN) architecture provides a flexibility and a suppleness in the deployment of smart parking systems that will be monotonous in the design and implementation, and will also be standardized in the development of applications and services for the different types and structures of existing car parks, bearing in mind that this solution creates a solid basis for the development and improvement of these systems in the future, as required.

The smart parking system proposed in this article is based on the implementation of two most recent technologies, such as WSN and RFID. The use of these two technologies only gives a plus compared to other parking management systems in terms of the implementation cost and also in terms of design quality.

Table 2. Advantages and disadvantages of different smart parking system.

Smart Parking Systems	Type of Parking System	Advantages	Disadvantages
S1: [5]	Interior parking, linear, no adaptable, single area	- Flexible and easy system implemented. - System is private with the spaces reservation via GSM before moving. - Less expensive system. - Security with a password received by the GSM.	- No application is developed for remote monitoring. - Access only to the driver who made a reservation a priori. - The blocking of the GSM system during mass access to the system. - No guidance and navigation system is used.
S2: [6]	Interior parking, linear, no adaptable, single area	- The system is simple and flexible. - The communication between the sensor nodes is wired. - Less costly system. - The system used valid for interior parking.	- Linear networking is used. - The system uses a display with a limited web application. - The system misses him the remote monitoring of the availability of available spaces in the car park.
S3: [7]	Interior parking, linear, no adaptable, single area	- Less expensive system. - The GSM system used to reserve free parking spaces. - The proposed system is valid for private indoor car parks with a gate and an entry and exit barrier.	- The system is limited for an improvement in the future in the implementation of the latter in outdoor linear car parks. - No mobile application is used for tracking vacant spaces remotely. - The GSM system used for reservation of spaces which can be blocked with multiple access.
S4: [8]	Interior parking, linear, no adaptable, single area	- System robust to communication interference between different nodes. - Hybrid system with RFID and wireless sensor. - RFID system for predefined parking.	- The system lacks him an application for the remote monitoring of free spaces. - No navigation system or additional services to increase the scalability of the latter. - The topology used is wired bus which limits the interoperability and the scalability of the system.
S5: [9]	Outdoor parking, Linear, no adaptable, single area	- Cloud system based on Google to manage mobile applications. - Use of NFC payment system. - Outdoor navigation based on the GOOGLE API. - Reservation system is deployed. - Management of spaces in an efficient way.	- The outdoor parking system which is valid only for linear car parks and not for mass car parks. - The payment is not checked. - Use of RFID only for certain parking spaces.
S6: [10]	Interior parking, mass, no adaptable, single area	- System based on ZigBee technology in the transmission of detected data. - Internal LCD-based guidance system. - The system is a mass car park that uses the cluster architecture in self-organization of the WSN. - Flexible and less expensive system.	- The system is not adaptable to linear parking. - The system lacks him a navigation mechanism or an external guidance system. - No payment system is implemented in this system.
S7: [11]	Interior parking, mass, no adaptable, multiarea	- The driver can know the empty spaces in the parking lot. - The system encompasses several car parks scattered throughout the city. - Drivers can detect parking spaces using a smartphone application.	- Light sensors are sensitive to detect the cars presence. - The system used is valid for private outdoor car parks and not for public. - The system has no navigation system to the car parks available in the city. - The driver cannot make remote payment.

Table 2. *Cont.*

Smart Parking Systems	Type of Parking System	Advantages	Disadvantages
S8: [12]	Interior parking, mass, no adaptable, single area	- The use of RFID to identify drivers and realize payment. - Less expensive system. - System is valid for indoor car parks. - The guiding system used indoors based on LCD screens.	- The system is valid only to mass parking. - No application is developed to facilitate the task for drivers when searching of available spaces.
S9: [13]	Outdoor parking, mass, no adaptable, single area	- The system is based on sending data over IPv6. - RFID system is deployed. - Anti-theft system based on sending GSM messages to the police. - The use of hybrid sensors in the indoor parking using barriers to manage inputs and outputs.	- The use of IR sensors that are sensitive to vehicle lights. - No security system at the exit. - No guidance or navigation system is used.
S10: [14]	Outdoor parking, mass, no adaptable, multiarea	- The system uses the tree topology for the deployment of sensors in the outdoor car parks. - Mobile application for drivers and agents. - The agents have an important role in monitoring the parking spaces in each area. - Using LEDs to display the number of empty spaces in each area.	- The system used is valid only for linear outdoor car parks.
S11: [15]	Interior parking, mass, no adaptable, single area	- Outdoor navigation implemented. - The security and payment system based on RFID. - The use of an application based on Google-MAP to locate all available parking spaces.	- The system is valid only for interior car parks. - The application is limited for the visualization of the free spaces in the interior.
S12: [16]	Interior parking, mass, no adaptable, single area	- The use RFID and ALPR for the identification and the security. - The use an application mobile to navigate to parking area and to locate available spaces. - The use NFC for online payment.	- The system is valid only to mass parking. - The topology created by the network is fixed.
S13: [17]	Outdoor parking, no adaptable, multiarea	- The use of powerful sensors. - The use of a mobile application (ParkX) to navigate to parking spaces. - The payment of parking fees is implemented.	- The sensors used are expensive. - No security system is implemented. - Booking in advance can create parking problems.
S14: [18]	Outdoor-indoor parking, no adaptable, single area	- The parking entrance and exit management is implemented using RFID. - The security and the spaces management are based on RFID.	- The use Wi-Fi multi-hop communication that consumes too much. - No guidance or navigation system is used. - No mobile application is used.
Proposed system	Outdoor-indoor parking, adaptable, multiarea	- Topology adaptable to any type of parking. - The use an application mobile to navigate to parking area and to locate available spaces. - RFID system is deployed. - Security and Reservation system is deployed. - The use of the online payment system.	

Table 3. Different technologies and services used in smart parking systems.

System: Ref	Communication Technology		Services						Connection Access			
	TS	TD	GD	PY	SE	RE	SG	AV	PS	IoT	SM	WA
S1: [5]		GSM			√	√	√	√				√
S2: [6]	ZigBee		√					√				√
S3: [7]	ZigBee	GSM		√	√	√			√		√	
S4: [8]		Bluetooth		√	√				√		√	
S5: [9]	ZigBee	Wi-Fi/3G	√	√				√		√	√	
S6: [10]	ZigBee		√									
S7: [11]	Wi-Fi	Wi-Fi/3G						√	√		√	√
S8: [12]	ZigBee		√				√					
S9: [13]				√			√	√	√	√	√	√
S10: [14]	ZigBee	Wi-Fi/3G	√		√		√	√	√	√	√	
S11: [15]				√	√				√		√	
S12: [16]	ZigBee			√	√			√	√		√	
S13: [17]	Wi-Fi		√	√		√	√	√		√	√	
S14: [18]	Wi-Fi				√							
Proposed system	ZigBee	Wi-Fi/3G	√	√	√	√	√	√	√	√	√	√

TS: technology used by sensor network; TD: technology used by the drivers; GD: guidance; PY: payment; SE: security; RE: reservation; IG: smart gateway; PS: parking management using smartphone; AV: availability checking over internet; IOT: Internet of Things; WA: web application; SM: smartphone; √: the technology or the service is used in the paper.

6. Conclusions

In this paper, we realised a thorough comparative study of different architectures and the different self-organization protocols used in the management of the different types of existing car parks in the cities. We have also proposed a new architecture of a new smart parking system based on the deployment and implementation of different technologies, such as WSN, IoT, RFID. This new architecture implements, on the one hand, a new hybrid and adaptable self-organization protocol for the deployment of sensor nodes in different environments in order to maximize the performance of the WSN and increase its longevity, and, on the other hand, uses existing technologies, such as WSN and RFID to minimize the cost of implementing the system and improve the quality of its design.

In future work, we will detail and develop this new adaptable self-organization protocol for wireless sensor networks by performing simulations in order to demonstrate its strength by comparing it with other existing self-organization protocols.

Author Contributions: The work presented here was carried out in collaboration between all authors. Adil Hilmani and Abderrahim Maizate contributed in the design and development of the smart parking system; Adil Hilmani wrote the paper. Aberrahim Maizate and Larbi Hassouni supervised the project.

Acknowledgments: The authors would like to thank the editor and anonymous referees for their valuable comments to improve the quality of this paper.

Conflicts of Interest: The authors declare no conflicts of interest.

References

1. Kalantary, S.; Taghipour, S. A survey on architectures, protocols, applications, and management in wireless sensor networks. *J. Adv. Comput. Sci. Technol.* **2014**, *3*, 1. [CrossRef]
2. Akyildiz, I.F.; Vuran, M.C. *Wireless Sensor Networks*; Wiley Publication: Hoboken, NJ, USA, 2010.
3. Akyildiz, I.F.; Su, W.; Sankarasubramaniam, Y.; Cayirci, E. A survey on sensor networks. *IEEE Commun. Mag.* **2002**, *40*, 102–114. [CrossRef]
4. Hilmani, A.; Maizate, A. A study of self-organization protocols in wireless sensor network. *Mediterr. Telecommun. J.* **2017**, *7*. N° 2.
5. Rahayu, Y.; Mustapa, F.N. A secure parking reservation system using GSM technology. *Int. J. Comput.* **2013**, *2*, 518. [CrossRef]
6. Yee, H.C.; Rahayu, Y. Monitoring parking space availability via ZigBee technology. *Int. J. Future Comput.* **2014**, *3*, 377.

7. Poojaa, A.; Glory, M.; Nathiya, P.; Ramya, R.; Sivasrinee, E.T. WSN based secure vehicle parking management and reservation system. In Proceedings of the National Conference on Research Advances in Communication, Computation, Electrical Scienceand Structures (NCRACCESS-2015), Deviyakurichi, India, 21 February 2015.

8. Karbab, E.M.; Djenouri, D.; Boulkaboul, S. Car park management with networked wireless sensors and active RFID. In Proceedings of the IEEE International Conference on Electro/Information Technology (EIT), Dekalb, IL, USA, 21–23 May 2015.

9. Mainetti, L.; Palano, L.; Patrono, L.; Stefanizzi, M.L.; Vergallo, R. Integration of RFID and WSN technologies in a smart parking system. In Proceedings of the 22nd International Conference on Software, Telecommunications and Computer Networks (SoftCOM), Split, Croatia, 17–19 September 2014.

10. Chen, M.; Chang, T. A parking guidance and information system based on wireless sensor network. In Proceedings of the IEEE International Conference on Information and Automation, Shenzhen, China, 6–8 June 2011.

11. Yang, J.; Portilla, J.; Riesgo, T. Smart parking service based on Wireless Sensor Networks. In Proceedings of the IECON 2012—38th Annual Conference on IEEE Industrial Electronics Society, Montreal, QC, Canada, 25–28 October 2012.

12. Patil, M.; Bhonge, V.N. Wireless sensor network and RFID for smart parking system. *Int. J. Emerg. Technol. Adv. Eng.* **2013**, *3*, 188–192.

13. Gandhi, B.M.K.; Rao, M.K. A prototype for IoT based car parking management system for smart cities. *Indian J. Sci. Technol.* **2016**, *9*. [CrossRef]

14. Quiñones, M.; Gonazález, V.; Quiñones, L. Design of a smart parking system using wireless sensor network. In Proceedings of the 10th Iberian Conference on Information Systems and Technologies (CISTI), Aveiro, Portugal, 17–20 June 2015.

15. Orrie, O.; Silva, B.; Hancke, G.P. A wireless smart parking system. In Proceedings of the IECON 2015—41st Annual Conference of the IEEE Industrial Electronics Society, Yokohama, Japan, 9–12 November 2015.

16. Chandra, H.; Hadisaputra, K.R.; Santoso, H.; Anggadjaja, E. Smart Parking Management System: An integration of RFID, ALPR, and WSN. In Proceedings of the IEEE 3rd International Conference on Engineering Technologies and Social Sciences (ICETSS), Bangkok, Thailand, 7–8 August 2017.

17. Gupta, A.; Kulkarni, S.; Jathar, V.; Sharma, V.; Jain, N. Smart Car Parking Management System Using IoT. *Am. J. Sci. Eng. Technol.* **2017**, *2*, 112–119.

18. Tsiropoulou, E.E.; Baras, J.S.; Papavassiliou, S.; Sinha, S. RFID-based smart parking management system. *Cyber-Phys. Syst.* **2017**, 1–20. [CrossRef]

19. Wagh, S.S.; More, A.; Kharote, P.R. Performance Evaluation of IEEE 802.15.4 Protocol under Coexistence of WiFi 802.11b. *Procedia Comput. Sci.* **2015**, *57*, 745–751. [CrossRef]

20. Olasupo, T.O.; Otero, C.E.; Otero, L.D.; Olasupo, K.O.; Kostanic, I. Path Loss Models for Low-Power, Low-Data Rate Sensor Nodes for Smart Car Parking Systems. *IEEE Trans. Intell. Transp. Syst.* **2017**. [CrossRef]

21. Shuaib, K.; Alnuaimi, M.; Boulmalf, M.; Jawhar, I.; Sallabi, F.; Lakas, A. Performance Evaluation of IEEE 802.15.4: Experimental and Simulation Results. *J. Commun.* **2007**, *2*, 29–37. [CrossRef]

Article

Priority-Based Machine-To-Machine Overlay Network over LTE for a Smart City

Nargis Khan [†], Jelena Mišić *,[†] [iD] and Vojislav B. Mišić [†] [iD]

Department of Computer Science, Ryerson University, Toronto, ON M5B 2K3, Canada;
nargis.khan@ryerson.ca (N.K.); vmisic@ryerson.ca (V.B.M.)
* Correspondence: jmisic@ryerson.ca
† These authors contributed equally to this work.

Received: 27 April 2018; Accepted: 10 July 2018; Published: 12 July 2018

Abstract: Long-Term Evolution (LTE) and its improvement, Long-Term Evolution-Advanced (LTE-A), are attractive choices for Machine-to-Machine (M2M) communication due to their ubiquitous coverage and high bandwidth. However, the focus of LTE design was high performance connection-based communications between human-operated devices (also known as human-to-human, or H2H traffic), which was initially established over the Physical Random Access Channel (PRACH). On the other hand, M2M traffic is mostly based on contention-based transmission of short messages and does not need connection establishment. As a result, M2M traffic transmitted over LTE PRACH has to use the inefficient four-way handshake and compete for resources with H2H traffic. When a large number of M2M devices attempts to access the PRACH, an outage condition may occur; furthermore, traffic prioritization is regulated only through age-based power ramping, which drives the network even faster towards the outage condition. In this article, we describe an overlay network that allows a massive number of M2M devices to coexist with H2H traffic and access the network without going through the full LTE handshake. The overlay network is patterned after IEEE 802.15.6 to support multiple priority classes of M2M traffic. We analyse the performance of the joint M2M and H2H system and investigate the trade-offs needed to keep satisfactory performance and reliability for M2M traffic in the presence of H2H traffic of known intensity. Our results confirm the validity of this approach for applications in crowd sensing, monitoring and others utilized in smart city development.

Keywords: LTE; RACH; PRACH; IEEE 802.15.4; IEEE 802.15.6; non-saturation operating regime; backoff error; smart city

---

1. Introduction

In many smart city application scenarios—from building monitoring and healthcare monitoring, through smart parking and smart city lighting, to crowd sensing and vehicular safety applications—a large number of smart devices send their messages to appropriate servers for further analysis and actions, as Figure 1 schematically shows. As monitoring and transmission oftentimes do not require human intervention, such communications are referred to as Machine-to-Machine (M2M) or Machine-Type Communications (MTC) [1]. Networks that support M2M traffic must provide broad coverage, but also message reliability and limited delay. In densely-populated urban areas, such requirements can be achieved through WiFi networks, but in sparsely-populated rural areas and along the highways, one must rely on cellular networks such as LTE/LTE-A (Long-Term Evolution and Long-Term Evolution-Advanced) [2].

In some M2M scenarios, messages arrive regularly with approximately constant inter-arrival times and thus can be transmitted using some kind of scheduled access; this is the case, for example, for healthcare applications, building monitoring and smart city lighting. In other cases such as crowd sensing and vehicular safety, messages arrive randomly and thus may be serviced through contention-based access. In both cases, messages are short, and typical interarrival periods are low when compared to other traffic such as video and data transmitted over LTE. As a result, M2M messages can be transmitted using LTE's Physical Random Access Channel (PRACH), which was originally intended to be used for initial access or area tracking by a terminal (User Equipment (UE)) that is not connected to the base station (eNodeB), for uplink synchronization of a UE that is connected to eNodeB, when a connected UE has to transmit uplink data or to acknowledge received data or when a UE needs to perform a handoff to the target cell [2]. The LTE standard prescribes that PRACH access be performed using a four-way handshake, which is contention-based (the details of random access are presented further in Section 2 below). If PRACH is congested due to a large number of M2M and/or H2H terminals attempting access concurrently, the SINR observed at the receiver (i.e., eNodeB) may be reduced to the extent that messages cannot be detected, and consequently, many of the access attempts will fail; this is denoted as the outage condition. In the past several years, a number of techniques to improve the performance of M2M traffic by alleviating outage due to congestion have been suggested:

1. UEs may be grouped into traffic classes for which random access may be delayed or temporarily blocked. This technique is known as access class barring (which is already supported for H2H calls) and extended access class barring [3].
2. Differentiation among traffic classes can be achieved by allowing different backoff windows for different classes of UEs [4].
3. Further differentiation among the classes can be achieved by allowing members of the traffic class to attempt access only in predefined time slots within specific LTE frames, using base station scheduling [5].
4. The base station can apply a suitable polling scheme (also known as pull-based scheme) to differentiate between UEs. In this scheme, M2M terminals initiate random access only after being paged by the eNodeB [6].
5. PRACH resource separation and dynamic PRACH resource allocation schemes allocate different PRACH resources such as preamble sequences and random access slots to different types of traffic (i.e., H2H and M2M) in a dynamic manner [7].
6. Traffic classes can be differentiated by using different power levels rather than using power ramping based on the age of the attempt [8].
7. Failed calls may be allocated a specific set of preambles to use for repeated access attempts [9].

Recently, an overlay network for M2M traffic was proposed that dedicates a portion of PRACH resources to M2M traffic [10]. The overlay network is based on the CSMA-CA mechanism similar to IEEE 802.15.4 [11] and allows M2M access to be completed without the four-way handshake. H2H traffic concurrently uses remaining resources and is coupled with M2M traffic through the SINR at the eNodeB. Further differentiation is possible using different and explicit power levels for M2M and H2H traffic [12].

However, this approach [10,12] does not address two important aspects of M2M communications. First, differentiation among different traffic classes in the M2M overlay network is needed. Second, SINR coupling between M2M and H2H traffic classes has been considered only at the packet reception level, but not at the level of listening to the medium during the CSMA-CA backoff process. This could produce incorrect durations of the backoff process and a too conservative estimate of the congestion at the overlay network.

In this work, we introduce priority differentiation in the overlay network by using the CSMA-CA similar to IEEE 802.15.6 [13] with modifications necessary to match the existing physical layer derived from PRACH. We model the medium access control algorithm including a model of imprecise listening outcome during the backoff process, which is shown to decrease the capacity of the overlay network to a non-negligible extent. We demonstrate the functionality and performance of our scheme using different schemes and bandwidths of PRACH, as well as PRACH design scenarios for micro- and macro-cells. Using an accurate characterization of noise and interference caused by other calls from the given cell, as well as from the surrounding cells (which is absent from other proposals), we show that the scheme is capable of achieving satisfactory performance, as well as sufficient differentiation between traffic classes. It is, thus, suitable for the massive Machine-Type Communications (mMTC) scenario—i.e., a large number of MTC devices with short messages and low arrival rates—which represents one of the major use cases for the development of 5G radio and network technology [14]. Furthermore, our scheme allows M2M terminals to actually transmit data during PRACH access, which in most cases should suffice given the short messages typical for M2M devices, whereas other schemes use random access to initiate a connection and send actual data only later, which increases message latency and leads to inefficient utilization of the available bandwidth.

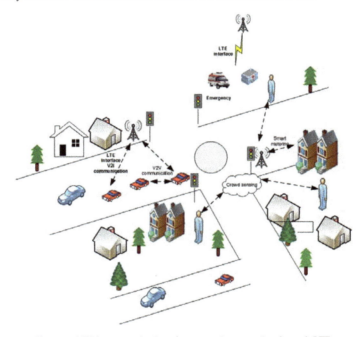

Figure 1. M2M communications for smart city scenarios through LTE.

The rest of the paper is organized as follows: In Section 2, we present the PRACH architecture and random access procedure. In Section 3, we present the M2M overlay network with the physical and MAC layer, preceded by a brief overview of earlier work on such overlays using different WLAN technologies. In Section 4, we present the random access model for H2H and PM2M traffic. The analytical model of PM2M with backoff error is discussed in Section 5. Performance evaluation of H2H and PM2M traffic (with and without the backoff error) is shown in Section 6. Finally, Section 7 concludes the paper.

2. PRACH Architecture and Random Access Procedure

The Physical Random Access Channel (PRACH) allows a UE to establish a connection with the base station (eNodeB) by sending a request to which the eNodeB will respond by scheduling appropriate resources for communications to and/or from the UE. Available bandwidth resources for LTE cell are divided in a time and frequency domain matrix. Time access is organized in frames that last 10 ms and that consist of 10 subframes with a duration of 1-ms each. Subframes can be divided into two 0.5-ms slots. In the frequency domain, resources are grouped in units of 12 OFDM subcarriers with a total bandwidth of 180 kHz. The basic access unit for either random or scheduled access is a Resource Block (RB), which consists of 12 subcarriers over one subframe. Cell bandwidth can be configured in frequency- or time-division duplex (i.e., FDD or TDD operation mode.

PRACH is carved out of the time and frequency domain matrix by dedicating a number of resource blocks in a number of consecutive LTE frames. The basic PRACH resource is composed of six resource blocks in frequency with a bandwidth of 1.080 MHz, for the duration of one subframe; higher traffic volume can be accommodated by allocating more resources, for a total of 16 configurations shown in Figure 2. For low traffic intensity and small system bandwidth, one PRACH resource per two frames may be sufficient (TDMA Configurations 0, 1, 2 and 15). As traffic increases, PRACH resources may be configured to occur once per frame (TDMA Configurations 3, 4 and 5), twice per frame (TDMA Configurations 6, 7 and 8) or even once every three subframes (TDMA Configurations 9, 10 and 11). These configurations avoid interference at a granularity of three neighbouring cells. However, higher traffic may require even more dense PRACH allocations, which brings the possibility of interference since the PRACH resource occurs on every second subframe (Configurations 12 and 13) or on every subframe in a frame (Configuration 14). In the discussions that follow, we will denote the number of PRACH subframes within the frame as configuration index c_f, where $c_f = k$ means that there are k PRACH subframes in the frame.

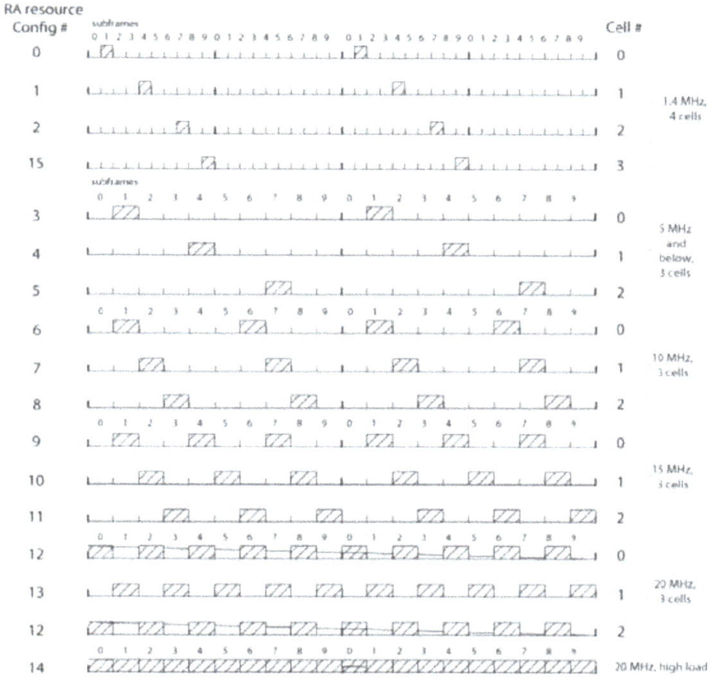

Figure 2. PRACH resource configurations, after [2].

Steps of the Random Access Procedure

The UE that wishes to establish communication with eNodeB needs to the perform random access procedure on PRACH [15] using the four-way handshake (Figure 3), which consists of the following steps:

Step 1: The terminal randomly selects the preamble from the available 54 preamble sequences and transmits it over PRACH to eNodeB.

Step 2: The eNodeB transmits an RA Response (RAR) to the terminal through the physical downlink shared channel (PDSCH). RAR contains temporary Cell Radio Network Temporary Identifier (CRNTI) identity information. It also contains scheduling information for the third step.

Step 3: Then, the terminal sends its CRNTI and scheduling information to eNodeB through the Physical Uplink Shared Channel (PUSCH) radio resources assigned in Step 2.

Step 4: Finally, the eNodeB responds with the confirmation of the identity of the terminal and finishes the contention procedure.

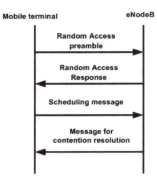

Figure 3. Four-way handshake between UE and eNodeB (after [15]).

Preambles are mutually-orthogonal Zadoff–Chu (ZC) sequences; by default, each cell has a pool of $N = 64$ preambles. A small number of preambles (typically, 10) is reserved for time critical actions like handoff, while the remaining 54 are available for random access. The duration of a preamble depends on the cell size since larger cells have higher signal attenuation and larger propagation delays. Signal attenuation can be countered by a longer preamble time (1600 μs, as opposed to the default value of 800 μs). Propagation delays can be countered by extending the time intervals. As a result, Preamble Format 0 fits in a single 1-ms subframe, Formats 1 and 2 fit into two consecutive subframes, while Format 3 fits into three consecutive subframes [2,15]. The structure of preamble formats is shown in Figure 4, and in the text that follows, we will refer to the format number as $PF = 0..3$.

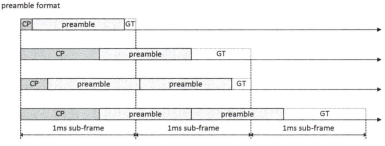

CP: cyclic prefix preceding the actual preamble
GT: guard time at the end of the sub-frame

Figure 4. Different preamble formats.

The rules for calculating preamble sequence length are based on optimizing the number of ZC sequences with respect to cross-correlation properties and minimizing interference from PUSCH in neighbouring cells [2,16,17]. For example, in a typical LTE system with a 5-MHz bandwidth, the bandwidth dedicated to the PRACH channel is $W = 1.08$ MHz. For Format 0, a preamble of total length $N_{ZC} = 839$ elements is transmitted within 800 μs, which gives the preamble element rate of $R = 1.048$ M elements per second.

Unfortunately, the first and third steps of handshaking are prone to collisions and the overload condition due to the limited number of preambles. The resulting low SINR value prevents completion of the RA handshake [10] in the case of high traffic volume, which is likely in the case of massive M2M access. In a nutshell, the use of the four-way handshaking procedure of LTE for massive network access is inefficient and leads to SINR outage at the eNodeB [2]. This has motivated our research efforts towards a PRACH overlay architecture.

3. PM2M Overlay Network over PRACH

3.1. Earlier Work on Overlays in LTE

In [18], an IEEE 802.15.4-based VANET was proposed for implementing the VANET Control Channel (CCH) in urban areas. IEEE 802.15.4 has a low power consumption feature, which is an advantage over IEEE 802.11p's high power consumption. In [19–21], a comparative study between IEEE 802.11p and LTE aimed to evaluate their suitability for different vehicular applications and finding, using analytical and simulation modelling, that the latter has a distinct advantage over IEEE 802.11p-based VANET for transmission of safety messages was shown [22]. Other studies have shown that LTE supports mobility and provides higher network capacity compared with IEEE 802.11p [20]. However, LTE was found not to provide sufficient reliability in terms of safety messages transmitted over PRACH, as the network can easily become overloaded [21,23]. The main culprit is the four-way handshake, which for small safety messages limits the capacity and increases the latency [10]. Additionally, the data rate for VANET safety messages remains constant regardless of the distance to eNodeB and the closeness of congestion, while in IEEE 802.11p, it can be adaptively adjusted according to the channel quality [24].

Before the introduction of the IEEE 802.15.6 standard, IEEE 802.15.4 and Bluetooth were considered as feasible physical and MAC layer protocols for healthcare applications. In [25], the authors did a comparative study between the IEEE 802.15.4 and IEEE 802.15.6-based MAC protocols for healthcare systems. The study showed that IEEE 802.15.4 cannot reliably transmit real-time medical data because it does not support high data rate applications and priority among traffic classes. The simulation study showed that IEEE 802.15.4 is suitable only for applications that require a data rate below 40 kbps, while applications requiring higher data rates should use the IEEE 802.15.6-based network. In [26], it was shown that there is no interference when WiMAX or LTE are integrated with IEEE 802.15.6. To enlarge the radio coverage, the authors in [27] integrated IEEE 802.15.6 with LTE because they showed that existing architectures were not suitable for the scenarios of high mobility due to the channel quality fluctuation.

The performance of a healthcare system through interconnecting IEEE 802.15.6 with IEEE 802.11e-based WLAN for a medical information system was studied in [28]. The proposed architecture used the RTS/CTS mechanism for accessing the medium in the WLAN, which caused overload in the network and coexistence issues. That work also did not consider the presence of backoff error due to the interference in the physical layer while accessing the medium to transmit the packets. In [26], it was shown that there is no interference when WiMax or LTE are integrated with the IEEE 802.15.6 network. It was proposed in [27] that LTE supports reliable data transmission with high data rates for real-time health messages over large coverage areas.

3.2. Superframe Structure of PM2M

The superframe structure of the proposed Priority-based Machine-to-Machine (PM2M) overlay network is shown in Figure 5. Time is organized in beacon-delineated superframes that start immediately after the reception of beacon; UEs send their messages in the CSMA-CA manner after completing the backoff procedure, as explained below. eNodeB has to acknowledge the message, otherwise the message will be retransmitted until the retransmission limit is reached. While H2H traffic will continue to follow the four-way handshake to access the network, the PM2M overlay network reduces four-way handshake to a simpler two-way one.

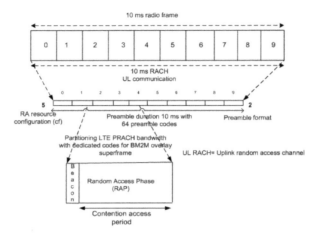

Figure 5. LTE and Priority-based Machine-to-Machine (PM2M) overlay superframe with PF = 2 (2-ms subframe).

3.3. Physical and MAC Layer

The physical layer of the M2M overlay network is implemented by selecting $N_M = 8$ of the 54 sequences available for contention-based access and dedicating them to M2M access. Data bits from the M2M stream are multiplexed on M2M preambles so that each sequence carries a single bit from each data byte. To transmit a single M2M data bit, $N_b = 16$ preamble elements are used as a kind of 'chipping' sequence, the size of which affects the performance as SINR increases by $10 \log_{10} N_b$. Higher SINR is needed for the detection of M2M data bits since an H2H preamble is detected based on the SINR over its entire duration, while only a portion of that duration is used by M2M packets.

Performance is also affected by the number of ZC codes dedicated to M2M, as these are bundled together so that each code carries $\frac{8}{N_M}$ bits of each user's byte. The physical layer data rate is, then, $R_M = \frac{RN_M}{N_b}$, where R is the preamble element rate.

In this scheme, each PRACH resource holds a single PM2M superframe, which makes CSMA-CA access possible. For the Medium Access Control (MAC) layer, PM2M access is configured as a CSMA-CA overlay. The time for preamble transmission becomes the superframe time for the PM2M overlay network. We consider the IEEE 802.15.6 beacon mode with beacon period boundaries where at the beginning of every superframe, a beacon is transmitted on the medium. The superframe time after the beacon is divided into slots each containing 20 bits. The superframe is divided into an Access Phase (AP) and Random Access Phase 1 (RAP1); all other access phases allowed by the standard will have zero length. We do not use the RTS/CTS handshake, nor the four-way handshake of LTE, as they would easily overload the PRACH.

CSMA-CA access in the superframe resembles the one used in the beacon-enabled IEEE 802.15.6. In the CSMA-CA overlay, one backoff period has 20 sequence elements, i.e., $tboff = 20/R = 18.51$ μs. To implement the overlay superframe, we use Preamble Format 2, where the preamble duration is 1.6 ms. Access in Format 2 is achieved by repeating the same preamble twice. Finally, to achieve a continuous superframe sequence without coordinated node sleeping, we assume configuration index $c_f = 5$.

3.4. Priority Mapping

IEEE 802.15.6 provides priorities through the Contention Window (CW) and Access Categories (AC). There are eight different ACs with different minimum and maximum CW values, which define User Priorities (UP) to access the medium, as shown in Table 1.

Table 1. IEEE 802.15.6 Access Categories (AC) with User Priorities (UP) and Contention Window (CW) values.

UP	Traffic	CW_{min}	CW_{max}
0	Background (BK)	16	64
1	Best Effort (BE)	16	32
2	Excellent Effort (EF)	8	32
3	Controlled Load (CL)	8	16
4	Video (VI)	4	16
5	Voice	4	8
6	Network control	2	8
7	Emergency or medical event data	1	4

4. Modelling PRACH for H2H and PM2M Traffic

We now present the analytical model of random access, beginning with H2H terminals. Although the population of H2H terminals in a single LTE/LTE-A cell is large, they attempt random access occasionally and infrequently, which means that we may assume that H2H requests arrive according to a Poisson distribution. The mean arrival rate λ_w of H2H traffic can be calculated for a single PRACH resource as, $\lambda_{WH} = (\lambda_w T_f)/c_f$, where T_f is the LTE superframe time and c_f determines the number of PRACH resource blocks per LTE frame.

LTE PRACH is overloaded by preamble transmissions with potential collisions and external interference caused by the random access in surrounding cells. To detect a signal successfully at the eNodeB, the Signal to Interference Noise Ratio (SINR) should exceed a certain threshold value as indicated in Figure 17.12 in [2]. For example, a threshold value of $18dB$ guarantees that the probability of preamble missed detection is smaller than 10^{-2} and the probability of false alarm is less than 10^{-3} for eNodeB. For H2H terminals, SINR is the ratio of preamble sequence energy over noise power density, for n H2H terminals concurrently performing access including initial and handoff requests. Assuming all transmissions use the same power level, the aforementioned ratio is:

$$E_{seq}/N_0 = \frac{\frac{P_{seq}I_1}{R}}{\frac{(n-1)I_1+N_M I_1+\eta_{p,1}+\eta_0 W}{W}}$$

$$= P_{seq}\frac{W/R}{n-1+N_M+\eta_{p,1}/I_1+\eta_0 W/I_1} \tag{1}$$

where
P_{seq} is the preamble sequence length in bits;
W is the LTE PRACH bandwidth;
R is the LTE PRACH preamble data rate;
I_1 is the received signal power;
$\eta_{p,1}$ is the power of external (Gaussian) interference;
η_0 is the spectral density of white noise; and
N_M is the number of preambles that are always active for the PM2M overlay.

The ratio of the outer cell interference and received signal power $\eta_{p,1}/I_1$ of PRACH follows a Gaussian distribution with mean and variance denoted by $k_{m,1}$ and $k_{v,1}$ [10]. In the case of the threshold being exceeded, the overload condition occurs, and the preamble cannot be detected successfully. The probability of PRACH overload in the first handshake step is:

$$O\_PRACH_n = P_r(n + \frac{\eta_{p,1}}{I_1} > \frac{W}{RT_1} - N_M - \frac{W\eta_0}{I_1}) \tag{2}$$

The PRACH overload for third handshake step for j concurrent H2H terminals is:

$$Q\_PRACH_j = P_r(j + \frac{\eta_{p3}}{I_3} > \frac{W_3}{R_3 T_3} - \frac{W_3 \eta_0}{I_3}) \tag{3}$$

We assume that spectral efficiency in the third handshake step is the same as the first step, $\frac{W_3}{R_3} = \frac{W}{R}$. The SINR threshold in this step is -5 dB because it is observed over a single bit. The ratio of the outer cell interference and received signal power $\frac{\eta_{p3}}{I_3}$ of PRACH follows a Gaussian distribution with mean and variance denoted by $k_{m,3}$ and $k_{v,3}$ [10].

4.1. H2H PRACH Overload/Outage during Preamble Collision

LTE PRACH may experience the outage condition by having large access traffic, possibly with preamble collisions. To calculate the probability of PRACH outage/overload, we need to know the total Poisson arrival rate of access on a single PRACH resource block including new, returning and handoff calls, $\lambda_{total} = \lambda + \lambda_{pc1} + \lambda_{pc3} + \lambda_h$. The probability of n arrivals is:

$$P_n = \frac{(\lambda_{total})^n}{n!} e^{-\lambda_{total}} \tag{4}$$

For n H2H access attempts in PRACH resources, from overload Equation (2), we obtain the overload probability as:

$$O\_PRACH_n = erfc(\frac{\frac{W}{R}\frac{1}{T_1} - \frac{W\eta_0}{I_1} - n + 1 - N_M - k_{m,1}}{\sqrt{k_{v,1}}}) \tag{5}$$

where $erfc$ is a complementary error function,

$$erfc(x) = \frac{2}{\sqrt{(\pi)}} \int_x^\infty e^{-\frac{t^2}{2}} dt \tag{6}$$

Thus, the total overload probability for the first handshake step due to collision and interference is obtained by averaging the H2H load as:

$$\begin{aligned} P_{O,1} &= \sum_{n=2}^{n_{max}} P_n O\_PRACH_n \\ &= \sum_{n=2}^{n_{max}} \frac{(\lambda_{total})^n}{n!} e^{-\lambda_{total}} O\_PRACH_n \end{aligned} \tag{7}$$

where n_{max} is a sufficiently large number.

For the third handshake step, the collision probability that H2H terminals collide when $j > 1$ is:

$$P_3(j) = e^{-\lambda_i, L_3} \frac{\lambda_{i,L_3}^j}{j!} \tag{8}$$

where λ_{i,L_3} denotes the arrival rate of the third step L_2/L_3 messages.

Now, to find the overload probability of the third handshake step, the overload probability of Equation (3) can be written for different values of bandwidth, spectral efficiency and SINR:

$$Q\_PRACH_j = erfc(\frac{\frac{W_3}{R_3}\frac{1}{T_3} - \frac{W_3\eta_0}{I_3} - j - k_{m,3}}{\sqrt{k_{v,3}}}) \tag{9}$$

Thus, the overall PRACH overload probability for the third handshake step with preamble collision and inter-cell interference is:

$$P_Q = \frac{\sum_{j=2}^{j} P_3(j)Q\_PRACH_j}{\sum_{j=2}^{j} P_3(j)} \tag{10}$$

4.2. PM2M Overload Calculation

The Bit Error Rate (BER) of the PM2M overlay depends on the interference caused by H2H traffic. We estimate the interference through the bit error rate BER experienced by PM2M traffic. To this end, we need to find the outage/overload probability of PM2M based on SINR requirements for PRACH, which can be expressed as:

$$E_b/N_0 = \frac{\frac{N_b I_1}{R}}{\frac{(n)I_1 + (N_M - 1)I_1 + \eta_{p,1} + \eta_0 W}{W}}$$
$$= N_b \frac{W/R}{n + N_M - 1 + \eta_{p,1}/I_1 + \eta_0 W/I_1} \tag{11}$$

where
N_b is the number of preamble elements;
W is the LTE bandwidth;
R is the LTE PRACH preamble data rate;
I_1 is the received signal power;
$\eta_{p,1}$ is the outer cell interference power; η_0 is the spectral density of white noise; and
N_M is the number of PM2M preamble codes that are always active.

The overload probability of PM2M data on each preamble can be derived analogously to Equations (2) and (5) as:

$$M\_oload_n = P_r(n + \frac{\eta_{p,1}}{I_1} > \frac{WN_b}{RT_M} - N_M - \frac{W\eta_0}{I_1})$$
$$= erfc(\frac{\frac{WN_b}{R}\frac{1}{T_M} - \frac{W\eta_0}{I_1} - n - N_M + 1 - k_{m,1}}{\sqrt{k_{v,1}}}) \tag{12}$$

Then, the total PM2M overload probability can be obtained as:

$$P_{M\_oload} = \sum_{n=0}^{\infty} P_n M\_oload_n$$
$$= \sum_{n=2}^{n_{max}} \frac{(\lambda_{total})^n}{n!} e^{-\lambda_{total}} M\_oload_n \tag{13}$$

Using the PM2M overload probability, we could approximate the BER as half of the overload:

$$BER_{PM2M} = 0.5 P_{M\_oload} \tag{14}$$

5. Modelling the PM2M Backoff Procedure with Backoff Error

Let us now present the analytical model for the CSMA-CA backoff procedure. We model backoff errors that occur when a UE incorrectly estimates the state of the channel. Our modelling is based on elements developed in [13] with necessary modifications regarding the superframe structure and coupling with the physical layer. The physical layer influences clear channel assessment at MAC. The latter comes due to SINR, which depends on H2H traffic and preambles belonging to the physical layer of the overlay network.

We consider a single-hop PM2M overlay network with H2H terminals in a single LTE/LTE-A cell. The system works in the non-saturation condition where the packet queue does not always have a packet to transmit and each UE experiences an idle period when its queue is empty. The model consists of two three-dimensional Discrete Time Markov Chains (DTMCs). Note that the physical layer of our proposed architecture is different from that in [13] since our physical layer is implemented with dedicated preambles and we do not use RTS/CTS to avoid creating extra overload on the PRACH.

We consider two user priorities, $UP_k, k = 0, 1$, where Indices 0 and 1 refer to lower and higher priority traffic class, respectively. All the time scales are presented in slots and modified according to the LTE time scale. The backoff value of a UP_k node is distributed uniformly over the interval $[1, CW_k]$. CW_k has the minimum value of $CW_{k,min} = W_{k,i}$ where $i = 0$. The maximum contention window value is $CW_{k,max} = W_{k,max_k}$, corresponding to the maximum number of retries $R = 7$. User priorities are differentiated according to the values of CW; see Table 1. We assume that a packet is dropped if the number of unsuccessful attempts exceeds the retry limit R. Contention window values for a user priority UP_k node for the i-th backoff phase are calculated as follows:

- Initially, $W_{k,i} = W_{k,min} = CW_{k,min}$, where $i = 0$.
- The contention window value doubles when, $W_{k,i} = min\{2W_{k,i-1}, CW_{k,max}\}$, for $2 <= i <= R$, if i is an even number
- The contention window value increases uniformly when, $W_{k,i} = W_{k,i-1}$, for $1 <= i <= R$, if i is an odd number.

We calculate the probability that neither the data nor the subsequent acknowledgement (ack) packet are corrupted by noise as:

$$\sigma = (1 - BER_{PM2M})^{dt_s + ak_s} \tag{15}$$

where BER_{PM2M} is the bit error rate caused by interference from H2H traffic and dt_s, ak_s represent the data and acknowledgement size in slots.

In IEEE 802.15.6, during the CSMA-CA medium access, a UE senses the medium before decrementing the backoff counter. If the medium is sensed as busy, the node will freeze the backoff counter until the medium is sensed to be idle. The UE senses the status of the medium in backoff periods equivalent to 20-bit periods. Listening in each bit period may give an erroneous result with the probability BER_{PM2M}. If more than half of the bits are wrong, the UE arrives at the wrong listening decision for a given backoff period with the probability of:

$$PB_{err} = \sum_{nb=11}^{20} \binom{20}{B} BER_{PM2M}^B (1 - BER_{PM2M})^{20-nb} \tag{16}$$

We develop a three-dimensional Discrete Time Markov Chain (DTMC) to model the backoff procedure of the CSMA-CA mechanism with backoff error only for two traffic classes and the Random Access Phase (RAP), as depicted in Figure 6. To calculate the average backoff time, we calculate all possible backoff phases during the CSMA-CA countdown and extend three-dimensional DTMCs to four-dimensional ones for all UPs, as shown in Figure 7.

The medium access probability τ_k of a UP_k node, where $k = 0, 1$ during RAP is calculated by solving the two dependent DTMCs derived by extending the framework from [13] with the probability of backoff error. The access probability is calculated only when the medium is idle and nodes are competing to get access. The incorrect idle medium probability in CSMA slots where all n_i nodes with priority i perform access is:

$$m\_idle_{Aerr} = \sum_{i=0}^{7} PB_{err}(1 - \tau_i)^{n_i} \tag{17}$$

and the probability that the medium is busy is:

$$m\_busy = 1 - m\_idle_{Aerr} \tag{18}$$

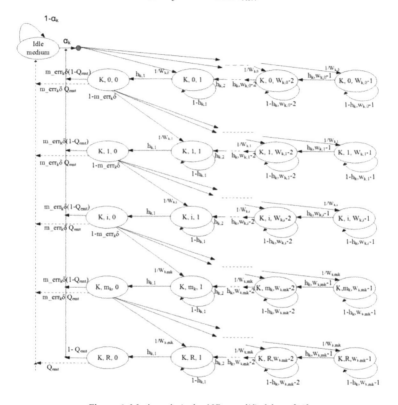

Figure 6. Markov chain for UP_k, modified from [13].

Then, we evaluate the probability of the medium being idle as observed by UE of class $k \in (0, 1)$ during the backoff countdown (which means that other nodes do not access the medium during the current RAP) as:

$$m\_err_k = \frac{m\_idle_{Aerr}}{1 - \tau_k} \tag{19}$$

During a given backoff countdown, there is a possibility that there is not enough time in the superframe (RAP) to complete the countdown and the transmission. The probability of this event is:

$$S\_time_k = \frac{1}{X_{RAP} - T_{succ} - C_k} \tag{20}$$

where
$T_{succ} = (data_s + ack_s + sifs)$ is the successful transmission time in slots;

$C_k = \frac{CW_{k,min} + CW_{k,max}}{4}$ is the approximate mean backoff counter value; and $T_{coll} = (data_s + ack_s + sifs)$ is the unsuccessful transmission time. In all cases, SIFS refers to short interframe space [11].

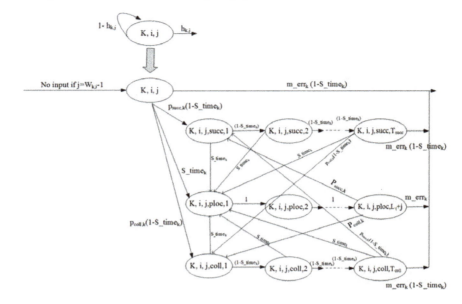

Figure 7. Extended Markov chain for UP_k modified from [13].

Now, we have to calculate the probability that the backoff counter value of a node will be unfrozen (i.e., decremented) for $j = 1 .. W_{k,m_k}$:

$$h_{k,j} = m\_err_k(1 - S\_time_k \frac{1 - m\_err_k^j}{1 - m\_err_k}) \tag{21}$$

The indices of state probabilities $b_{k,i,j}$ of the Markov chain as shown in Figure 6 are $k = 0 \ldots 1$, $i = 0 \ldots R$ and $j = 0 \ldots W_{k,i}$. The medium access probability is calculated as $\tau_k = \sum_0^R b_{k,i,o}$.

We have to calculate the zeroth backoff phase, which depends on the probability of the CSMA slot being in the idle state, the probability that the queue is empty due to successful transmission or dropped because of the exceeded retry limit. In our model, we adopt the expression for the probability of the queue being empty Q_{emt} from [13]. Then, the probability of being in the idle state may also refer to the wrong medium status in the presence of backoff error. Assuming that the probability of the data frame arrival during the interval between two successive Markov points is denoted as α, the probability of the idle state is calculated as:

$$S_{idle,k} = PB_{err} \frac{\tau_k m\_err_k \sigma_k Q_{empt}}{\alpha_k (1 - (1 - m\_err_k \sigma_k)^{R+1})} \tag{22}$$

Thus, the sum of all DTMC states belonging of the zeroth backoff phase for traffic class k is:

$$Z_{boff,k} = \frac{\tau_k m\_err_k \sigma_k (1 - Q_{emt}) + S_{idle,k} \alpha}{1 - (1 - m\_err_k \sigma_k)^{R+1}(1 - Q_{emt})} \tag{23}$$

The normalization condition for DTMCs of each class requires that the sum of all the state probabilities is one. By solving the system of equations belonging to the DTMC of each traffic class and coupling the equation for the behaviour of medium, we calculate the medium access probability for each traffic class with backoff error, $\tau_k, k = 0, 1$, during RAP as:

$$1 = S_{idle,k} + Z_{boff} \sum_{i=0}^{R} (1 - m\_err_k)^i (1 + \sum_{j=1}^{W_{k,i}} \frac{W_{k,i} - j + 1}{W_{k,i} m\_err_k \sigma_k}) \tag{24}$$

During the CSMA-CA mechanism when a node tries to get access to the medium, it has to backoff and lock the backoff counter if the channel is busy due to a transmission by another node, be it ultimately successful or not; or there is not enough time in the current superframe to complete the frame transmission.

The node unlocks the backoff counter again when the channel is idle for the SIFS period within the superframe time, and the current superframe has enough time to complete the frame transaction.

All of the above conditions work fine in the absence of backoff error. However, in the presence of backoff error, the node could decide that the medium is idle and unlock the backoff counter when the medium is actually busy, which could lead to excessive collisions in the overlay network. Alternatively, the node may freeze the backoff counter when it should not; this leads to longer backoffs and possibly to relegating a transmission to the next superframe.

We added the backoff error in the DTMC for the backoff procedure for traffic class k, as shown in Figure 7, and calculated the Probability Generating Functions (PGFs) of times for the important phases:

- $Ebfsucc_{k,j}(z)$, the time period between the locking and unlocking of the backoff counter due to successful transmission by another node.
- $Ebfcoll_{k,j}(z)$, the duration of unsuccessful transmission.
- $Ebfploc_{k,j}(z)$, the time between locking and unlocking when there is not enough time for completing a packet transmission.

All of the above conditions are modelled for the RAP access phase with two traffic classes $k = 0, 1$, with $j = 1 .. W_{k,m_k}$ being the backoff counter value for the locked condition. We calculate the PGFs for the three periods stated above as:

$$Ebfsucc_{k,j}(z) = S\_time_k Ebfp_{k,j}(z) \frac{1 - (1 - S\_time_k)^{T_{succ}} z^{T_{succ}}}{(1 - (1 - S\_time_k)z)} + (1 - S\_time_k)^{T_{succ}} m\_err_k z^{T_{succ}}$$
$$+ (1 - S\_time_k)^{T_{succ}} (p_{succ,k} Ebfsucc_{k,j}(z) + p_{coll,k} Ebfcoll_{k,j}(z)) \tag{25}$$

$$Ebfcoll_{k,j}(z) = S\_time_k Ebfp_{k,j}(z)(1 - (1 - S\_time_k)^{T_{coll}} z^{T_{coll}}) / (1 - (1 - S\_time_k)z))$$
$$+ (1 - S\_time_k)^{T_{coll}} m\_err_k z^{T_{coll}} + (1 - S\_time_k)^{T_{coll}} (p_{succ,k} Ebfsucc_{k,j}(z) \tag{26}$$
$$+ p_{coll,k} Ebfcoll_{k,j}(z))$$

$$Ebfploc_{k,j}(z) = z^{L_{t,k}+j} (m\_err_k z + (p_{succ,k} Ebfsucc_{k,j}(z) + p_{coll,k} Ebfcoll_{k,j}(z))) \tag{27}$$

where the parameters used in the derivations are as follows:

S_time_k is the probability that there is not enough time to complete a frame transaction in the current RAP;

$T_{succ} = (data + ack + 3sifs)$ is the successful transmission time in slots;

T_{coll} is the unsuccessful transmission time in slots;

$P_{succ,k}$ is the probability of locking the backoff counter due to successful transmission by others;

$P_{coll,k}$ is the probability of locking the backoff counter due to unsuccessful transmission by others; and

$L_t = (X_{RAP} + data + ack + 3sifs)$ is the number of CSMA slots when the backoff counter must be locked due to insufficient time for completing the transaction.

All of the above equations are solved to compute the values of unknown variables and model the duration of periods when the backoff counter is locked on the transition probabilities of the Markov chain with backoff error. Then, we proceed to find the mean number of backoff attempts in the presence of the backoff evaluation error, which, for traffic class k, has the probability $b_{attmp,k} = m\_err_k \sigma[k]$.

The duration of the backoff process has a truncated geometric distribution with respect to the number of backoff phases, and we need to find the scaling factor, which corresponds to the probability that the backoff process does not complete within R attempts:

$$P_{scale} = 1 - B_{attmp}(X = R) = 1 - \sum_{R=1}^{7} (b_{attmp,k}(1 - b_{attmp,k})^R) \tag{28}$$

which gives:

$$B_{att,k}(z) = \frac{(b_{attmp},z)(1 - ((1 - b_{attmp,k}z))^{R+1})}{(1 - (1 - (b_{attmp,k}z)))P_{scale}} \tag{29}$$

Then, the mean number of backoff attempts ($B\_N_{amp,k}$) for the traffic class $k \in (0,1)$ node before a successful access to the medium is:

$$B\_N_{attmp,k} = \frac{\partial}{\partial z} B_{att,k}(z)|_{z=1} \tag{30}$$

6. Performance Evaluation

6.1. Performance of H2H Traffic in the Presence of the Overlay Network

We consider the LTE cells with a mix of H2H and M2M traffic, using the PRACH and PM2M overlay parameters given in Table 2.

Table 2. Parameters of PRACH and the PM2M overlay network.

Parameter	Value
codes per cell, N	64
codes for H2H traffic, N_i	46
codes for PM2M overlay traffic, N_M	8
LTE frame duration	540 overlay backoff periods
LTE system bandwidth	5 MHz
PRACH bandwidth	$W = 1.08$ MHz
preamble length	839 elements
preamble duration	1600 μs
preamble elements	$N_b = 16$
preamble format	2
RACH configuration index	$c_f = 5$
preamble element rate	$R_p rate = 1.048$ M elements
traffic class	TC_0 and TC_1
one backoff period	18.51 μs
superframe beacon interval	540 backoff periods
PM2M superframe duration	410 backoff periods
PM2M MAC data packet size	150 bytes with header
Maximum number of attempts to transmit the packet, R	7

We first evaluate the performance of H2H traffic in the presence of PM2M overlay. The H2H request arrival rate was varied between 20 and 220 requests per second. Figure 8a shows the H2H probability of success, which remains within 99% up to 220 H2H calls/s. The collision probability shown in Figure 8b is only 0.0045, which validates the probability of success. The presence of the overlay network is not overloading the cell with respect to H2H traffic, as shown in Figure 8c, where we observe that, for the H2H arrival rate up to 220 calls/s, the overload probability for H2H traffic is only 0.00065, which is very low indeed. The mean access delay (Figure 8d) is essentially flat, with only a slight increase from 14.500 ms–14.556 ms in the observed range. Note that these performance limits would apply to M2M devices in case they use regular LTE access on PRACH: in other words, the random access procedure on PRACH is able to accommodate only about 220 calls per second, be they posted by H2H or M2M users.

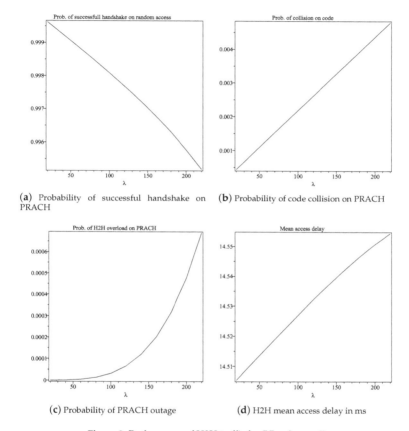

(**a**) Probability of successful handshake on PRACH

(**b**) Probability of code collision on PRACH

(**c**) Probability of PRACH outage

(**d**) H2H mean access delay in ms

Figure 8. Performance of H2H traffic for $PF = 2$, $c_f = 5$.

6.2. Performance of the PM2M Overlay Network without Backoff Error

We evaluate the performance of the PM2M overlay network for two traffic classes and for the contention-based RAP, with and without the backoff error, for H2H traffic intensity set to 100 calls/s. We consider the non-saturation condition, which means that the UE buffer will not always have a data frame to transmit. We assume that the data packet size is 30 bytes, including MAC headers of 10 bytes (where the cell and node ID should be) and the remaining 20 bytes used for MAC data.

We first investigate the capacity of the PM2M overlay network on PRACH by neglecting the error in clear channel assessment. The packet arrival rate per M2M node was set in the range between 0.4 and two packets/s, while the number of PM2M nodes was varied between 300 and 1560. The upper bound for the number of nodes was selected so as to capture reasonable decline in transmission success probability.

Figures 9a and 10a show the probability of successful packet transmission for Traffic Classes 0 and 1. We notice that Traffic Class 1 achieves a 5% higher success probability than Traffic Class 0 for 1560 nodes. The mean backoff time for Classes 0 and 1, for 1560 nodes, was 98 and 35 backoff periods, respectively, as shown in Figures 9b and 10b. This is reasonable since lower the priority traffic class with a higher contention window value has to backoff for a longer period of time than the higher priority class with shorter contention window. Medium access probabilities are shown in Figures 9c and 10c. We notice that Traffic Class 1 has up to a 15% higher access probability.

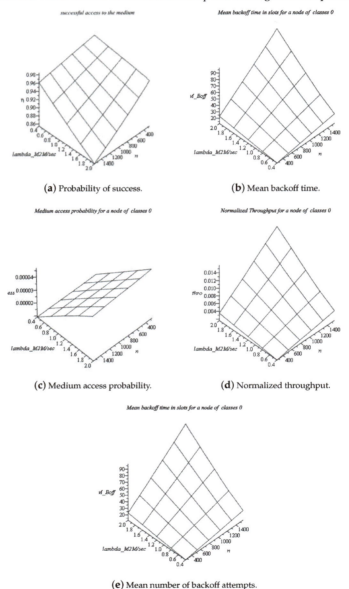

(**a**) Probability of success.

(**b**) Mean backoff time.

(**c**) Medium access probability.

(**d**) Normalized throughput.

(**e**) Mean number of backoff attempts.

Figure 9. Performance of the PM2M overlay for Traffic Class 0 without backoff error.

We calculate the normalized throughput for each node, which was defined as the fraction of time in which the channel is used to transmit the frames' payload. Figures 9d and 10d show that the throughput of TC_1 is almost three-times higher than TC_0 for 1560 PM2M nodes and the highest data arrival rate. The mean number of backoff attempts is shown in Figures 9e and 10e for Traffic Classes 0 and 1, respectively; again, we note the slight disadvantage of Traffic Class 0 with respect to Class 1.

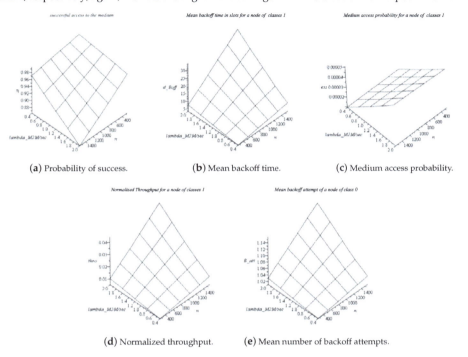

(**a**) Probability of success.　　(**b**) Mean backoff time.　　(**c**) Medium access probability.

(**d**) Normalized throughput.　　(**e**) Mean number of backoff attempts.

Figure 10. Performance of the PM2M overlay for Traffic Class 1 without backoff error.

6.3. Performance of the PM2M Overlay with Backoff Error

We evaluate the performance of PM2M with backoff error for both traffic classes under the same conditions as in the previous experiment, except that the number of nodes was ranging between 300 and 1320. As before, these values were chose to result in the decrease of the probability of successful access to the medium in the range similar to the case without backoff error, as considered in the previous subsection.

We found that we can accommodate up to about 1320 nodes for each traffic class in the same range of transmission success probability, which represents a 12% decrease of overlay network capacity. The transmission success probability for 1320 nodes and a packet arrival rate of two packets per second is close to 0.83 and 0.87 for Traffic Classes 0 and 1, respectively. The mean number of backoff periods in slots for Classes 0 and 1, shown in Figures 11b and 12b, reaches 33 slots and 100 slots, respectively, under the highest load. The medium access probability (Figures 11c and 12c) is about 10–15% lower for class TC_0 than for the higher priority class TC_1. Figure 12d shows that the throughput of TC_1 is almost three-times higher than TC_0 (Figure 11d) under the highest load. Regarding the mean number of backoff attempts, Figure 11e shows that lower traffic class TC_0 has to perform slightly more backoff attempts than higher priority traffic class TC_1 (Figure 12e), as we expected with the presence of backoff error.

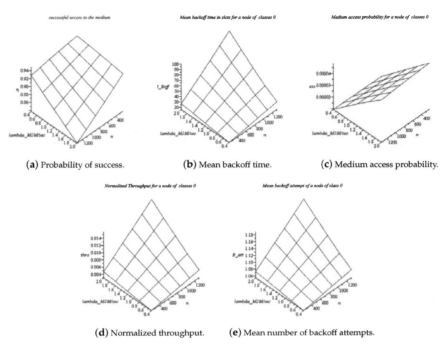

(**a**) Probability of success. (**b**) Mean backoff time. (**c**) Medium access probability.

(**d**) Normalized throughput. (**e**) Mean number of backoff attempts.

Figure 11. Performance of the PM2M overlay for traffic class TC_0 with backoff error.

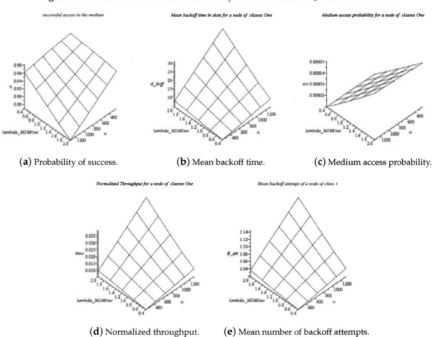

(**a**) Probability of success. (**b**) Mean backoff time. (**c**) Medium access probability.

(**d**) Normalized throughput. (**e**) Mean number of backoff attempts.

Figure 12. Performance of the PM2M overlay for traffic class TC_1 with backoff error.

6.4. Discussion

It may seem that 1320 and 1560 M2M calls per second, obtained through the use of the PM2M overlay, are not that impressive a performance limit. However, it is known that there are "major difficulties in carrying the M2M traffic of more than 2000 UEs with an acceptable success ratio, even when all the 64 available preambles are dedicated TO M2M contention-based access" [29]. Improvements are reported when more preambles are used, up to 500 in [29], even though this is highly unrealistic. Namely, ZC sequences are mutually orthogonal, but they nonetheless cause interference with each other and decrease the achievable SINR. An increased number of preambles thus leads to increased error probability and degraded performance.

On the contrary, the PM2M overlay described here achieves this level of performance by using only eight out of 54 available ZC preambles, as explained in Section 3.3, which leaves the remaining 46 free for use with H2H traffic (10 preambles are set aside for handoff H2H calls); when 16 preambles are used, our CSMA overlay scheme can accommodate up to 2000 devices [12], which clearly shows its superiority over plain LTE random access for M2M calls.

A different scheme has been recently proposed that tries to resolve collisions and, presumably, improve performance by reassigning a subset of available preambles to calls that failed an access attempt [9]. However, they use a simplified error calculation based on slotted ALOHA, which does not account for interference caused by simultaneous random access attempts and/or other channels in the neighbouring cells. Moreover, their scheme requires modification of PRACH handling for M2M traffic, as all M2M nodes are required to listen to eNodeB announcements through which the subset of preambles used for repeated access is publicized, as it changes from one PRACH resource to the next one.

Unlike those schemes, our analysis uses the SINR calculation given in [2], which explicitly models the interference from other random access attempts both in the given and surrounding cells, which allows for more accurate and more realistic results. Furthermore, we model the impact of errors made during the medium sensing process, which no other scheme takes into account.

Finally, we note that all other schemes use random access just to initiate connection and obtain resources, as is common for H2H calls, and the actual data are sent later. In contrast, our scheme allows short messages typical for M2M devices to be actually transmitted during random access, which would lead to reduced latency and improved performance.

7. Conclusions

In this work, we have presented an IEEE 802.15.6-based overlay network that allows the LTE network to support massive M2M traffic with priorities over PRACH. The PM2M overlay operates by dedicating a number of available preambles to the physical layer of the overlay network; the remaining preambles can be used for LTE-prescribed random access by regular LTE UEs. We have modelled the performance of the overlay, as well as the mutual interference of H2H and PM2M traffic when both are present in the LTE cell and the performance of the PM2M overlay with and without the errors in the clear channel sense performed during the backoff countdown. Our results indicate, first, that the H2H traffic still enjoys fair access to the PRACH despite the presence of the PM2M overlay. Second, the PM2M overlay is capable of accommodating up to about 1500 M2M devices in a single cell with default LTE capacity. Third, the backoff error reduces this capacity by about 12% compared to the case with perfect channel sensing. In both cases, the PM2M overlay is capable of providing sufficient differentiation between low- and high-priority traffic classes given the backoff period. Our results show that including backoff error decreases overlay capacity by approximately 12% compared to the perfect clear channel assessment. We have also evaluated priority differentiation in the overlay network using different sizes of backoff windows. Therefore, we could consider a higher priority traffic class for more critical mMTC applications, such as vehicular safety, and a lower priority traffic class for applications with less stringent requirements, such as crowd sensing, thus making it suitable for a wide range of smart city applications.

Author Contributions: J.M. did the conceptualization and designed the methodology. N.K. did the investigation and adapted the methodology under the supervision of J.M. Validation was performed by J.M. and V.B.M. Original draft was written by N.K., and subsequently reviewed and edited by J.M. and V.B.M.

Funding: This research was funded by National Science and Engineering Research Council of Canada (NSERC) through Discovery Grant program.

Conflicts of Interest: The authors declare no conflict of interest. The founding sponsors had no role in the design of the study; in the collection, analyses, or interpretation of data; in the writing of the manuscript, and in the decision to publish the results.

References

1. Mišić, V.B.; Mišić, J. (Eds.) *Machine-to-Machine Communications—Architectures, Technology, Standards, and Applications*; CRC Press: Boca Raton, FL, USA, 2014.
2. Sesia, S.; Toufik, I.; Baker, M. *LTE, the UMTS Long Term Evolution: From Theory to Practice*; John Wiley & Sons: Hoboken, NJ, USA, 2009.
3. Lien, S.Y.; Liau, T.H.; Kao, C.Y.; Chen, K.C. Cooperative access class barring for machine-to-machine communications. *IEEE Trans. Wirel. Commun.* **2012**, *11*, 27–32. [CrossRef]
4. Cheng, J.P.; Lee, C.; Lin, T. Prioritized Random Access with Dynamic Access Barring for RAN Overload in 3GPP LTE-A Networks. In Proceedings of the 2011 IEEE GLOBECOM Workshops (GC Wkshps), Houston, TX, USA, 5–9 December 2011; pp. 368–372.
5. Wu, H.; Zhu, C.; La, R.; Liu, X.; Zhang, Y. FASA: Accelerated S-ALOHA Using Access History for Event-Driven M2M Communications. *IEEE/ACM Trans. Netw.* **2013**, *21*, 1904–1917. [CrossRef]
6. 3GPP. *3GPP TS 37.868 V11.0. Study on RAN Improvements for Machine Type Communications*; Technical Report; 3GPP: Valbonne, France, 2011.
7. Lo, A.; Law, Y.W.; Jacobsson, M.; Kucharzak, M. Enhanced LTE-Advanced Random-Access Mechanism for Massive Machine-to-Machine (M2M) Communications. In Proceedings of the 27th Meeting of Wireless World Research Forum (WWRF), Düsseldorf, Germany, 23–25 October 2011.
8. Mišić, J.; Mišić, V.B.; Ali, M.Z. Explicit power ramping during random access in LTE/LTE-A. In Proceedings of the IEEE Wireless Communications and Networking Conference, San Francisco, CA, USA, 19–22 March 2017.
9. Ali, M.S.; Hossain, E.; Kim, D.I. LTE/LTE-A random access for massive machine-type communications in smart cities. *IEEE Commun. Mag.* **2017**, *55*, 76–83. [CrossRef]
10. Mišić, J.; Mišić, V.; Khan, N. Sharing It My Way: Efficient M2M Access in LTE/LTE-A Networks. *IEEE Trans. Veh. Technol.* **2017**, *66*, 696–709.
11. Mišić, J.; Mišić, V. *Wireless Personal Area Networks—Performance, Interconnections and Security with IEEE 802.15.4*; John Wiley and Sons: Hoboken, NJ, USA, 2008.
12. Mišić, J.; Mišić, V. Adapting LTE/LTE-A to M2M and D2D Communications. *IEEE Netw.* **2017**, *31*, 63–69. [CrossRef]
13. Rashwand, S.; Mišić, J.; Mišić, V.B. Analysis of CSMA/CA Mechanism of IEEE 802.15.6 under Non-Saturation Regime. *IEEE Trans. Parallel Distrib. Syst.* **2016**, *27*, 1279–1288. [CrossRef]
14. Boccardi, F.; Heath, R.W.; Lozano, A.; Marzetta, T.L.; Popovski, P. Five disruptive technology directions for 5G. *IEEE Commun. Mag.* **2014**, *52*, 74–80. [CrossRef]
15. 3GPP. *3GPP TS 36.321 V10.1.0. Medium Access Control (MAC) Protocol Specifications*; Technical Report; 3GPP: Valbonne, France, 2011.
16. 3GPP. *3GPP TS 36.331 V10.1.0. Radio Resource Specifications*; Technical Report; 3GPP: Valbonne, France, 2011.
17. Dahlman, E.; Parkval, S.; Skold, J. *4G: LTE/LTE-Advanced for Mobile Broadband*; Academic Press: Cambridge, MA, USA, 2011.
18. Wan, J.; Li, D.; Zou, C.; Zhou, K. M2M Communications for Smart City: An Event-Based Architecture. In Proceedings of the 2012 IEEE 12th International Conference on Computer and Information Technology, Chengdu, China, 27–29 October 2012; pp. 895–900, doi:10.1109/CIT.2012.188. [CrossRef]
19. Araniti, G.; Campolo, C.; Condoluci, M.; Iera, A.; Molinaro, A. LTE for vehicular networking: A survey. *IEEE Commun. Mag.* **2013**, *51*, 148–157. [CrossRef]
20. Mir, Z.H.; Filali, F. LTE and IEEE 802.11p for vehicular networking: A performance evaluation. *EURASIP J. Wirel. Commun. Netw.* **2014**, *1*, 89.

21. Vinel, A. 3GPP LTE Versus IEEE 802.11p/WAVE: Which Technology is Able to Support Cooperative Vehicular Safety Applications? *IEEE Wirel. Commun. Lett.* **2012**, *1*, 125–128. [CrossRef]
22. Arora, A.; Rakesh, N.; Mishra, K.K. Analysis of Safety Applications in VANET for LTE Based Network. In *Networking Communication and Data Knowledge Engineering*; Perez, G.M.E., Ed.; Springer: Singapore, 2018; pp. 141–154.
23. Abid, H.; Chung, T.C.; Lee, S.; Qaisar, S. Performance Analysis of LTE Smartphones-Based Vehicle-to-Infrastructure Communication. In Proceedings of the 2012 9th International Conference on Ubiquitous Intelligence and Computing and 9th International Conference on Autonomic and Trusted Computing, Fukuoka, Japan, 4–7 September 2012; pp. 72–78.
24. Campolo, C.; Molinaro, A. Data rate selection in WBSS-based IEEE 802.11p WAVE vehicular ad hoc networks. In Proceedings of the 2010 7th International Symposium on Communication Systems, Networks and Digital Signal Processing, Newcastle upon Tyne, UK, 21–23 July 2010; pp. 412–416.
25. Zaouiat, C.; Latif, A. Performances Comparison of IEEE 802.15. 6 and IEEE 802.15. 4. *IJACSA Int. J. Adv. Comput. Sci. Appl.* **2017**, *8*, 461–467.
26. Hu, L.; Dung, O.M.; Liu, Q.; Han, T.; Sun, Y. Integration of Wireless Body Area Networks (WBANs) and WAN, WiMAX and LTE. *KSII Trans. Internet Inf. Syst.* **2013**, *7*, 980–997.
27. Castel, T.; Lemey, S.; Agneessens, S.; Torre, P.V.; Rogier, H.; Oestges, C. LTE as a potential standard for public safety indoor body-to-body networks. In Proceedings of the 2015 IEEE Symposium on Communications and Vehicular Technology in the Benelux (SCVT), Luxembourg, 24 November 2015; pp. 1–6.
28. Rashwand, S. Efficient Wireless Communication in Healthcare Systems; Design and Performance Evaluation. Ph.D. Thesis, The University of Manitoba, Winnipeg, MB, Canada, 2012.
29. Cherkaoui, S.; Keskes, I.; Rivano, H.; Stanica, R. LTE-A random access channel capacity evaluation for M2M communications. In Proceedings of the 8th IFIP Wireless Days (WD 2016), Toulouse, France, 23–25 March 2016.

Journal of
Sensor and
Actuator Networks

Article

Trajectory-Assisted Municipal Agent Mobility: A Sensor-Driven Smart Waste Management System

Ahmed Omara [1,†], **Damla Gulen** [2,†], **Burak Kantarci** [1,*,†] and **Sema F. Oktug** [2,*,†]

1   School of Electrical Engineering and Computer Science, University Ottawa, Ottawa, ON K1N 6N5, Canada; aomar020@uottawa.ca
2   Department of Computer Engineering, Faculty of Informatics, Istanbul Technical University, 34469 Istanbul, Turkey; gulenda@itu.edu.tr
*   Correspondence: burak.kantarci@uottawa.ca (B.K.); oktug@itu.edu.tr (S.F.O.); Tel.: +1-613-562-5800 (ext. 6955) (B.K.); +90-212-285-3584 (S.F.O.)
†   All authors contributed equally to this work.

Received: 12 June 2018; Accepted: 19 July 2018; Published: 21 July 2018

Abstract: Ubiquity, heterogeneity and dense deployment of sensors have yielded the Internet of Things (IoT) concept, which is an integral component of various smart spaces including smart cities. Applications and services in a smart city ecosystem aim at minimizing the cost and maximizing the quality of living. Among these services, waste management is a unique service that covers both aspects. To this end, in this paper, we propose a WSN-driven system for smart waste management in urban areas. In our proposed framework, the waste bins are equipped with sensors that continuously monitor the waste level and trigger alarms that are wirelessly communicated to a cloud platform to actuate the municipal agents, i.e., waste collection trucks. We formulate an Integer Linear Programming (ILP) model to find the best set of trajectory-truck with the objectives of minimum cost or minimum delay. In order for the trajectory assistance to work in real time, we propose three heuristics, one of which is a greedy one. Through simulations, we show that the ILP formulation can provide a baseline reference to the heuristics, whereas the non-greedy heuristics can significantly outperform the greedy approach regarding cost and delay under moderate waste accumulation scenarios.

Keywords: wireless sensor networks; Internet of Things; smart cities; waste management; urban planning; optimization

---

1. Introduction

Smart cities operate on the foundation of information and communication technologies in order to bridge citizens and technology with the ultimate goal of improving quality of life and sustainability [1]. Moreover, smart cities manage city assets including, but not limited to, the local departments, information systems, libraries, schools, hospitals, waste management systems and transportation systems [2]. The most commonly-known smart city services are smart transportation, smart grid, smart parking, smart health and smart lighting [3]. Wireless Sensor and Actuator Networks (WSAN) facilitate the manageability and efficiency of smart city services [4–7]. Most researchers define the smart city paradigm as an application of the Internet of Things (IoT) concept [8]. Besides, the high penetration rate of the IoT technologies, which are used in all the activities of everyday life, is significantly increasing [9].

The Internet of Things (IoT) has been one of the major research topics in the Information and Communication Technology (ICT) field in various applications [9]. Indeed, IoT and WSAN play the key roles in the realization of smart cities, and as stated in [10], a smart city is comprised of water, energy, waste, transportation and information and communication aspects, which are orthogonal to each other. One of the key areas to build sustainable cities is waste management, which stands for acquiring the waste status in the bins through volumetric sensors [11]. Waste accumulation is inevitable in any life cycle [12]. Therefore, waste management is considered to be a factor that directly impacts the quality of living for citizens. Recent research reports that the growth rate of the Municipal Solid Waste (MSW) amount is higher than the urbanization growth rate [13]. In developing countries, the increase of the municipal solid waste generation is correlated with rapid urbanization, an increase in the population and living standards [14]. In the field of waste management, there have been several studies focused on different aspects and challenges [13–19]. To enable dynamicity in the garbage collection, garbage truck fleet management and determining collection routes, IoT is pointed out as an inseparable component of a waste management system in a smart city infrastructure [20]. To ensure the effectiveness of waste management services, the IoT and WSAN data regarding the waste levels throughout a municipal region call for effective and efficient decision-making systems [21].

In this paper, we propose a WSN-driven smart waste management solution for a smart city setting. To this end, we propose a heuristic method for efficient planning of waste collection routes in the presence of a WSN that raises a set of alarms to initiate/trigger waste collection. We compare the heuristic to a baseline approach, which plans waste management solely based on the next closest location in town. The baseline approach is called Closest Vehicle First (CVF). Two heuristic solutions are developed to improve the naïve approach: (1) Collect based on Upper Threshold (CUT) and (2) Collect based on Upper and Lower Threshold (CULT). The two approaches work similarly; however, CUT keeps adding all the bins to the truck list even if they have not triggered the alarms, whereas CULT aims to collect only the bins with waste levels higher than the lower threshold. Besides, the CUT approach utilizes an upper threshold for the load level of waste bins, whereas the second heuristic takes upper and lower load thresholds into consideration. Through simulations, we show that CUT and CULT improve the baseline solution by up to 16.7% and 8.3% in terms of management cost and by 4.6% and 3% regarding collection delay, respectively. Furthermore, to evaluate the optimality of our heuristic methodology, we formulate an optimization model for the planning of optimal routes for waste collection. Under various small-scale scenarios with different pre-determined sensor-driven alarm thresholds, we show that the proposed heuristic solution can achieve the operation within 85.75% of the solution in real time. The proposed approaches, for the first time, consider the waste arrival rate so as to improve the waste management routing problem. Moreover, considering the waste arrival implicitly gives an indication of the behaviour of filling up the waste bins. Hence, the truck can be directed to collect the bins even if they have not triggered the alarms. Furthermore, the penalty cost considered in the model plays a key role along with the waste arrival rate because overflowed bins are penalized, which would lead to a significant increase in the cost.

This work is organized as follows. In Section 2, we briefly discuss the state of the art in WSN-based waste management in smart cities. Section 3 describes the system model and defines the smart waste management problem. Section 4 provides a thorough explanation of the optimization model for WSN-driven waste management in a smart city setting, while Section 5 presents the baseline approach to address waste management and our proposed heuristic in detail. Section 6 shows numerical results under various test cases by comparing the heuristic to the baseline solution and the optimization model. Finally, Section 7 concludes the article and gives future directions.

2. Related Work and Motivation

Waste management has been of interest for various researchers in the sustainability and smart cities research field. Urban populations are increasing and causing a change in the consumption patterns. Increasing urbanization speed and scale has caused at least 50% of the global population to reside in urban regions. Moreover, by the year 2050, this ratio is expected to be 86% and 64% of the population for developed and developing countries, respectively [22]. Some studies evaluated different scheduling and routing approaches and their relationships to the fundamental characteristics of the solid waste management system [23]. A comprehensive review of waste management systems for residential units was presented in [24]. Utilization of sensors is particularly considered for monitoring critical parameters such as moisture and temperature instead of the load or residual capacity of waste bins. Such a system can be extended to a city-/municipality-wide monitoring and actuation system through networked sensors and by exploiting the benefits of computational and storage capabilities in the cloud. To this end, we identify the study in [12] as the closest work to ours from the architectural standpoint. In the reference study, a cloud-based waste management system was introduced with the objective of reducing gas/fuel consumption and improving efficiency (i.e., total delay). According to the proposed system, waste bins in a metropolitan area are equipped with sensors that sense and communicate the load levels of the bins to the cloud platform for further processing and decision making. The decision-making module of the proposed system resides in the cloud and provides services for waste collection, route optimization, recycling and disposal, food industry, taxation and even energy generation through waste.

In [20], high priority areas were formed, e.g., schools and hospitals, and priority was given to the bins close to those areas when collecting waste. A dynamic routing process was employed to serve high priority bins immediately. The authors studied four models, namely: (1) the dedicated truck model, (2) detour model, (3) minimum distance model and (4) reassignment model. In the same study, a sector-based approach was formed to partition the area into sectors to which bins and trucks were assigned. However, in some models, trucks can be allowed to serve bins that are located in other sectors. The models listed above were studied under real and synthetic data obtained from the municipality of Saint Petersburg, Russia. The performance of the models was presented with respect to CPU time to form the routes, collected load, distance, routing time, response time and fuel quantity. The results were obtained by varying the number of sectors, prioritizing bins under various scenarios, number of trucks per sector and truck capacity. The study reported that in most cases, the reassignment model outperformed its counterparts regarding the above-mentioned performance metrics. It is worth noting that if a waste management cost function was formulated by incorporating all these metrics, the performance evaluation could be more useful for the overall system.

In [25], the problem of waste management was addressed by planning vehicle routes to collect solid waste in a municipality in Finland. The trucks that collected the bins had capacities that could not be exceeded. In the region under consideration, 30,000 bins were considered to be located in densely- and sparsely-populated districts. Furthermore, different types of municipal solid waste and bins were also considered.

Among the researchers who have contributed to the field of waste management and monitoring, there are exemplary ones who have applied machine learning approaches to their proposals. In [26], level detection for solid waste bins was proposed along with a grey level co-occurrence-based classification.

In [27], the authors aimed to locate an optimal landfill site to achieve minimum economical and socio-environmental effects and cost for the waste management system in the city of Regina (SK, Canada) by integrating Multi-Criteria Decision Analysis (MCDA) with Inexact Mixed Integer Linear Programming (IMILP).

In [28], a real-time framework was developed to monitor the bin status and condition. The monitoring application was based on decision algorithms for sensing solid waste arrival. The route optimization for waste management was envisioned to translate into the minimization of cost and carbon emissions. The authors aimed to minimize the collection cost by performing route optimization in Municipal Solid Waste Collection (MSWC) [29]. The data used in the optimization study was obtained from 39 districts in the city of Trabzon, Turkey. The experiments involve multimedia data that were acquired through video cameras installed in the vehicles. The integration of the Route View Pro™ optimization tool with the Geographic Information System (GIS) enabled finding the shortest route. The proposed approach was shown to reduce the total solid waste collection by 24% via route optimization.

The authors in [30] proposed to utilize bins' sensors to transmit real-time data of the bins' fill-level to overcome the uncertainty regarding the amount of waste in the bins. In order to ensure improved efficiency for waste collection, three different operational management approaches were presented: (1) the limited approach, which was based on a cluster first-route heuristic, where the visited bins were selected by their minimum fill-level threshold in each day; after the selection of bins to be collected was defined, a Capacitated Vehicle Routing Problem (CVRP) model was run to optimize each vehicle route in order to achieve minimum transportation cost; (2) the smart collection approach, in which an MILP formulation determined the best collection sequence of bins on each day based on the maximization of the profit; (3) the smarter collection approach, where a heuristic was integrated with the same MILP model to choose the best days that maximized the profit. Out of these approaches, the study concluded that the smart collection was the most efficient and generic one. It is worth noting that the MILP model can also be improved by considering the waste arrival rate and/or a penalty cost that may be applied to the overflowed bins, which can significantly affect the profit.

In [31], Wireless Monitoring Units (WMU) were installed in the waste bins where each WMU was equipped with wireless sensors that monitored the remaining capacity of each bin and reported it to the wireless access points for further processing in a central monitoring station. It was shown that the remaining capacity of a waste bin could be predicted with an accuracy of 98.3%, where a wireless access point could serve a set of WMUs that resided within the coverage of 27 m in diameter.

It is worth noting that data analytics and artificial intelligence methods play a crucial role in profiling the waste arrival, collection and accumulation processes. Therefore, sensory data need to be coupled with data analytics solutions and methodologies. However, this is included in our future agenda. A thorough survey of data analytics approaches for management and profiling of waste management in smart cities was presented in [32].

From the standpoint of the methodology, the study in [30] presented the closest concept to our approach in this article. In the cited work, the authors tackled the problem of obtaining actual load levels in the waste bins through the use of sensors and feeding the information into an optimization model or a sub-optimal heuristic. To this end, three solutions were formulated, where: the first one applied a naive minimum load threshold; the second one aimed to obtain the best collection order of the bins; as an alternative, the authors introduced a further improved model that considered the time dimension, i.e., when and in what order to collect the bins. One of the open issues, as stated by the authors, in their proposed model was the utilization of the waste arrival and accumulation in the bins in the problem. Furthermore, as suggested by the authors, cost factors may vary in time and type. With these in mind, in this article, we incorporate various cost factors into the optimal waste collection model, as well as estimated load levels in the bins.

3. System Model

The waste management problem addressed by our proposed model uses real-time information of the waste fill-levels of the bins to define dynamic routes for each truck. This problem has the following components and inputs: given a complete undirected graph with a set of M waste bins and a distance of Δ_{ij} between any two bins, a central station with a set of N trucks where all the trucks start and end their routes and a disposal area where the trucks dump the waste collected from the bins. Before proceeding with the details of the model, it is worth presenting the notation of the system.

Each waste bin i is defined with a maximum capacity Λ_i and is equipped with communication capability to transmit the real-time waste level of the bin measured by an ultrasonic sensor. The sensors inside the waste bins transmit the fill-levels of the bins in m^3s, which is then transformed into kilograms. Furthermore, this particular study is considered for urban areas; thus, it is reasonable to model the waste arrival rate by the Poisson distribution in the cities. Moreover, we present in the Result Section the performance of the system under aggressive arrival rates. However, under significantly light arrival rates, CUT ensures that all the bins on the same assigned route of a truck will be collected regardless of whether or not they have raised an alarm. In the case of an overflow at bin i, a penalty fee of ρ_i is applied. Moreover, each truck t has a pre-determined number of workers (h_t) and a maximum capacity (C_t). All trucks are equipped with two-way communication capability with the base station.

The system model described in Figure 1 shows that all the trucks are initially located in the central station. Once the waste arrival to bin i accumulates and reaches a pre-defined threshold Ψ_i, an alarm denoting the call for waste collection is triggered and sent to the base station. The base station communicates with the cloud to process the data and to find the optimal route to collect the waste in loaded bins including the bin that alarmed. The cloud sends the optimal route to truck t through the base station. At the end of the collection, all trucks stop at the disposal area to empty the waste collected from the bins. The objective is to obtain a list of waste bins that are potentially to be visited, and to obtain the optimal visiting trajectory for each truck t, which will minimize the cost value, as well as the collection delay. Referring to the description of the problem, three dynamic waste collection methods are presented in Section 5.

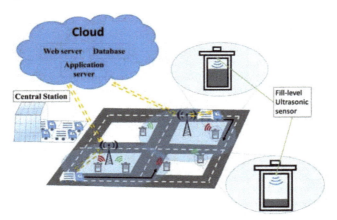

Figure 1. An overview of the system model.

4. Optimization Model for WSN-Based Waste Management in Smart Cities

This section formulates an Integer Linear Programming (ILP) model for the optimal waste management in a smart city in the presence of coordinated wireless sensors for monitoring the waste status at multiple locations. Before we proceed with the details of the optimization, it is worth presenting the notation of the model. The inputs, variables and outputs used in the MILP model are listed and detailed in Table 1.

Table 1. Basic notations used in the system description. Notations are grouped into three categories: Constants, inputs and variables.

Notations	Equations	Sections	Definition
D	2; 43	4.1; 5.1	Cost of (un)dumping per bin (from a bin to a truck) (€)
H	2; 43	4.1; 5.1	Cost of human resource (€)/h
G	2; 43	4.1; 5.1	Cost of gas mileage (€)/km
S	6; 26; 47	4.1; 4.2; 5.1	Average speed in the town (km/h)
W	2; 26	4.1; 4.2	Time needed to collect waste from a bin (minutes)
N	2	4.1	Total number of trucks
M	2; 13; 36; 43	4.1; 4.2; 5.1	Total number of bins
UB	21; 38	4.1; 4.2	The upper bound of variable P_i
Ψ_i	-	5	Upper threshold for the waste amount of bin i
ϕ_i	-	5	Lower threshold for the waste amount of bin i
ρ_i	2; 43	4.1; 5.1	Penalty of bin i per kg (€)
R_t	6; 26; 47	4.1; 4.2; 5.1	Time needed to empty truck t at the dumping area and prepare it for the next trip (minutes)
h	5; 26; 47	4.1; 4.2; 5.1	Distance from the dumping area to the central station (meters)
Δ_{ij}	5	4.1	Distance between bin i and bin j (meters)
t_{ij}	20; 26	4.2	Time needed to move from bin i to bin j (minutes)
Δ_i	8; 32	4.2	Distance from bin i to the dumping area (meters)
r_i	7; 33	4.2	Distance from the central station to bin i (meters)
λ_i	17; 23; 37	4.1; 4.2	Average waste arrival at bin i (kg)
h_t	2; 43	4.1; 5.1	Number of workers in truck t
Λ_i	2; 43	4.1; 5.1	Capacity of bin i (kg)
δ_i	17; 37	4.1; 4.2	Initial load for bin i (kg)
C_t	17; 37	4.1; 4.2	Capacity of truck t (kg)
T_i	20	4.1	Time from the central station to first bin i (minutes)
c_t	-	5	Initial load of truck t (kg)
K	-	5	Threshold for the count of bins that have alarmed
k	-	5	Number of bins that have alarmed
A_i	-	5	Alarm status of bin i
B	-	5	List of bins that have alarmed
Z_t	-	5	Route of truck t
L_{ij}	-	5	List of bins on the shortest path between bin i and j

Table 1. Cont.

Notations	Equations	Sections	Definition
Q_{in}^t	7–21; 27–29; 31–38	4.1; 4.2	The binary variable is one if bin i is the n-th collected bin by truck t
X_{ij}^{tn}	5; 9; 10; 11; 16; 26–30	4.1; 4.2	The binary variable defines the multiplication of Q_{in}^t by Q_{jn+1}^t
H_{ij}^t	17; 18; 19; 37; 38; 39	4.1; 4.2	The integer variable defines the multiplication of P_i by Q_{in}^t
V_{jn}^{tn}	20; 21; 22; 23	4.1	The integer variable defines the multiplication of P_i by Q_{jn-1}^t
d_t	2; 3; 5; 6; 44	4.1; 5.1	The integer variable defines the total distance covered by truck t (meters)
d	2; 3; 43; 44	4.1; 5.1	The integer variable defines the total distance covered by Ntrucks (meters)
I_t	2; 47	4.1; 4.2; 5.1	The integer variable defines the distance from the central station to first bin of truck t (meters)
$\hat{I}_t$	2; 47	4.1; 4.2; 5.1	The integer variable defines the distance from last bin of truck t to the dumping area (meters)
τ_t	4; 6	4.1	The integer variable defines the total time of truck t (minutes)
τ	2; 4; 43; 45	4.1; 5.1	The integer variable defines the total time of the Ntrucks (minutes)
b_t	15; 16; 30; 34; 45	4.1; 4.2; 5.1	The integer variable defines the total number of bins collected by truck t
F_i	2; 23; 43	4.1; 5.1	The integer variable defines the final load of bin i (kg)
P_i^t	18; 20; 21; 23; 38–41	4.1; 4.2	The integer variable defines the pick up time of bin i (minutes)
Y_t	-	5	List of visited bins by truck t

4.1. Cost-Based Optimization Model

The objective of the cost-based optimization model is to minimize the cost of waste collection. The objective function in Equation (1) is broken down into the cost components in the set of constraints starting Equation (2). The following parameters contribute to the cost of waste collection: gas mileage, human resource and penalty due to excessively-loaded bins.

$$Minimize\ Cost \tag{1}$$

subject to

$$Cost - G \cdot d - \tau \cdot H \cdot h_t - \sum_{i=1}^{M} (F_i - \Lambda_i) \cdot \rho_i = H \cdot W \cdot M \cdot N \cdot h_t + D \cdot M \tag{2}$$

$$d - \sum_{t=1}^{N} d_t = 0 \tag{3}$$

$$\tau - \sum_{t=1}^{N} \tau_t = 0 \tag{4}$$

$$d_t - \sum_{n=1}^{M} \sum_{i}^{M} \sum_{j \neq i}^{M} \Delta_{ij} X_{ij}^{nt} = \widehat{I}_t + I_t + \hbar, \ \forall t \in N \tag{5}$$

$$\tau_t - d_t / S = R_t, \forall t \in N \tag{6}$$

$$I_t - \sum_{i=1}^{M} Q_{i1}^{t} \cdot r_i = 0, \ \forall t \in N \tag{7}$$

$$\widehat{I}_t - \sum_{n=1}^{M} \sum_{i=1}^{M} (Q_{i+1,n+1}^{t} - Q_{in}^{t}) \cdot \Delta_i = 0, \ \forall t \in N \tag{8}$$

Equations (3)–(8) formulate the distance-related constraints. Equations (3) and (4) define the total distance and total collection time (i.e., route length), respectively. In addition, Equations (5) and (6) define the distance and time covered by each truck. The next constraint in Equation (7) represents the distance from the central station to the first bin. Finally, the constraint in Equation (8) formulates the disposal distance from the last bin to the disposal area.

$$X_{ij}^{nt} - Q_{in}^{t} \leq 0, \forall j \in M, \forall n \in M, \forall t \in N \tag{9}$$

$$X_{ij}^{nt} - Q_{jn+1}^{t} \leq 0, \forall j \in M, \forall n \in M, \forall t \in N \tag{10}$$

$$Q_{in}^{t} + Q_{jn+1}^{t} - X_{ij}^{nt} \leq 1, \forall j \in M, \forall n \in M, \forall t \in N \tag{11}$$

The optimization model requires formulating the conditional variable that denotes whether bins i and j are picked up by truck t at the n-th and $(n+1)$-th order, respectively. This can be formulated as the multiplication of the two variables, i.e., $(Q_{in}^{t} \times Q_{in+1}^{t})$. The non-linearity in $Q_{in}^{t} \times Q_{in+1}^{t}$ is linearized by the constraints in (9)–(11). The first two inequalities ensure that X_{ij}^{nt} will be zero if either Q_{in}^{t} or Q_{in+1}^{t} is zero. The last inequality ensures that X_{ij}^{nt} will be equal to one, only if both binary variables are one. However, this will linearize X_{ij}^{nt} without violating any of the other constraints.

$$\sum_{n=1}^{M} \sum_{t=1}^{N} Q_{in}^{t} = 1, \forall i \in M \tag{12}$$

$$\sum_{n=1}^{M} \sum_{i=1}^{M} \sum_{t=1}^{N} Q_{in}^{t} = M \tag{13}$$

$$\sum_{i=1}^{M} Q_{in}^t \leq 1, \forall n \in M, \forall t \in N \tag{14}$$

$$\sum_{n=1}^{M} \sum_{i=1}^{M} Q_{in}^t - b_t = 0, \forall t \in N \tag{15}$$

$$\sum_{n=1}^{M} \sum_{i=1}^{M} X_{ij}^{nt} = b_t - 1, \forall t \in N \tag{16}$$

$$\sum_{n=1}^{M} \sum_{i=1}^{M} (Q_{in}^t \cdot \delta_i + \lambda_i \cdot H_{in}^t) \leq C_t, \forall t \in N \tag{17}$$

$$P_i - (1 - Q_{in}^t) \cdot UB \leq H_{in}^t, \forall i \in M, \forall n \in M, \forall t \in N \tag{18}$$

$$H_{in}^t \geq 0, \forall i \in M, \forall n \in M, \forall t \in N \tag{19}$$

The next set of equations denotes the capacity constraints: Equation (12) ensures that bin *i* can be collected only by one truck. Equation (13) guarantees that all bins must be collected; and the constraint in Equation (14) ensures the following: given truck *t*, order *n* can be set to bin *i* at most once. The constraint set in Equations (12)–(14) ensures that all bins can be visited only once in consecutive order.

The constraint in Equation (15) defines the number of collected bins by each truck, whereas the constraint (16) defines the number of trips made between two consecutive bins. The constraint in Equation (17) ensures that the total bins collected by truck *t* will not exceed the truck capacity. Similar to the constraints above, the product of the binary variable Q_{in}^t with the integer variable P_i (pickup time of bin *i*) is linearized where H_{in}^t denotes the product, i.e., $H_{in}^t = Q_{in}^t \times P_i$. Equation (18) ensures that H_{in}^t will have the same value as P_i if Q_{in}^t is one, and zero otherwise. Equation (19) ensures that H_{in}^t will have a non-negative value. Similarly, Equations (21) and (22) solve the non-linearity in Equation (20) the same as the way Equations (18) and (19) do.

Equation (20) formulates the pickup time of bin *i* by summing the time distance between bins *i* and *j* (i.e., t_{ij}), pickup time of the previous bin P_j and the time needed to reach the first bin from the central station. Equation (23) defines the final load of bin *i* by adding the current load (i.e., the multiplication of the pickup time and arrival rate) of the bin to the initial load.

$$P_i - \sum_{j \neq i}^{M} (X_{ij}^{nt} \cdot t_{ij}) - \sum_{j \neq i}^{M} V_{jn}^t - (Q_{i1}^t \cdot T_i) = 0, \ \forall t \in N, \forall i \in M, \forall n \in M, n > 1 \tag{20}$$

$$P_i - (1 - Q_{in-1}^t) \cdot UB \leq V_{jn}^t, \forall i \in M, \forall n \in M, \forall t \in N \tag{21}$$

$$V_{jn}^t \geq 0, \forall i \in M, \forall n \in M, \forall t \in N \tag{22}$$

$$F_i - (P_i \cdot \lambda_i) = \delta_i, \forall i \in M \tag{23}$$

4.2. Delay-Based Optimization Model

In the delay-based ILP model, the constraints in Equations (27)–(42) share the same functionality as the cost model constraints. However, Equation (26) defines the objective function to minimize the truck delay based on the travel time between two consecutive bins, travel time from the central station to the first bin, travel time from the last bin to the dumping area, travel time from the dumping area to the central station, the time needed to empty the bins and time required to unload the truck in the dumping area.

$$Minimize \ Delay \tag{24}$$

subject to

$$Delay - \sum_{t=1}^{N} Delay_t = 0 \tag{25}$$

$$Delay_t - \sum_{n=1}^{M} \sum_{i}^{M} \sum_{j \neq i}^{M} t_{ij} X_{ij}^{nt} - b_t W = (I_t + \widehat{I_t} + \hbar)/S + R_t, \forall t \in N \tag{26}$$

$$X_{ij}^{nt} \leq Q_{in}^{t}, \forall i \in M, \forall j \in M, \forall n \in M, \forall t \in N \tag{27}$$

$$X_{ij}^{nt} \leq Q_{jn+1}^{t}, \forall i\ M, \forall j \in M, \forall n \in M, \forall t \in N \tag{28}$$

$$Q_{in}^{t} + Q_{jn+1}^{t} - X_{ij}^{nt} \leq 1, \forall i \in M, \forall j \in M, \forall n \in M, \forall t \in N \tag{29}$$

$$\sum_{n=1}^{M} \sum_{i=1}^{M} X_{ij}^{nt} = b_t - 1, \forall t \in N \tag{30}$$

$$\sum_{n=1}^{M} \sum_{t=1}^{N} Q_{in}^{t} = 1, \ \forall i \in M \tag{31}$$

$$\widehat{I_t} = \sum_{n=1}^{M} \sum_{i=1}^{M} (Q_{i+1,n+1}^{t} - Q_{in}^{t}) \cdot \Delta_i, \ \forall t \in N \tag{32}$$

$$I_t = \sum_{i=1}^{M} Q_{i1}^{t} \cdot r_i, \ \forall t \in N \tag{33}$$

$$\sum_{n=1}^{M} \sum_{i=1}^{M} Q_{in}^{t} = b_t, \forall t \in N \tag{34}$$

$$\sum_{i=1}^{M} Q_{in}^{t} \leq 1, \forall n \in M, \forall t \in N \tag{35}$$

$$\sum_{n=1}^{M} \sum_{i=1}^{M} \sum_{t=1}^{N} Q_{in}^{t} = M \tag{36}$$

$$\sum_{n=1}^{M} \sum_{i=1}^{M} (Q_{in}^{t} \cdot \delta_i + \lambda_i \cdot H_{in}^{t}) \leq C_t, \forall t \in N \tag{37}$$

$$P_i - UB(1 - Q_{in}^{t}) \leq H_{in}^{t}, \forall i \in M, \forall n \in M, \forall t \in N \tag{38}$$

$$H_{in}^{t} \geq 0, \forall i \in M, \forall n \in M, \forall t \in N \tag{39}$$

$$P_i - \sum_{j \neq i}^{M} (X_{ij}^{nt} \cdot t_{ij}) - \sum_{j \neq i}^{M} V_{jn}^{t} - (Q_{i1}^{t} \cdot T_i) = 0, \ \forall t \in N, \forall i \in M, \forall n \in M, n > 1 \tag{40}$$

$$P_i - (1 - Q_{in-1}^{t}) \cdot UB \leq V_{jn}^{t}, \forall i \in M, \forall n \in M, \forall t \in N \tag{41}$$

$$V_{jn}^{t} \geq 0, \forall i \in M, \forall n \in M, \forall t \in N \tag{42}$$

5. Heuristics for WSN-Based Waste Management in Smart Cities

This section describes three heuristic solutions addressing the efficient waste management problem, namely: (1) Closest Vehicle First (CVF), (2) Collect based on Upper Threshold (CUT) and (3) Collect based on Upper and Lower Threshold (CULT). The notations for the constants and inputs presented in Table 1 are also used while describing the heuristics.

5.1. Closest Vehicle First: A Locality-Based Baseline Solution

The CVF model is constructed to address the problem of the waste management by providing an efficient route for the given set of bins that reached their thresholds and raised alarms. In this approach, bins are visited if and only if they raised alarms, so as to reduce the cost by not visiting unnecessary bins that contain an insignificant amount of waste.

The CVF model works as follows: Trucks remain in ready mode to pick up bins until an alarm is raised. Bin i triggers the alarm when the waste level reaches the upper threshold Ψ_i. When the number of raised alarms reaches K, the cloud constructs a route (B) between the triggered bins and sends it to a truck t through the base station. The route construction is based on Dijkstra's shortest path algorithm. The constructed route is assigned to an available truck. However, if there is no available truck, the cloud assigns the route to the closest truck. The formed route is appended to the selected truck's current route. The truck goes directly to the disposal area when it reaches the capacity C_t and stays ready for the next trip. When the truck goes to the disposal area, if there are bins that are assigned to it, but not served, those bins are assigned to the other trucks. If the load of the truck has not reached C_t and all bins have been visited on the route, a new route is constructed from the list B and assigned to the truck considering the current load of the truck. The flowchart of this model is presented in Figure 2.

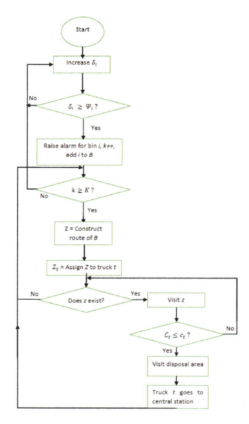

Figure 2. Closest Vehicle First (CVF) flowchart.

5.2. Proposed Nearly-Optimal Heuristics

In order to address the problem of the waste management, two other nearly optimal heuristics, CUT and CULT, are introduced, and details are given in this section.

5.2.1. Collect Based on Upper Threshold

The CUT model is constructed to address the problem of the waste management by providing an efficient route differently than CVF. This approach tries to reduce the cost by making the route more optimal. In this approach, visited bins are not only the ones that raised alarms, but also the ones that are on the assigned route and have not triggered the alarms. The reason behind this is to reduce the unnecessary trips of a truck to collect the waste from the bins.

The first part of CUT is constructed in the same way as CVF, which was presented earlier. Until the construction of the first route, the algorithm behaves in the same manner. While the CVF approach collects the closer bins that raised the alarms, the CUT method aims to collect the bins that are on the same assigned route even though they have not triggered the alarms. Trucks that visit the disposal area or that are assigned new routes operate in the same manner as in CVF. The flowchart of the CUT is presented in Figure 3.

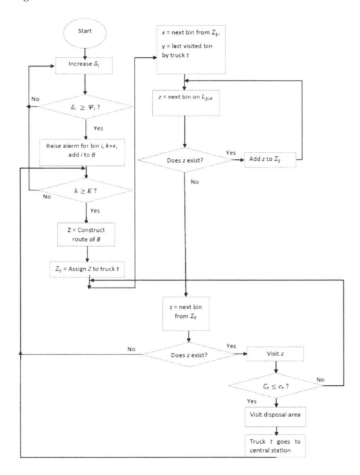

Figure 3. Collect based on Upper Threshold (CUT) flowchart.

5.2.2. Collect Based on Upper and Lower Threshold

The CULT model is developed to address the problem of the waste management by improving the efficiency of the route construction that was presented by the previous approaches. This approach tries to reduce the cost by making the route more optimal and removing unnecessary visits to the bins with an insignificant amount of waste. In this approach, visited bins are not only the ones that raised alarms, but also the ones that are on the way to the bins that generated alarms. However, different from the CUT approach, there is a decision point in order to visit a bin, which has not triggered an alarm. The reason behind this behaviour is to reduce the unnecessary service given to the passed-by bins that contain a negligible amount of waste. Hence, it aims at cost reduction. For the mentioned decision, a new parameter defining a lower threshold value for the waste amount (ψ_i) is introduced.

CULT is constructed in the same manner as the CUT model presented previously. However, when truck i is assigned a route, it checks the bins that are accessible on the way from the current location to the next bin on the route. However, the decision about whether or not to add new bins on-the-fly depends on their current waste levels. Only the bins that are on the way and having a waste amount higher than ψ_i are candidates for pick up by truck i. Trucks visiting the disposal area or those being assigned new routes follow the same steps as CVF and CUT. The flowchart of CUT is presented in Figure 4.

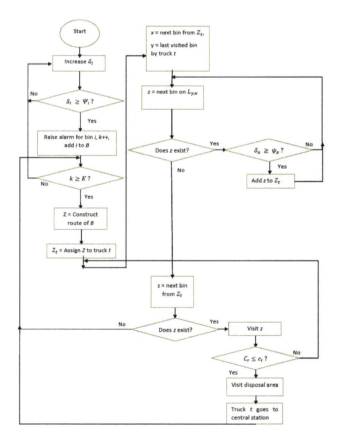

Figure 4. Collect based on Upper and Lower Threshold (CULT) flowchart.

6. Performance Evaluation

The optimization toolbox in MATLAB has been used to solve both MILP models (cost and delay) [33]. The simulation environment for heuristic methods that are presented in this paper is a Java-based home-grown simulator. It is worth noting that the optimization models aim to provide a performance guideline for the heuristics and are not envisioned to be run in real-time scenarios. As a matter of fact, large map scenarios such as those with more than 15 bins would require fast heuristics as opposed to optimization models due to the high computational complexity of those formulations. In the next two subsections, detailed settings and results are presented along with a thorough discussion.

6.1. Simulation Settings

The simulation settings are given in Table 2, and they describe the values used in the optimization models. The central station, which is the start and end point, hosts two trucks that participate in the waste collection process. Each truck has $h_t = 3$ workers, who get paid $H = 39$ €/h, and moves with speed $S = 20$ km/h. In addition, the workers collect waste from a bin in W = 2.5 min with a cost $D = 1.62$ €/bin. Moreover, the truck gas mileage costs 20 €/km (i.e., G). Each truck goes to the landfill to empty the collected waste and prepare for the next bins' alarm in 12 min (i.e., R_t). The distance from the landfill area to the central station ($\hbar$) is set to 250 m. In the case of an overflowed bin, an additional cost of $\rho_i = 5$ € is added as a penalty. However, a small map scenario with M = {5, 10, 15} bins and waste arrival rate $\lambda_i = \{1, 3, 5, 7\}$ kg/5 min was considered in order to compare the proposed approaches with both optimization models (cost and delay), as shown in Section 6.2.1. In the given scenario, the truck and the bin have a maximum capacity $C_t = 400$ kg and $\Lambda_i = 20$ kg, respectively. On the other hand, the larger map scenario considers $M \in \{20, 40\}$ bins, a waste arrival rate of $\lambda_i = \{3$ kg/5 min, 5 kg/5 min} and a bin capacity $\Lambda_i \in \{20$ kg, 30 kg}, while the truck capacity (C_t) takes its value from the set {400, 600} kg, as given in Section 6.2.2. Furthermore, in order to present our approaches' suitability for the real case scenarios, the test scenarios are enhanced by getting results with larger maps considering $M = \{80, 160\}$, a waste arrival rate of $\lambda_i = 3$ kg/5 min, $\Lambda_i = 30$ kg, while a truck capacity (C_t) = 600 kg, as given in Section 6.2.2.

Table 2. Performance evaluation settings.

Notations	Value
Cost of emptying bin (D)	1.62 €/bin
Cost of human resource (H)	39 €/h
Cost of gas mileage (G)	20 €/km
Average speed in the town (S)	20 km/h
Time needed to collect waste from a bin (W)	2.5 min
Total number of trucks (N)	2
Total number of bins (M)	{5, 10, 15, 20, 40, 80, 160}
The upper bound of variable P_i (UB)	10^{15}
The upper threshold for the waste amount of bin i (Ψ_i)	[10–15] kg
The lower threshold for the waste amount of bin i (ψ_i)	[5–8] kg
Penalty of the overflowed bin (ρ_i)	5 €/kg
Time needed to empty truck t at the dumping area and prepare it for the next trip (R_t)	12 min
Distance from the dumping area to the central station ($\hbar$)	2500 m
Distance between bin i and bin j (Δ_{ij})	[200–2300] m
Time needed to move from bin i to bin j (t_{ij})	[0.6–6.9] min
Distance from bin i to the dumping area (Δ_i)	[400–2300] m
Distance from the central station to bin i (r_i)	[200–2300] m
Average waste arrival rate at a bin (λ_i)	{1, 3, 5, 7} kg/5 min
Number of workers in a truck (h_t)	3
Maximum capacity of a bin (Λ_i)	{20, 30} kg
Initial load for bin i (δ_i)	[0–30] kg
Maximum capacity of a truck (C_t)	{400, 600} kg
Time from the central station to the first bin i (T_i)	[0.6–6.9] min
Initial load of a truck t (c_t)	[0–600] kg
Threshold for the count of bins that have alarmed (K)	{1,2,3}
Number of bins that have alarmed (k)	[0–160]
Alarm status of bin i (A_i)	{On, Off}

6.2. Simulation Results

In this section, the proposed waste collection approaches are evaluated to investigate how well the proposed solutions align with the optimization model results. The first subsection compares the two heuristics and the optimization model results for some small-scale scenarios. However, due to the inefficiency of the ILP solver under large maps, the second subsection shows more complex scenarios using larger maps and the comparison of the proposed heuristic approaches.

6.2.1. Optimality Assessment of the Heuristics

In order to evaluate the optimality of the proposed approaches, a comparison among the optimization model, CVF and CUT approaches is presented. Two criteria were considered in the comparison, namely the total cost and delay, as shown in Figures 5 and 6, respectively. Moreover, the comparison shows the influence of changing the number of bins and the waste arrival rate on the cost value and delay time. Figure 5 presents the total cost for three different bin scenarios (i.e., the number of bins is either 5, 10 or 15) and four different waste arrival rates starting from lighter values to more aggressive values (1 kg/5 min, 3 kg/5 min, 5 kg/5 min and 7 kg/5 min). The results show that the cost increased either when the number of bins increased or the waste arrival rate became more aggressive. However, the CVF and CUT approaches became very close to the cost optimization result with an arrival rate of 1 kg/5 min for all bin scenarios. With higher waste arrival rates, the penalty value increased since the bins could end up overflowing rapidly. Hence, the gap between the optimal solution and the two heuristic approaches became larger particularly under the arrival rate of 5 kg/5 min and 7 kg/5 min. It is definitely not realistic to have such high arrival rates, so we would like to present how aggressive arrival rates significantly increased the cost due to the penalties.

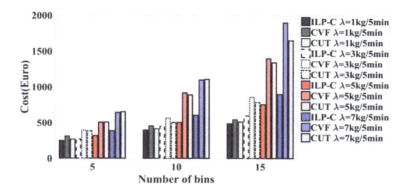

Figure 5. An overview of the system model.

A second criterion used to evaluate the proposed approaches was delay. To be coherent with the other performance comparisons, we considered the same bin scenarios (i.e., the number of bins is either 5, 10 or 15) and the same waste arrival rates (1, 3, 5 and 7) kg/5 min. Figure 6 shows the total delay of both trucks that participated in the waste collection process. In contrast to the cost model, the delay value was poorly affected by varying the waste arrival rate; however, varying the number of bins increased the total delay since the trucks needed more time to empty all the bins. The comparison shows that CUT had better results compared to CVF, particularly under the scenario with a higher number of bins. As a conclusion, both figures show that CUT is a better candidate in waste collection operation.

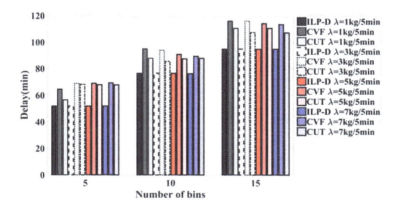

Figure 6. An overview of the system model.

6.2.2. Feasibility Study of Heuristics

In order to compare the effectiveness and efficiency of the heuristic methods, several scenarios were applied to the simulation environment. In the simulation environment, the arrival process of the waste was formulated based on the Poisson distribution. Under multiple runs, distinct instances of the bins were obtained. For each scenario, the results were calculated as the average of five different runs.

For the comparisons, two maps, which included 20 and 40 bins, were used. The map containing 40 bins was two-times larger than the 20-bin map. The map with 40 bins is presented in Figure 7. On the map, the central truck station is where the trucks start their routes, and the disposal area is the point where trucks visit upon reaching their capacity upper limit. Each vertical segment of the grid is 200 m long, and each horizontal segment is 300 m long. Bins are marked with red rectangles on the map. In each scenario, two trucks were employed. Three different arrival rates, which were 1 kg per 5 min, 3 kg per 5 min and 5 kg per 5 min, were used. For these settings, increasing the bin capacity from 20 kg to 30 kg and increasing the truck capacity from 400 kg to 600 kg were observed separately. Each scenario was solved by the CVF, CUT and CULT methods. In order to compare these three methods, cost, delay per route and the number of trips values were used. Total cost was obtained for 12 h. Delay per route was obtained by dividing the total time that trucks needed to visit the bins by the route count for 12 h. Instead of total delay, the delay per route metric was employed.

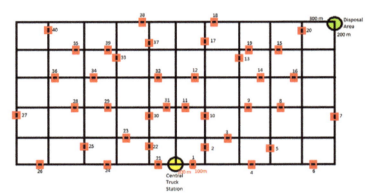

Figure 7. Bin deployment map.

In the first two figures, Figures 8 and 9, cost values are observed under the arrival rate of 3 kg per 5 min. In the first figure, Figure 8, the change is observed for bin capacity being increased from 20 kg to 30 kg. In Figure 9, the impact of truck capacity being increased from 400 kg to 600 kg is depicted. The increase in the bin count improved CUT when compared to CULT and CVF. For the 20-bin case, both methods similarly increased their performance in comparison to CVF in terms of cost. Under the 40-bin case, CUT and CULT performed better than CVF and provided a more efficient solution in terms of cost. However, increasing bin capacity did not introduce further improvements to the performance CUT and CULT in comparison to CVF. CUT provided a 14% better solution than CVF, whereas CULT provided a 0.07% better solution than CVF. When the bin capacity increased, the difference between the threshold value that triggered the alarm and the bin capacity increased, as well. This resulted in trucks having a longer period of time to visit that bin before the waste started to spread and caused the penalty. Collecting the waste from the bins that have not yet triggered alarms caused longer delay values for the ones that had alarmed to be collected. This increased the penalty for CUT and CULT. When there was not enough time between the alarm threshold being reached and bin capacity being met, the decision mechanism can affect the solution by decreasing the total cost, and vice versa.

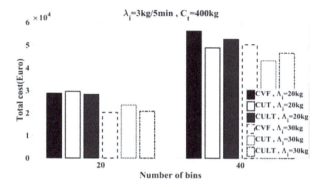

Figure 8. Cost: bin count when the bin capacity was increased.

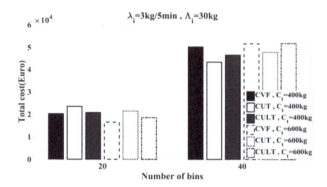

Figure 9. Cost: bin count when the truck capacity was increased.

When increasing truck capacity under the 20-bin case in Figure 9, all three methods provided reasonable solutions. CVF performed the best, and for CUT and CULT, the difference from CVF increased in a negative way. Under the 40-bin case, CUT performed the best, and increasing truck capacity made CULT perform worse than CVF. Under the lower truck capacity, both CUT and CULT performed better than CVF. Moreover, the improvement of CVF by CUT decreased when the truck capacity was increased. Increasing truck capacity was expected to decrease the total cost in general depending on the trip count decrease and observed as expected for the map with 20 bins. However, when there were 40 bins on the map, increasing truck capacity caused higher cost values. This was due to the more non-optimal routes. The distance between bins could be higher in the wider area, and when the truck could not reach its capacity, it needed to wait for new triggers to be generated. This led to longer distances for the trucks to visit. Moreover, visiting further bins caused other bins on the route to spread waste around and cause penalties.

In the following two figures, Figures 10 and 11, the change in bin capacity and truck capacity is studied under the arrival rate of 5 kg per 5 min. When the arrival rate increased, the results became closer to each other. The bins that did not trigger, but on the way of a truck that was assigned a route were highly probable to have generated a trigger at the next arrival of waste. Therefore, adding these kinds of bins independently of ψ_i to the route increased the efficiency in terms of cost and delay. Moreover, selecting closer Λ_i, λ, Ψ_i and ψ_i resulted in similar cost and delay results. In the scenarios applied, ψ_i was set to $\Lambda_i/4$ and Ψ_i was set to $\Lambda_i/2$. For $\Lambda_i = 20$, and $\lambda = 5$ kg/5 min, $\psi_i = 5$; when a bin received an amount of waste, it reached the ψ_i directly. This removed the difference between CUT and CULT methods in this scenario. For the 5 kg/5 min arrival rate scenario, increasing bin capacity decreased the total cost for all methods, but did not have a significant impact on the comparison of the three algorithms.

However, increasing truck count caused a more significant impact on the cost values, which can be seen from Figure 11. Increasing truck capacity increased the total cost in general for both maps containing 20 and 40 bins. However, in the 40-bin case, the improvement of the CUT and CULT according to CVF increased. They both performed better in each situation, but they increased the efficiency percentages that they provided when compared to CVF.

The change in the settings provided less difference in delay when compared to cost values. Delay per route values was effected by how well the route was optimized and how close the visiting bins were. When the delay was decreased, it could be said that the route was more optimized in those simulations with the provided configuration settings. The following four figures are presented to show the comparison in terms of delay per route.

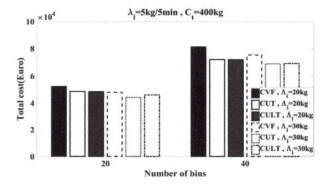

Figure 10. Cost: bin count when the bin capacity was increased.

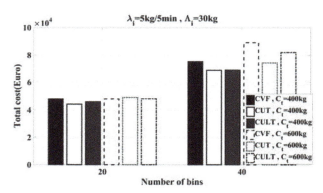

Figure 11. Cost: bin count when the truck capacity was increased.

In Figure 12, the increasing bin capacity affect can be seen for the 20-bin and 40-bin maps with the arrival rate of 3 kg per 5 min. The impact was very small; however, in general, the CVF provided the shortest and CUT provided the longest delay per the route values. It is seen in Figure 8 that CUT was the most effective among the three algorithms on the 40-bin map. Therefore, CUT can be chosen as a solution when the time is not important, but the cost efficiency is more important. When time is the most important metric, CVF can be chosen. This was the result of CUT providing more optimal routes for each truck. Since trucks visited any other bin on the way to the alarmed bins, trucks did not have to go further first and come back again for the bins that they passed by before. Furthermore, when the bin count was increased, the delay per route values decreased, and this meant that the algorithms could work better and manage more optimal routes when the area was wider and there were more triggers coming from the bins in a time window. When there were less bins on the map, the possibility of getting many triggers at the same time decreased, and getting less triggers would cause the bins to be added on the route in an unoptimized manner.

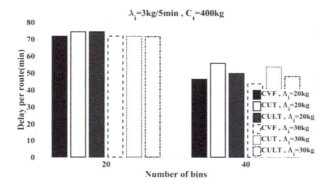

Figure 12. Delay per route: bin count when the bin capacity was increased.

In Figure 13, the increase in truck capacity can be seen at the arrival rate of 3 kg per 5 min. It is observed that when the truck capacity was increased, the delay per route increased. This is precisely the expected result to be observed, since there was more capacity that one truck could collect, and it visited more bins in a route. Moreover, increasing truck capacity resulted in more effective performance of CVF and less effective performance of CULT, which was the opposite condition of the lower truck capacity scenario.

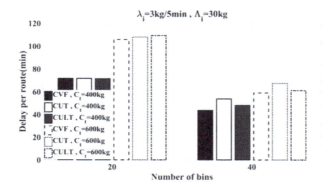

Figure 13. Delay per route: Bin count when the truck capacity was increased.

In the following figures, Figures 14 and 15, the scenarios where the arrival rate was 5 kg/5 min are presented. The delay per route values was smaller in general when compared to Figures 12 and 13.

Since the arrival rate was increased, the collected bins had higher amount of wastes stored in them. This resulted in a shorter time for the trucks reaching their capacity. In Figure 14, the affect of bin capacity increase is shown. Increasing the truck capacity effected smaller map scenarios more than the wider area map. In the first section on the left, the biggest impact can be observed by the CULT, and while CULT and CVF were performing better, CUT increased the delay per route value for the smaller area case. For the wider area, all the methods performed better and provided smaller delay values when the bin capacity was increased.

In Figure 15, the effect of truck capacity increase is shown. The increase in delay per route values in all cases where the truck capacity was increased independently of other configuration settings was the natural result. For this figure, where the arrival rate was 5 kg/5 min and the bin capacity was 30 kg, increasing the truck capacity from 200 kg to 400 kg did not change the order of the effectiveness of the three algorithms. CVF provided the smallest delay per route values, and CUT provided the longest ones.

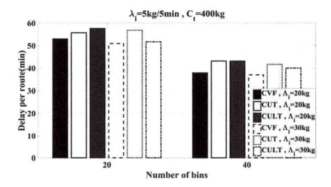

Figure 14. Delay per route: bin count when the bin capacity was increased.

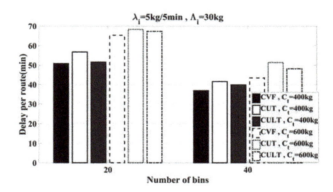

Figure 15. Delay per route: bin count when the truck capacity was increased.

As the last comparison metric, the number of routes in each scenario are shown in the following four figures.

In Figures 16 and 17, the arrival rate is 3 kg/5 min, and the simulation is observed for 20 bins and 40 bins maps. First, in Figure 16, the increase in bin capacity is presented. The highest route number was always in CVF, and the lowest was in CUT. However, the difference between the methods is more visible and observable when the wider map was used. Route count being small meant that each trip took a longer time for that method, and a trip took longer when the bins either had a small amount of waste inside in each collection or the routes that the trucks were assigned to were not that optimal. The increase in the bin capacity increased the number of routes in both cases when there were 20 or 40 bins. The reason behind this behaviour was that the thresholds were set according to the bin capacities (Λ_i's), which is $\Lambda/2$. Once an alarm has been triggered, the bin had a greater amount of waste to be collected. This consumed the truck capacity more quickly and resulted in higher values of route counts.

In Figure 17, the increase in the truck capacity is presented. In this figure, like the previous one, CUT had the smallest number of routes, and CVF had the most number of routes. Again, the difference among them is more visible when the map has 40 bins. For both maps, when the truck capacity increased, the route number decreased. With the increased truck capacity, one truck could hold more waste in a single trip, which precisely resulted in the decrease in the number of routes.

For the following two figures, Figures 18 and 19, the arrival rate is set to 5 kg/5 min, and the maps with 20 and 40 bins are observed under increasing bin capacity or truck capacity. First, in Figure 18, the increase in the bin capacity is observed.

In Figure 19, the increase in the truck capacity is tested under the 5 kg/5 min arrival rate setting. The increase in the truck capacity decreased the count of routes as explained before. For these scenarios, again, the highest number of routes was observed by applying CVF, whereas the lowest number of routes were observed under CUT and CULT.

In the following Table 3, total cost, delay per route and number of route counts are presented when $\lambda = 1$ kg/5 min. The applied scenarios are the same as the previous cases. The increase in Λ_i and C_i were tested on two maps containing 20 and 40 bins.

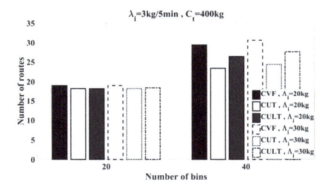

Figure 16. Number of routes: bin count when the bin capacity was increased.

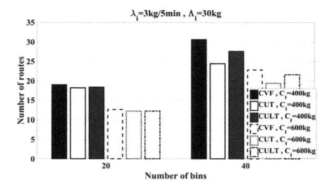

Figure 17. Number of routes: bin count when the truck capacity was increased.

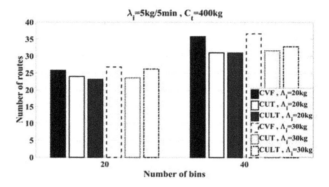

Figure 18. Number of routes: bin count when the bin capacity was increased.

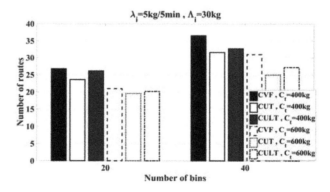

Figure 19. Number of routes: bin count when the truck capacity was increased.

Table 3. Cost when $\lambda = 1$ kg/5 min.

Method	Bin Count	Bin Capacity (kg)	Truck Capacity (kg)	Cost (€)	Delay per Route	No. of Routes
CVF	20	20	400	5354.16	193.78	5.8
CUT	20	20	400	6246.67	205.16	6
CULT	20	20	400	5542.85	199.41	5.8
CVF	20	30	400	4343.99	155.17	5.8
CUT	20	30	400	4953.32	187.85	5.6
CULT	20	30	400	4229.57	143.68	6.2
CVF	20	30	600	4189.10	305.8	2.8
CUT	20	30	600	4936.05	345.12	3
CULT	20	30	600	4134.74	330.23	2.6
CVF	40	20	400	11,188.28	109.36	12
CUT	40	20	400	14,950.88	126.79	10
CULT	40	20	400	11,801.55	112.27	11.6
CVF	40	30	400	5926.93	104.85	12
CUT	40	30	400	11,722.18	116.95	10.4
CULT	40	30	400	6634.55	104.22	12
CVF	40	30	600	5665.45	158.35	8
CUT	40	30	600	11,579.94	17,726	7
CULT	40	30	600	6066.07	157.86	8

In Table 3, the first part presents the results on the map with 20 bins. When Λ_i and C_i were lower, the CVF results were more efficient in terms of cost. However, increasing these parameters separately resulted in more efficient solutions when compared to CULT. Since λ was small, there was enough time for the trucks to visit bins that had alarmed and collect the ones on their way according to the decision mechanism in CULT. Delay per route values were similar for CVF and CULT in most cases. As the truck capacity increased, the difference between them started to become wider. In addition, CUT yielded longer durations for a single trip in each scenario on the smaller map. The number of routes was quite similar on the smaller map. Comparing the methods for this particular performance metric on the wider map was more worthwhile.

When the simulation scenarios were tested on the map with 40 bins, CVF demonstrated the most competent performance, whereas CUT resulted in the worst solutions in terms of cost. Increasing Λ_i and C_i also increased the gap between CVF and its counterparts. Delay per route under CVF and that under CULT on the wider map were quite similar. CUT exhibited a longer delay time per route, which meant adding new bins on-the-fly ended up increasing the delay by collecting waste from bins that did not have a significant amount of waste accumulated. Delay per route may not significantly change when the bin capacity was increased. Thus, trip durations mostly depended on the truck capacity. Similar to the delay performance, the number of routes that trucks had in a single simulation run was smaller under CUT. Since trucks travelled longer in a single trip and the total delay did not change significantly, the number of routes was smaller under CUT. Moreover, the route numbers almost never changed under CVF and CULT. Besides, increasing the truck capacity had a direct impact on the route count, but not the bin capacity.

In order to present our approaches' suitability to real-life scenarios, the test scenarios were modified to show results with larger maps that contained more bins. Three additional larger maps were used: (1) the map given in Figure 7 for the 40-bin scenario was modified, and 40 more bins (total of 80 bins) were deployed to the region; (2) the map given in Figure 7 was duplicated in terms of the area and the number of bins; moreover, a third map of 160 bins was constructed. All three approaches (i.e., CVF, CUT and CULT) were tested using these three maps with the following parameter settings: bin capacity ($\Lambda_i = 30$ kg), truck capacity ($C_t = 600$ kg), waste arrival rate ($\lambda_i = 3$ kg/5 min) and the number of trucks ($N = 2$). These scenarios were compared based on their total cost, delay per route and the number of routes. The results are presented in Figures 20–22.

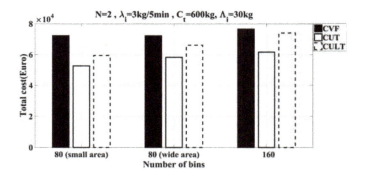

Figure 20. Cost: bin count as the number of bins increased.

Figure 20 shows the total cost obtained under these three scenarios. CUT outperformed its counterparts, CULT and CVF. As mentioned earlier in this section, under the moderate arrival rate, as the map became larger, CUT tended to provide more cost-efficient solutions. As expected, increasing map size and the number of bins increased the total cost for all methods. Definitely, the higher the number of bins, the higher the number of triggers during a certain period of time. On the other hand, by considering more triggers when making decisions, the routes could be constructed more efficiently (leading to consecutively visited bins becoming closer). Hence, better cost values were achieved, and as we increased the area, we did not observe a remarkable increase in the total cost values obtained.

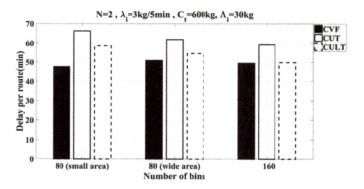

Figure 21. Delay per route: bin count as the number of bins increased.

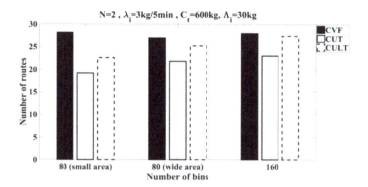

Figure 22. Number of routes: bin count as the number of bins increased.

Figures 21 and 22 present the delay per route and the number of routes, respectively, calculated for the same three scenarios. In terms of total delay, CUT provided the most efficient results for all three scenarios with two trucks. However, the number of routes was the lowest for CUT and highest for CVF. Moreover, total delay did not change significantly as observed for the previous cases. Hence, CVF resulted in the smallest delay per route. Previously, it was observed that the delay per route decreased as the area became larger due to the increase in the route counts. The results of 80-bin and 160-bin scenarios also supported this. As the number of routes increased, shorter routes were established since collected bins became closer to each other and the trucks reached their capacity limits quickly.

As for the complexities of these three methods, the Big O notation is applied. All three methods use Dijkstra's algorithm to generate the shortest path from the given weighted adjacency matrix. The weights are the distances between the nodes, which represent the bins. Dijkstra's algorithm calculates the shortest distance, but does not calculate the path information. It is modified for the simulation environment to show the shortest path between any given two nodes for the methods CUT and CULT. At the beginning of the simulation, Dijkstra's algorithm runs and constructs a matrix representing the distances between any two points. For CUT and CULT, an additional matrix representing the path information between any two nodes is constructed. Dijkstra's algorithm is not covering to negative weighted edges, and Bellman–Ford algorithm can be used in that case and improve the constructed route for a truck in the simulation environment. The time complexity of Dijkstra's algorithm is $O(V^2)$, where V denotes the number of vertices in a connected graph.

If binary heap representation were used, it might have improved the complexity and have reduced it to $O(E \log V)$, E being the edge count and V being the number of vertices. This complexity is for constructing the matrices at the beginning. Time complexity for adding a bin to the route is $O(M)$, M representing the bin count. Time complexity for checking the bins on the shortest path in CUT and CULT is $O(M)$. In summary, all three methods have the time complexity of $O(V^2)$, where V denotes the number of vertices in a connected graph.

According to the results, when the bin capacity and bin threshold's (Ψ_i, δ_i) had a high difference compared to each other, in the small sized area with smaller arrival rates (λ), CVF gave a more efficient solution compared to CUT and CULT. This means there was enough time for the trucks to reach the bins that raised alarms before waste was spread on the ground. The penalty values for spread waste affected the total cost in terms of the spread waste amount. In this situation, collecting the waste from the bins that did not raise an alarm, even if they were on the way of the truck, increased the total cost and delay values since dumping a single bin had its own cost and time consumption. CUT gave the least efficient solution among them. CULT provided a better solution and became closer to the the solution of CVF if the truck capacity also increased. This was the result of a decrease in the number of trips to the disposal area. When truck capacity was higher, the trucks could pick up more bins in one trip. The additional bins that did not raise an alarm, but were picked up on the way did not occupy a significant amount of space in the truck when C_i was higher. It is worth noting that the longest path was the ones between the disposal area and the central station (h), and also, the most time-consuming activity was emptying the waste at the disposal area and making the truck ready for the next trip (R_t), so increasing the trip count increased the cost and delay significantly.

In larger maps, with higher Λ_i and proportional λ, the proposed heuristic CULT provided more efficient solutions regarding cost and delay. However, when the constants became closer and the map became smaller, CVF and CUT tended to ensure better solutions. The increase in the C_i had more impact on the results when the map and the λ were larger.

7. Conclusions

Wireless sensor and actuator networks in smart cities are essential for acquiring unique data that should be processed, analysed and used for decision-making/support systems that can improve the quality of life for the citizens. Among smart city services and applications, waste management has been challenging, and emergent, since its impacts are two-fold: quality of living and municipal costs.

In this paper, we have proposed a framework that aims at providing a sensor-driven waste management system by mainly providing trajectory assistance for the municipal agents (i.e., vehicles such as trucks) that are deployed for waste collection. In the proposed waste management system, a passive sensor is deployed in a particular bin to monitor the waste level. Besides the dedicated sensors, a cloud platform is responsible for the collection of the acquired sensor data, pre-processing, analysing and possibly presenting them to the end user. In the case of an exceeded threshold of the waste level, an actuator raises an alarm indicating the need to schedule a pickup. The pickup process is not as straightforward due to the following reasons: (1) Alarms may be triggered by multiple actuators; thus, the cloud platform, where sensory reports, as well as alarms are received and processed, is expected to run a schedule. (2) As the deployment of municipal agents is a costly process, the platform has to decide on whether or not to collect the waste in the bins that have not reached the pickup threshold yet. To address these problems, we have formulated two ILP models to form lower bounds in terms of the delay and cost performance. Furthermore, in order to emulate the behaviour of the ILP formulations, a greedy algorithm, Closest Vehicle First (CVF), and two heuristic solutions have been proposed, namely Collect based on Upper Threshold (CUT) and Collect based on Upper and Lower Threshold (CULT). The former defines an empirical upper threshold for collections, whereas the latter further checks whether the load level of a bin is below a lower threshold so as to postpone the collection process to an upcoming alarm. Through simulations, we have shown that the ILP formulations can provide cost and delay lower bounds for all three algorithms. Furthermore, the proposed heuristics CUT and CULT can reduce the cost under the greedy pickup schedule by (up to) 16.7% and 8.3% in the presence of a small number of bins. Moreover, under the same settings, we have also shown that CUT and CULT can reduce the delay of the greedy pickup by 4.6% and 3% in terms of delay, respectively. Last but not least, the greedy heuristic CVF is more favourable in large-scale scenarios when the covered region has 20 of more bins regardless of the waste arrival rate. As mentioned earlier, the optimization models are employed in urban areas, relying on reasonable waste arrival rates for the cities. Therefore, it is rare to have accumulative wastes in the bins for multiple consecutive days. Furthermore, Equations (13) and (36) ensure that all bins must be collected. Moreover, CUT ensures that all the bins, regardless of having raised alarms, on the same assigned route to the truck will be collected along with those residing on the same route. However, the model can be extended to include rural areas with very low arrival rates by adding a time counter for those bins that have not been collected for more than T days, where T can be set by the operator.

Our ongoing and future agenda includes multiple directions. Currently, we are working on building a multi-objective optimization and heuristics to meet various targets with the same decision support system. In the medium run, we will also integrate the latency and reliability of communication between the dedicated sensors and the cloud platform. In a longer time frame, we will develop an all-in-one integrated system that takes communication constraints, as well as financial- and user experience-related parameters into account. Moreover, the model can be extended to include rural areas with very low arrival rates by adding a time counter for those bins that have not been collected for more than T days, where T can be set by the operator.

Author Contributions: A.O. and D.G., B.K. and S.F.O., conceived of and pursued the literature survey on WSAN-based waste management in smart cities. D.G. worked on the heuristic implementation, while A.O. worked on formulating and solving the optimizations. Simulations and optimizations have been verified by S.F.O. and B.K. All authors wrote the paper collaboratively. A.O. and D.G. created the illustrative images.

Funding: This research was funded by [Natural Sciences and Engineering Research Council of Canada (NSERC) Discovery Program] grant number [RGPIN-2017-04032] and [Turkish Ministry of Development] grant number [ITU-AYP-2016-8].

Conflicts of Interest: The authors declare no conflict of interest.

References

1. Habibzadeh, H.; Qin, Z.; Soyata, T.; Kantarci, B. Large Scale Distributed Dedicated- and Non-Dedicated Smart City Sensing Systems. *IEEE Sens. J.* **2017**, *17*, 7649–7658. [CrossRef]
2. Shyam, G.K.; Manvi, S.S.; Bharti, P. Smart waste management using Internet-of-Things (IoT). In Proceedings of the 2nd International Conference on Computing and Communications Technologies (ICCCT), Chennai, India, 23–24 February 2017; pp. 199–203.
3. Habibzadeh, H.; Boggio-Dandry, A.; Qin, Z.; Soyata, T.; Kantarci, B.; Mouftah, H.T. Soft Sensing in Smart Cities: Handling 3Vs Using Recommender Systems, Machine Intelligence, and Data Analytics. *IEEE Commun. Mag.* **2018**, *56*, 78–86. [CrossRef]
4. Page, A.; Hijazi, S.; Askan, D.; Kantarci, B.; Soyata, T. Research Directions in Cloud-Based Decision Support Systems for Health Monitoring Using Internet-of-Things Driven Data Acquisition. *Int. J. Serv. Comput.* **2016**, *4*, 18–34.
5. Pouryazdan, M.; Kantarci, B.; Soyata, T.; Song, H. Anchor-Assisted and Vote-Based Trustworthiness Assurance in Smart City Crowdsensing. *IEEE Access* **2016**, *4*, 529–541. [CrossRef]
6. Pouryazdan, M.; Kantarci, B. The Smart Citizen Factor in Trustworthy Smart City Crowdsensing. *IT Prof.* **2016**, *18*, 26–33. [CrossRef]
7. Hijazi, S.; Page, A.; Kantarci, B.; Soyata, T. Machine Learning in Cardiac Health Monitoring and Decision Support. *IEEE Comput.* **2016**, *49*, 38–48. [CrossRef]
8. Silva, B.N.; Khan, M.; Han, K. Towards sustainable smart cities: A review of trends, architectures, components, and open challenges in smart cities. *Sustain. Cities Soc.* **2018**, *38*, 697–713. [CrossRef]
9. Atzori, L.; Iera, A.; Morabito, G. Understanding the Internet of Things: Definition, potentials, and societal role of a fast evolving paradigm. *Ad Hoc Netw.* **2017**, *56*, 122–140. [CrossRef]
10. Strzelecka, A.; Ulanicki, B.; Koop, S.; Koetsier, L.; van Leeuwen, K.; Elelman, R. Integrating Water, Waste, Energy, Transport and ICT Aspects into the Smart City Concept. *Procedia Eng.* **2017**, *186*, 609 – 616. [CrossRef]
11. Gruler, A.; Quintero-Araújo, C.L.; Calvet, L.; Juan, A.A. Waste collection under uncertainty: A simheuristic based on variable neighbourhood search. *Eur. J. Ind. Eng.* **2017**, *11*, 228–255. [CrossRef]
12. Aazam, M.; St-Hilaire, M.; Lung, C.H.; Lambadaris, I. Cloud-based smart waste management for smart cities. In Proceedings of the IEEE 21st International Workshop on Computer Aided Modelling and Design of Communication Links and Networks (CAMAD), Toronto, ON, Canada, 23–25 October 2016; pp. 188–193.
13. Coban, A.; Ertis, I.F.; Cavdaroglu, N.A. Municipal solid waste management via multi-criteria decision making methods: A case study in Istanbul, Turkey. *J. Clean. Prod.* **2018**, *180*, 159–167. [CrossRef]
14. Minghua, Z.; Xiumin, F.; Rovetta, A.; Qichang, H.; Vicentini, F.; Bingkai, L.; Giusti, A.; Yi, L. Municipal solid waste management in Pudong New Area, China. *Waste Manag.* **2009**, *29*, 1227–1233. [CrossRef] [PubMed]
15. Fussa, M.; Barros, R.T.V.; Poganietz, W.R. Designing a framework for municipal solid waste managementtowards sustainability in emerging economy countries—An application to a case study in Belo Horizonte (Brazil). *J. Clean. Prod.* **2018**, *178*, 655–664. [CrossRef]
16. Ikhlayel, M. Development of management systems for sustainable municipal solid waste in developing countries: A systematic life cycle thinking approach. *J. Clean. Prod.* **2018**, *180*, 571–586. [CrossRef]

17. Guerrero, L.A.; Maas, G.; Hogland, W. Solid waste management challenges for cities in developing countries. *Waste Manag.* **2013**, *33*, 220–232. [CrossRef] [PubMed]
18. Marshall, R.E.; Farahbakhsh, K. Systems approaches to integrated solid waste management in developing countries. *Waste Manag.* **2013**, *33*, 988–1003. [CrossRef] [PubMed]
19. Henry, R.K.; Yongsheng, Z.; Jun, D. Municipal solid waste management challenges in developing countries—Kenyan case study. *Waste Manag.* **2006**, *26*, 92–100. [CrossRef] [PubMed]
20. Anagnostopoulos, T.; Kolomvatsos, K.; Anagnostopoulos, C.; Zaslavsky, A.; Hadjiefthymiades, S. Assessing dynamic models for high priority waste collection in smart cities. *J. Syst. Softw.* **2015**, *110*, 178–192. [CrossRef]
21. Manqele, L.; Adeogun, R.; Dlodlo, M.; Coetzee, L. Multi-objective decision-making framework for effective waste collection in smart cities. In Proceedings of the Global Wireless Summit (GWS), Cape Town, South Africa, 15–18 October 2017; pp. 155–159.
22. UNEP—United Nations Environment Programme. Municipal Solid Waste: Is It Garbage or Gold? 2013. Available online: https://na.unep.net/geas/getUNEPPageWithArticleIDScript.php?article_id=105 (accessed on 10 March 2018).
23. Johansson, O.M. The effect of dynamic scheduling and routing in a solid waste management system. *Waste Manag.* **2006**, *26*, 875–885. [CrossRef] [PubMed]
24. Jouhara, H.; Czajczyńska, D.; Ghazal, H.; Krzyzynska, R.; Anguilano, L.; Reynolds, A.; Spencer, N. Municipal waste management systems for domestic use. *Energy* **2017**, *139*, 485–506. [CrossRef]
25. Nuortioa, T.; Kytöjoki, J.; Niskaa, H.; Braysy, O. Improved route planning and scheduling of waste collection and transport. *Expert Syst. Appl.* **2006**, *30*, 223–232. [CrossRef]
26. Arebey, M.; Hannan, M.; Begum, R.; Basri, H. Solid waste bin level detection using gray level co-occurrence matrix feature extraction approach. *J. Environ. Manag.* **2012**, *104*, 9–18. [CrossRef] [PubMed]
27. Chenga, S.; Chanb, C.; Huang, G. An integrated multi-criteria decision analysis and inexact mixed integer linear programming approach for solid waste management. *Eng. Appl. Artif. Intell.* **2006**, *16*, 543–554. [CrossRef]
28. Mamun, M.A.A.; Hannan, M.A.; Hussain, A.; Basri, H. Theoretical model and implementation of a real time intelligent bin status monitoring system using rule based decision algorithms. *Expert Syst. Appl.* **2016**, *48*, 76–88. [CrossRef]
29. Apaydin, O. Route optimization for solid waste collection: Trabzon (Turkey) case study. *Glob. NEST J.* **2007**, *9*, 6–11.
30. Ramos, T.R.P.; de Morais, C.S.; Barbosa-Póvoa, A.P. The smart waste collection routing problem: Alternative operational management approaches. *Expert Syst. Appl.* **2018**, *103*, 146–158. [CrossRef]
31. Ramson, S.J.; Moni, D.J. Wireless sensor networks based smart bin. *Comput. Electr. Eng.* **2017**, *64*, 337–353. [CrossRef]
32. Data analytics approach to create waste generation profiles for waste management and collection. *Waste Manag.* **2018**, *77*, 477–485.
33. MATLAB Optimization Toolbox, version 8.0 (MATLAB R2017b). Available online: https://www.mathworks.com/products/optimization.html (accessed on 10 March 2018).

Article

Activity Recognition Using Gazed Text and Viewpoint Information for User Support Systems

Shun Chiba †, Tomo Miyazaki [ID], Yoshihiro Sugaya [ID] and Shinichiro Omachi * [ID]

Graduate School of Engineering, Tohoku University, Aoba 6-6-05, Aramaki, Aoba-ku, Sendai 980-8579, Japan; chiba@iic.ecei.tohoku.ac.jp (S.C.); tomo@iic.ecei.tohoku.ac.jp (T.M.); sugaya@iic.ecei.tohoku.ac.jp (Y.S.)

* Correspondence: machi@ecei.tohoku.ac.jp
† Current address: Future Architect, Inc., 1-2-2 Osaki, Shinagawa-ku, Tokyo 141-0032, Japan.

Received: 30 June 2018; Accepted: 31 July 2018; Published: 2 August 2018

Abstract: The development of information technology has added many conveniences to our lives. On the other hand, however, we have to deal with various kinds of information, which can be a difficult task for elderly people or those who are not familiar with information devices. A technology to recognize each person's activity and providing appropriate support based on that activity could be useful for such people. In this paper, we propose a novel fine-grained activity recognition method for user support systems that focuses on identifying the text at which a user is gazing, based on the idea that the content of the text is related to the activity of the user. It is necessary to keep in mind that the meaning of the text depends on its location. To tackle this problem, we propose the simultaneous use of a wearable device and fixed camera. To obtain the global location of the text, we perform image matching using the local features of the images obtained by these two devices. Then, we generate a feature vector based on this information and the content of the text. To show the effectiveness of the proposed approach, we performed activity recognition experiments with six subjects in a laboratory environment.

Keywords: activity recognition; eye tracker; fisheye camera; viewpoint information

---

1. Introduction

Advanced information technology and various information devices have made the environment where we live remarkably convenient. On the other hand, society is becoming more complicated because we have to deal with various kinds of information. It might be difficult for elderly people or those who are not familiar with information devices to enjoy the merits of the advanced informationization of modern society. Consider a case where you are at a station and are traveling to a destination by train. If you are not good at handling information devices, the first thing you have to do is look at a route map and find the destination station. Then, you will need to find the route information from the current station to your destination: the first railway line where you take a train, transit station, railway line after transit, and so on. Next, you will need to find an appropriate ticket vending machine and purchase a ticket for that destination. Then, it is necessary to find the ticket gate where you catch the train. This procedure will continue until you arrive at your destination. However, such necessary information can be easily provided by information devices. If it was possible to recognize each person's fine-grained activity and provide appropriate support based on that activity, this could be a useful technology for smart cities, where all people, including the elderly, can enjoy the benefits of advanced information technology.

In this paper, we propose a novel fine-grained activity recognition method for user support systems that focuses on identifying the text at which a user is gazing. Text exists everywhere around us and provides various kinds of useful information. Our proposal is based on the idea that the content of the text is related to the activity of the user.

However, it is necessary to keep in mind that using only the content of gazed text is insufficient to estimate the activity. The meaning of the text depends on its location and situation. For example, if the gazed text is a number, you cannot judge whether the user is checking a price when shopping or looking at a sign indicating the distance to a destination. To tackle this problem, we propose the simultaneous use of a wearable device and fixed camera as sensors. These two are assumed to be Internet of things (IoT) devices and are connected to each other. Using these devices, we propose a method to simultaneously obtain the content of the text at which the user is gazing and its global location. Then, the activity of the user is recognized by a machine learning method using this information.

To achieve this, we use an eye tracker as a wearable device and a fisheye camera as a fixed camera. The eye tracker is used to measure the viewpoint of the user and acquire an image of the area around that viewpoint. Recognition of the gazed text of the user is possible by utilizing the eye tracker. The fisheye camera is capable of acquiring a 360° image of the area around the camera with a fisheye lens. The global location of the user's viewpoint is estimated by matching the images acquired with these devices. Finally, the user's activity is recognized using a feature vector calculated from the acquired features. The effect of the proposed approach was tested in the situation where a user buys a ticket at a ticket vending machine in a station.

The main contribution of this paper is twofold. First, we propose a general idea of an activity recognition algorithm utilizing content and location of the text at which a user is gazing. By using text information, more detailed activities can be recognized compared to the target activities of the existing methods described in the next subsection. Second, we construct a system with a wearable device and fisheye camera based on the proposed algorithm, and the effect of the system is experimentally shown. The results show the feasibility of the user support system mentioned above. To the best of our knowledge, this is the first attempt at using the content and global location of the text at which a user is gazing for activity recognition.

Related Work

Many studies on activity recognition have been carried out. One of the typical approaches is to recognize activities using fixed cameras, and this approach has a long history. Polana and Nelson defined activities to be temporally periodic motions possessing a compact spatial structure [1]. They used a periodicity measure for detecting an activity and classified the activity by a feature vector based on motion information. Yamashita et al. proposed a method for human body detection, posture estimation, and activity recognition using an image sequence acquired by a fixed camera [2]. Human body detection and posture estimation were performed using a single frame, and the activity was recognized by combining the information of several frames. Chen et al. used a panoramic camera located at the center of a living room to classify activities [3]. Moving subjects and TV switching were detected by background subtraction. It should also be noted that the method that uses a fixed camera can also be applied to recognize the activities of a group of people. The method proposed by Gárate et al. was used for the tracking and activity recognition of a moving group in a subway station [4]. This method had the advantages of robustness, the ability to process the data for a long video, and the ability to simultaneously recognize multiple events.

Using wearable sensors is another option for activity recognition. Ouchi and Doi proposed a method of utilizing the sound acquired by a microphone, in addition to data from an acceleration sensor [5]. In this method, a user's activity is first roughly classified into resting, walking, or performing an activity using an accelerometer. If it is classified as performing an activity, a more detailed work analysis is conducted using the sound. Because this method uses sound, it is not possible to classify work that has no distinctive sound, and it cannot perform accurate classification in places with loud noises. Zeng et al. proposed a method for recognizing activity by convolutional neural networks using mobile sensors [6]. In their method, the local dependency and scale invariant characteristics could be extracted. Pham used an acceleration sensor in a smart phone or wristwatch-type mobile device [7]. Real-time activity recognition was performed by data processing, segmentation, feature extraction, and classification. Xu et al. introduced the Hilbert–Huang transform to handle nonlinear and non-stationary signals [8]. They proposed a method for extracting multiple features to improve the effect of activity recognition. Liu et al. focused on housekeeping tasks and developed a wearable sensor-based system [9]. In their method, the activity level was also evaluated for each task. Rezaie and Ghassemian focused on the lifetime of sensor nodes considering the actual use situation [10]. Their approach nearly doubled the system lifetime. Twomey et al. conducted a survey of activity recognition methods that use accelerometers [11]. They selected six important aspects of human activity recognition and discussed these topics. In terms of devices, Wang et al. reviewed the wearable sensors for activity recognition [12].

Among the approaches using wearable sensors, the technique of using a wearable camera to recognize the environment and user's activity is called a first-person vision or an egocentric vision method, and has been attracting attention in recent years [13]. Yan et al. proposed a multitask clustering framework to classify daily activities [14]. They introduced two novel clustering algorithms to determine partitions that are coherent among related tasks. Abebe and Cavallaro proposed the use of a long short-term memory network to encode temporal information [15]. They derived a stacked spectrogram representation for global motion streams so that 2D convolutions could be used for learning and feature extraction. Noor and Uddin used the information of objects to increase the accuracy of activity recognition [16]. They showed that adding object information not only improved the accuracy but also increased the training speed. Nguyen et al. reviewed daily living activity recognition methods that used egocentric vision [17].

Examples of the target activities mentioned in the above references are summarized in Table 1.

Table 1. Example of target activities.

Method	Devices	Target Activities
Polana [1]	Fixed camera	walking, running, swinging, skiing, exercising, and jumping
Yamashita [2]	Fixed camera	walking, picking, bending, boxing, clapping, waving, jogging, running, and walking
Chen [3]	Fixed camera	standing, walking, sitting, falling, and watching television
Ouchi [5]	Wearable sensor	washing dishes, ironing, vacuuming, brushing teeth, drying hair, shaving, flushing the toilet, and talking
Zeng [6]	Wearable sensor	jogging, walking, ascending stairs, descending stairs, sitting, and standing
Pham [7]	Wearable sensor	running, walking, sitting, standing, jumping, kicking, going-up stairs, going down-stairs, laying, and unknown activities
Xu [8]	Wearable sensor	lying, sitting, standing, walking, running, cycling, nordic walking, watching television, computer work, driving a car, ascending stairs, descending stairs, vacuuming, ironing, folding laundry, house cleaning, playing soccer, and rope jumping
Liu [9]	Wearable sensor	hanging clothes, folding clothes, wiping furniture, sweeping floor, mopping floor, vacuuming floor, scrubbing floor, digging, filling, moving items (on the floor), moving items (upstairs), and moving items (downstairs)
Rezaie [10]	Wearable sensor	standing, sitting, lying down, brushing, eating, walking, and running
Twomey [11]	Wearable sensor	walking, ascending stairs, descending stairs, sitting, standing, lying down, working at computer, walking and talking, standing and talking, sleeping, etc.
Yan [14]	Wearable camera	reading a book, watching a video, copying text from screen to screen, writing sentences on paper, and browsing the internet
Abebe [15]	Wearable camera	going upstairs, running, walking, sitting/standing, and static
Noor [16]	Wearable camera	reaching, sprinkling, spreading, opening, closing, cutting, etc.

However, it is difficult to realize the above-mentioned user support system using these existing approaches. When using the approaches with fixed cameras and wearable sensors, it is difficult to recognize activities other than the motion of the whole body. For example, assuming that the user stands in front of a ticket vending machine at a station, the necessary information is quite different depending on whether the user watches the route map or instructions for the ticket vending machine. It is difficult to distinguish these activities using wearable acceleration sensors or fixed cameras because there is almost no movement of the body. As for the first-person vision approach, it is not easy to obtain the global location of the user, which is also important information for user support. These problems can be solved by using the content and location of the text at which the user is gazing. Textual information exists everywhere around us, and the possibility of looking at text is considered to be high not only when reading a book but also when users are engaged in other activities. The textual information provides a good clue to recognize the user's activity.

2. Materials and Methods

2.1. Proposed Method

The outline of the proposed method is shown in Figure 1. A wearable eye tracker and fixed fisheye camera are used as input devices. For convenience, the images obtained from the eye tracker and fisheye camera are called the eye-tracker image and fisheye image, respectively. Information about the user's viewpoint can also be obtained from the eye tracker. The text at which the user is gazing is detected using the eye-tracker image and viewpoint information. This text is regarded as the text of interest, and it is recognized by an optical character reader (OCR). On the other hand, the eye-tracker and fisheye images are matched to calculate the user's viewpoint in the fisheye image. Hence, the global location of the gazed text is detected. Then, the activity of the user is estimated using the information about the text and its location. Note that the fisheye camera has a drawback that the acquired image is distorted and its resolution is low, which makes image recognition difficult. Therefore, the fisheye image is only used to detect the user's viewpoint, and text recognitoin is performed using the eye-tracker image.

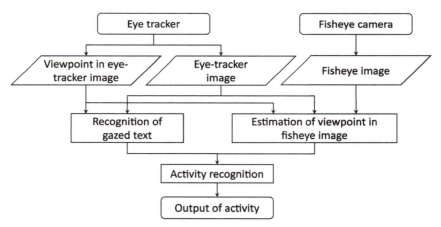

Figure 1. Outline of the proposed method.

2.1.1. Recognition of Gazed Text

An image of the area around the viewpoint is segmented from the eye-tracker image and is binarized. Then, the text recognition is performed using the Tesseract-OCR [18]. When a text is detected in the image, the coordinates of a rectangle surrounding the recognized text area, the recognition result, and its reliability are output. The distance between the recognized text and the viewpoint position is calculated, and the nearest text is regarded as the gazed text. If the segmented image does not include any text, it is judged that the user is not gazing at any text.

Then, the recognized text is matched using a text database prepared in advance. This database consists of a set of texts and their categories. For the purpose of database construction and text matching, we used SimString [19]. The category of the text is determined through the matching with the database. If there is no matched text in the database, the recognized text is used as is and its category is determined to be *others*.

2.1.2. Estimation of Viewpoint in the Fisheye Image

In order to estimate the user's viewpoint in the fisheye image, image matching is performed between the fisheye image and the eye-tracker image. Because the distortion of the fisheye image is different from that of the eye-tracker image, we adopt two-stage matching. First, the eye-tracker image is used as is to roughly detect the region. Then, the eye-tracker image is converted according to the detected location, and it is used for precise detection. We use the speeded-up robust features (SURF) [20] as the feature for image matching.

In the first stage, we extract the keypoints of SURF from each image and perform feature matching. An example is shown in Figure 2a. The large image is the fisheye image, and the small image at the upper-right corner is the eye-tracker image. The matched keypoints are connected by lines. Each extracted keypoint has information about the rotation angle and scale. Using this information, the scale and difference in the rotation angles between the two images are adjusted. The position of the eye-tracker image in the fisheye image is estimated by searching for the position that minimizes the sum of the distances between matched feature points. An example of a roughly detected region is shown in Figure 2b.

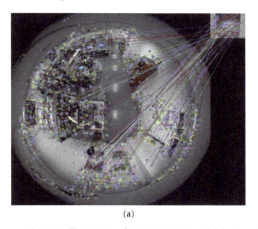 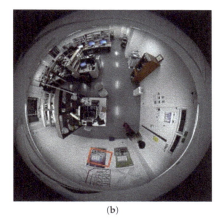

(a)   (b)

Figure 2. First stage of image matching. (**a**) feature point matching. The large image is the fisheye image, and the small image at the upper-right corner is the eye-tracker image. (**b**) roughly detected region. This region that corresponds to the eye-tracker image is indicated as a red rectangle in the fisheye image.

The accuracy of this matching is not very high because the distortion of the fisheye lens is not taken into account. Therefore, we convert the eye-tracker image so that the distortion is the same as that at the detected position in the fisheye image by calculating the corresponding points of these images [21]. Then, the image matching of the second stage is performed using the converted image. Figure 3 shows an example of the result of the second-stage image matching. It can be confirmed that the accuracy was much improved compared with the first stage matching (Figure 2a). Finally, we calculate the viewpoint position in the fisheye image using the positional relationship obtained by the image matching.

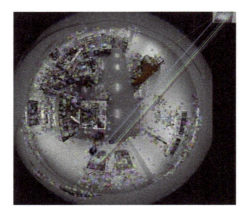

Figure 3. Second stage of image matching.

2.1.3. Activity Recognition

Activity recognition is performed using the acquired gazed text and viewpoint location in the fisheye image. The accuracy of the eye-tracker varies depending on the user or misrecognition of the text. Therefore, we adopt the random forest [22] method, which is less sensitive to noise, as the classification algorithm. In the training phase, subsamples are selected from the training data by random sampling to construct decision trees. These decision trees are used for classification.

We use six-dimensional feature vector (x, y, n, t, d, c) as the feature vector. The meaning of each element is listed in Table 2. The number of characters is used for distinguishing long and short texts, which normally represents guidance and place names, respectively. The average of character codes is used for distinguishing between numbers and alphabets. The distance between the viewpoint and the gazed text is used to judge whether or not the user is really gazing at the text.

Table 2. Elements of feature vector.

Element	Meaning
x	x-coordinate of the viewpoint location in the fisheye image
y	y-coordinate of the viewpoint location in the fisheye image
n	number of characters in the gazed text
t	average of character codes in the gazed text
d	distance between the viewpoint and the gazed text
c	category of the gazed text

2.2. Experiment

2.2.1. Equipment

As a wearable eye tracker, we used SMI eye tracking glasses (https://www.smivision.com/). This device is equipped with a camera for obtaining an infrared image of the eyes of the user, and a camera for obtaining the field of view of the user. This makes it possible to record the field of view and viewpoint of the user at the same time. Because the frame rates for the field of view and viewpoint are 24 fps and 30 fps, respectively, synchronization is required.

As a fixed fisheye camera, we used the Kodak PIXPRO SP360 4K (https://www.kodak.com/). This is an omnidirectional camera equipped with one fisheye lens. It is possible to acquire an image that covers 360° in the horizontal direction and 235° in the vertical direction.

2.2.2. Experimental Environment

We constructed an experimental environment to simulate a ticket vending machine in a station. An image of a ticket vending machine and route map was printed on paper and affixed to the wall to reproduce the vicinity of the ticket vending machine. The constructed environment is shown in Figure 4a. A portion of the text database used is listed in Table 3.

In order to reproduce the surveillance camera in the station, we installed the fisheye camera on the ceiling. It was installed in front of the ticket vending machine, about 2.5 m away from the wall. A fisheye image acquired by the fisheye camera is shown in Figure 4b.

 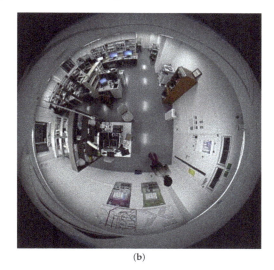

(a)   (b)

Figure 4. Experimental environment. (**a**) printed image of ticket vending machine and route map affixed to wall; (**b**) omnidirectional image acquired by fisheye camera.

Table 3. Portion of text database.

Category	Texts
Guidance	Touch the button, Tozai Line, Nanboku Line,...
Station name	Aobayama, Sendai, International Center,...
Price	200, 250, 300,...

2.2.3. Training Data

The training data were constructed as follows. First, a subject was asked to stand in the experimental environment. Then, he or she was asked to look at the ticket vending machine and route map by moving their viewpoint (see Figure 5). We simultaneously recorded the viewpoint information and video of the field of view. Frames were extracted by synchronizing these data, and feature vectors were created with the values described in Section 2.1.3. The length of the captured video was approximately 110 s, and the number of feature vectors was 2040.

A label describing the user's activity was manually assigned to each feature vector. Considering the gazed text and location of the text, the activity was classified into the following eight types:

- Looking at the route map to check the price,
- Looking at the route map to check the station name,
- Looking at the route map to look for guidance,

- Looking at the ticket vending machine to check the price,
- Looking at the ticket vending machine to check the station name,
- Looking at the ticket vending machine to look for guidance,
- Operating the ticket vending machine,
- Others.

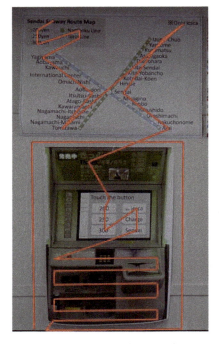

Figure 5. Viewpoints of training data.

3. Results and Discussion

3.1. Experimental Results

First, the accuracy of the proposed method was verified. We conducted the experiment with six subjects in the constructed experimental environment. The subjects were instructed to move their viewpoint to purchase a ticket for Aobayama Station while assuming that they were currently at Sendai Station. Because the distance to the ticket vending machine was not provided, each subject took the usual distance. The method used to create the experimental data was the same as that used to create the training data. The activity in each frame was recognized by the proposed method.

The number of video frames for each subject, number of correctly recognized frames, and recognition accuracy are listed in Table 4. The accuracy calculated with all the frames of all the subjects was 75.4%. Note that this is the accuracy for individual frames. Considering that recognition using several frames and recognition results in a time series can also be used when the method is actually used for user support, it is considered that activity recognition was possible by the proposed method under the experimental environment. There was a difference of more than 20 percentage points in the recognition accuracy, and it could be confirmed that there were variations among the subjects.

Table 4. Experimental results.

Subject	Number of Frames	Number of Correctly Recognized Frames	Accuracy
1	903	668	74.0%
2	620	403	65.0%
3	750	558	78.4%
4	717	462	64.4%
5	441	344	78.0%
6	1314	1141	86.9%
Total	4745	3576	75.4%

3.2. Discussion

Next, we analyze the causes of recognition failures and show improvement plans. The causes of recognition failures were roughly classified into two types. The first was the motion blur that occurred during movement of the viewpoint, as shown in Figure 6. There are two ways to move the viewpoint: moving only the eyes without moving the head, and rotating the head without moving the eyes. Motion blur frequently occurs in the experimental data acquired from subjects who frequently rotate their head. As a result, both the text recognition accuracy and image matching deteriorated. To overcome this problem, it will be useful to use an eye tracker with a higher frame rate.

Figure 6. Example of failure caused by motion blur.

The second reason was the error of the viewpoint location detected by the eye tracker. If the gazed text was incorrectly detected, the activity of the user was not correctly recognized. An example of this is shown in Figure 7. Although the subject was looking at the guidance of the "Sendai Subway Route Map", the detected viewpoint was slightly shifted downward. As a result, the activity was incorrectly recognized as "Looking at the route map to check the price". The eye tracker used in this experiment has the characteristic that the viewpoint location to be detected tends to be shifted when looking at the edge of the field of view. Therefore, if the subject moves only their eyes without moving their head, the detected location of the viewpoint is greatly shifted. To solve this problem, using multiple texts included in a wide area around the viewpoint will be effective.

Figure 7. Example of failure caused by misdetection of viewpoint. Although the subject was looking at the guidance of the "Sendai Subway Route Map", the detected viewpoint was slightly shifted downward.

4. Conclusions

We proposed a fine-grained activity recognition method that uses a wearable eye tracker and fixed fisheye camera. The information about the text at which the user is gazing is utilized based on the idea that the content of the text is related to the activity. The proposed activity recognition method consists of three processes: the gazed text recognition, estimation of the viewpoint in the fisheye image, and classification of the activity using the feature vector. To obtain the global location of the text, we performed image matching of the images obtained by these two devices. We demonstrated that activity recognition was possible under the experimental environment created by simulating the vicinity of a ticket vending machine in a station.

Although only an experiment in this limited environment was conducted at this time, we believe that the proposed approach can be applied for various purposes. In order to recognize activities in various situations, it will be necessary to further select and add features. Then, the method can be applied to recognize the activities in stores and libraries, in addition to stations. It is also important to construct a concrete user support system with the proposed approach.

Author Contributions: Funding acquisition, S.O.; Methodology, S.C.; Project administration, S.O.; Software, S.C.; Supervision, T.M. and Y.S.; Validation, T.M. and Y.S.; Writing—Original draft, S.C.; Writing—Review & editing, S.O.

Funding: This work was partially supported by JSPS KAKENHI Grant Numbers JP16H02841, JP16K00259.

Conflicts of Interest: The authors declare no conflict of interest.

References

1. Polana, R.; Nelson, R. Recognizing activities. In Proceedings of the 12th International Conference on Pattern Recognition, Jerusalem, Israel, 9–13 October 1994; Volume 1, pp. 815–818.
2. Yamashita, T.; Yamauchi, Y.; Fujiyoshi, H. A single framework for action recognition based on boosted randomized trees. *IPSJ Trans. Comput. Vision Appl.* **2011**, *3*, 160–171. [CrossRef]

J. Sens. Actuator Netw. **2018**, *7*, 31

3. Chen, O.T.-C.; Tsai, C.-H.; Manh, H.H.; Lai, W.-C. Activity recognition using a panoramic camera for homecare. In Proceedings of the 14th IEEE International Conference on Advanced Video and Signal Based Surveillance, Lecce, Italy, 29 August–1 September 2017; pp. 1–6.
4. Gárate, C.; Zaidenberg, S.; Badie, J.; Brémond, F. Group tracking and behavior recognition in long video surveillance sequences. In Proceedings of the 2014 International Conference on Computer Vision Theory and Applications, Lisbon, Portugal, 5–8 January 2014.
5. Ouchi, K.; Doi, M. Smartphone-based monitoring system for activities of daily living for elderly people and their relatives etc. In Proceedings of the 2013 ACM Conference on Pervasive and Ubiquitous Computing Adjunct Publication, Zurich, Switzerland, 8–12 September 2013; pp. 103–106.
6. Zeng, M.; Nguyen, L.T.; Yu, B.; Mengshoel, O.J.; Zhu, J.; Wu, P.; Zhang, J. Convolutional neural networks for human activity recognition using mobile sensors. In Proceedings of the 2014 6th International Conference on Mobile Computing, Applications and Services, Austin, TX, USA, 6–7 November 2014; pp. 197–205.
7. Pham, C. MobiRAR: Real-time human activity recognition using mobile devices. In Proceedings of the 2015 Seventh International Conference on Knowledge and Systems Engineering, Ho Chi Minh City, Vietnam, 8–10 October 2015; pp. 144–149.
8. Xu, H.; Liu, J.; Hu, H.; Zhang, Y. Wearable sensor-based human activity recognition method with multi-features extracted from Hilbert-Huang transform. *Sensors* **2016**, *16*, 2048. [CrossRef] [PubMed]
9. Liu, K.-C.; Yen, C.-Y.; Chang, L.-H.; Hsieh, C.-Y.; Chan, C.-T. Wearable sensor-based activity recognition for housekeeping task. In Proceedings of the 2017 IEEE 14th International Conference on Wearable and Implantable Body Sensor Networks, Eindhoven, Netherlands, 9–12 May 2017; pp. 67–70.
10. Rezaie, H.; Ghassemian, M. An adaptive algorithm to improve energy efficiency in wearable activity recognition systems. *IEEE Sens. J.* **2017**, *17*, 5315–5323. [CrossRef]
11. Twomey, N.; Diethe, T.; Fafoutis, X.; Elsts, A.; McConville, R.; Flach, P.; Craddock, I. A comprehensive study of activity recognition using accelerometers. *Informatics* **2018**, *5*, 27. [CrossRef]
12. Wang, Y.; Cang, C.; Yu, H. A review of sensor selection, sensor devices and sensor deployment for wearable sensor-based human activity recognition systems. In Proceedings of the 10th International Conference on Software, Knowledge, Information Management & Applications, Chengdu, China, 15–17 December 2016; pp. 250–257.
13. Kanade, T.; Hebert, M. First-person vision. Proc. IEEE. **2012**, *100*, 2442–2453. [CrossRef]
14. Yan, Y.; Ricci, E.; Liu, G.; Sebe, N. Egocentric daily activity recognition via multitask clustering. *IEEE Trans. Image Process.* **2015**, *24*, 2984–2995. [CrossRef] [PubMed]
15. Abebe, G.; Cavallaro, A. A long short-term memory convolutional neural network for first-person vision activity recognition. In Proceedings of the 2017 IEEE International Conference on Computer Vision Workshops, Venice, Italy, 22–29 October 2017; pp. 1339–1346.
16. Noor, S.; Uddin, V. Using context from inside-out vision for improved activity recognition. *IET Comput. Vision* **2018**, *12*, 276–287. [CrossRef]
17. Nguyen, T.-H.-C.; Nebel, J.-C.; Florez-Revuelta, F. Recognition of activities of daily living with egocentric vision: A review. *Sensors* **2016**, *16*, 72. [CrossRef] [PubMed]
18. Smith, R. An overview of the Tesseract OCR engine. In Proceedings of the Ninth International Conference on Document Analysis and Recognition, Parana, Brazil, 23–26 September 2007; pp. 629–633.
19. Okazaki, N.; Tsujii, J. Simple and efficient algorithm for approximate dictionary matching. In Proceedings of the 23rd International Conference on Computational Linguistics, Beijing, China, 23–27 August 2010; pp. 851–859.
20. Bay, H.; Ess, A.; Tuytelaars, T.; Van Gool, L. Speeded-up robust features (SURF). *Comput. Vision Image Underst.* **2008**, *110*, 346–359. [CrossRef]
21. Mori, T.; Tonomura, M.; Ohsumi, Y.; Goto, S.; Ikenaga, T. High quality image correction algorithm with cubic interpolation and its implementations of dedicated hardware engine for fish-eye lens. *J. Inst. Image Electron. Eng. Jpn.* **2007**, *36*, 680–687.
22. Breiman, L. Random Forests. *Mach. Learn.* **2001**, *45*, 5–32. [CrossRef]

Article

Instrumented Wireless SmartInsole System for Mobile Gait Analysis: A Validation Pilot Study with Tekscan Strideway

Faisal Arafsha [1,*] ![ORCID], **Christina Hanna** [2], **Ahmed Aboualmagd** [2], **Sarah Fraser** [2] and **Abdulmotaleb El Saddik** [1] ![ORCID]

1   Multimedia Communications Research Laboratory, School of Electrical Engineering and Computer Science,
    University of Ottawa, 800 King Edward Ave, Ottawa, ON K1N 6N5, Canada; elsaddik@uottawa.ca
2   Interdisciplinary School of Health Sciences, University of Ottawa, 200 Lees Ave,
    Ottawa, ON K1S 5S9, Canada; chann072@uottawa.ca (C.H.); amahm036@uottawa.ca (A.A.);
    sarah.fraser@uottawa.ca (S.F.)
*   Correspondence: farafsha@uottawa.ca

Received: 30 June 2018; Accepted: 15 August 2018; Published: 20 August 2018

Abstract: A SmartInsoles Cyber-Physical System (CPS) is designed and implemented for the purpose of measuring gait parameters of multiple users in a restriction-free environment. This CPS comprises a master software installed on a computer and numerous multi-sensory health devices in the form of smart insoles. Each of these insoles contains 12 Force-Sensitive Resistor (FSR) sensors, an Inertial Measurement Unit (IMU), a WiFi-enabled microcontroller and a battery to power all components. A validation pilot study was completed in collaboration with the Interdisciplinary School of Health Sciences at the University of Ottawa by performing 150 trials on 15 healthy subjects. Each subject performed 10 walks on the Tekscan Strideway gait mat system, while simultaneously wearing the designed SmartInsoles CPS. Spatiotemporal data for over 450 unique steps were collected by both systems. These data were analyzed carefully, and a thorough comparison was performed between the results from the two systems. Seven parameters were analyzed in this study: stride time, stance time, swing time, double support time, step time, cadence and gait time. Detailed results in the form of tables, scatterplots, histograms and Bland–Altman graphs were generated. Analysis of the results shows high agreement between the values of the two systems and suggests high accuracy of the implemented CPS as a multi-device, multi-sensory system for gait measurement and analysis.

Keywords: smart insole; gait analysis; wireless cyber-physical system; Internet of Things; mHealth

1. Introduction

Recording detailed foot kinetics and pressure point data can be beneficial in performance enhancement applications such as in sports and physiotherapy. Research in post-routine analysis for medical and rehabilitation applications is still lacking an optimal solution that can record gait data to be used for fall prediction, detection and avoidance [1]. Solutions to this problem are especially imperative for people who have a high risk of serious injuries as a result of falling or tripping [2].

Nonetheless, many of the validated tools used to collect mobility data (i.e., walkways/gait mats, force plates, cameras) provide excellent data on several gait parameters, but can be expensive to use and involve stationary or in-floor systems that limit the measurement of gait parameters to constrained research environments (laboratory) or in clinical settings (hospital corridors) [3].

Novel technological advances in IoT, including wireless technology and sensors, allow for the possibility of building low-cost, wearable insoles that can collect continuous measurements. These measurements can be acquired while a given participant is performing an everyday activity in naturalistic conditions (e.g., going up and down stairs, crossing a road, etc.). Furthermore, these advances provide an opportunity for mobility monitoring (over time and in different contexts) and measurement of improvements after rehabilitation within and outside a clinical setting [4].

A recent review by Muro-de-la-Herran and colleagues [5] provided an overview of the advantages and disadvantages of wearable versus non-wearable technologies to measure mobility. Each technique has its advantages and disadvantages, and the authors concluded that the choice of technology really depends on the research question and applications [5]. In the current validation study, we aimed to validate data from lightweight, low-cost, recently engineered wireless shoe insoles against a standard walkway system (Strideway by Tekscan), in order to use these insoles for mobility tasks in naturalistic settings. The gait mat system used in this study costs approximately $25,000, while each SmartInsole, in its current prototype state, costs less than $200.

2. Background

Force plates, accelerometers and camera systems have been widely used to quantify gait [5]. Fixed plantar pressure measurement systems provide very high performance and accurate measurements. The Italian National Institute of Health has been conducting studies that involve the design, validation, implementation and performance testing of plantar Pressure Measurement Devices (PMD) [6,7]. A thorough study was also conducted to test five commercial PMDs for accuracy in pressure force measurement, hysteresis, creep and Center of Pressure (CoP) estimation [8]. They discussed and compared the main characteristics of the five PMDs, the technologies used, calibration, and accuracy through several tests. Wired insoles used for gait analysis have also been used successfully to acquire different parameters of gait for over 30 years [9,10]. More recently, in the last 15 years, many have moved away from wired devices to gait mat technology that allows people to walk freely without wearing any technology, but this mat technology is limited to a fixed distance [11,12]. Components of the mat technology (i.e., pressure sensors), accelerometers and insole technology have advanced rapidly, allowing for smaller, more robust sensors that can be used with wireless technology in a shoe insole format. The main advantages of the wireless shoe insole format are that they can be used in naturalistic settings, can monitor changes in gait overtime in these settings and can be used in conjunction with other wireless technologies to track an individual in real time.

Different approaches were taken in recent studies to design shoe insoles for gait measurement and analysis: some use pre-fabricated pressure sensors, while some fabricated their own, and some studies added inertial measurement (i.e., accelerometers and gyroscopes) to get more information that could assist in analyzing the users' gait characteristics. With respect to the development and testing of insoles, Howell et al. [13,14] developed an insole with 32 Force-Sensitive Resistor (FSR) sensors to find the most effective number of sensors and their optimum locations in an insole. They derived a 12-sensor insole by analyzing force data acquired by the 32-sensor insole. This 12-sensor insole was then validated by comparing results with an established gait analysis system at the Physical Therapy Department at the University of Utah. Results showed high agreement and correlation between the two systems. Tan et al., on the other hand, developed an insole with piezoelectric transducers to measure and analyze gait and discussed the need for a low-cost wireless solution for that purpose [15,16]. They focused on plantar pressure calculation using the designed low-cost system and compared their results with the Kistler Force Plate.

A different approach was taken by Motha et al. [17], who fabricated a rubber insole with a focus on plantar pressure. They used Interdigitated Capacitors (IDC) as pressure sensors due to their high pressure sensitivity, amongst other reasons, as reported by [18]. The insole they designed has pressure sensors embedded in three areas: forefoot, midfoot and hind-foot. Their studies demonstrate how different postures present different responses from these three pressure areas. Crea et al. also designed an insole that embeds a grid of 64 pressure sensing elements that use LED and light sensor pairs to measure pressure distribution and center of pressure [19]. They also explained the possibility for estimating walking speed based on the distribution of detected pressure and the number of detected steps. Barun et al., on the other hand, combined 13 capacitive pressure sensors with a 3D accelerometer [20] embedded in their insole and recorded data internally in a flash storage, which can then be loaded into a computer for analysis.

Jagos et al. developed the eSHOE, which has all components embedded in the shoe. Components in the eSHOE include a three-axis accelerometer and a three-axis gyroscope, in addition to four FSR sensors [21]. Their main goal was to validate the eSHOE by comparing acquired gait parameters with the results obtained from the GAITRite walkway [22], which is a plantar pressure and gait analysis system developed by CIR Systems. The GAITRite is an electronic 6-m mat with embedded pressure sensors capable of measuring spatiotemporal gait characteristics. Results from both systems show high similarity, which signifies the possibility of replacing the gold standard GAITRite with the low-cost eSHOE. The process followed by Jagos et al. [21] to validate their eSHOE was very thorough and produced noteworthy results.

With the same embedded structure as the eSHOE, Hafidh et al. started the development of the SmartInsole© in 2013, which is a gait measurement insole device with the complete circuit embedded within the insole [23]. The embedded circuitry includes 12 FSR sensors, an accelerometer, a microcontroller, a Bluetooth modem and a 3.3-Vcell battery. Over the past five years, many versions of the SmartInsole have been designed. The smart insoles used in this study are enhanced versions of Hafidh's SmartInsole, with modifications in many aspects including the number of sensors, power and communication mechanisms, in addition to using the insoles as smart measurement instruments within a much bigger context.

In this study, we use a Cyber-Physical System (CPS), developed in-house, that performs distributed processing within the instrumented SmartInsoles. These insoles wirelessly transmit gait data to a centralized master machine that performs more processing including parameter calculations, event detection and real-time visualization, in addition to communicating historical data to a cloud database for storage. The SmartInsoles are standalone sensing devices that are interconnected via the developed CPS. Each of them can measure the specified gait parameters by itself. However, we developed the CPS to have most of the processing load happen in a remote machine. This, in fact, helps in achieving a higher data collection rate and allows for more sensory details to be transmitted to the cyber system installed on the centralized master machine. The cyber system will handle all the processing and provide feedback in real time. A CPS setup also allows for multiple SmartInsole devices to stream simultaneously, which can be very helpful in group activity measurements such as sports or physiotherapy. In order to carefully validate this smart insole, we chose to test the data from our system against the data from a Tekscan Strideway gait mat system. As Jagos et al.'s work [21] is one of the most comprehensive evaluations of new insole technology for gait measurement purposes, we will use a similar approach to compare several gait parameters acquired by the SmartInsole (within our CPS) and the Strideway.

3. Materials and Methods

3.1. SmartInsoles CPS: Wireless Gait Activity Monitoring System

Cyber-physical systems are systems engineered to seamlessly integrate computational components, networking and physical processes in a well-defined context to serve a specific purpose. The implemented system used in this study is a CPS designed for gait activities' measurement and analysis. It collects sensory data from numerous multi-sensory SmartInsole devices and transmits them to a central system that performs live visualization and data storage operations. The whole operation process including collecting data and streaming sensory information is done over conventional IEEE802.11 WiFi. Using WiFi allows for more user movement freedom and higher transmission range in comparison to Bluetooth. It also allows for multiple devices to communicate concurrently and enables device mobility. These are important characteristics that help subjects perform tests in a realistic and non-confined environment.

Several pairs of insoles were developed for different shoe sizes and following the exact same design. Each developed insole includes 12 FSR sensors Model FSR-402 from Interlink electronics [24], as well as an Inertial Measurement Unit (IMU) containing an MPU-9250 chip [25] that is capable of measuring 3D gyro, 3D accelerometer and 3D compass data. The circuitries are printed on flexible Printed Circuit Boards (PCB) for improved durability and controlled using an ESP-8266 microcontroller breakout board, which has WiFi capabilities [26,27]. All sensors are embedded in these insoles following the exact same layout, while the WiFi-enabled microcontroller and the 3.3-VLi-ion battery were placed in an external rubber case. Each flexible PCB is padded with a 2 mm-thick foam sheet and placed inside a size-adjustable sandal (Figure 1).

Figure 1. (**Left**) Flexible PCB with embedded sensors and the control pack containing the WiFi-enabled microcontroller and the 3.3-VLi-ion battery; (**Right**) a user showing the padded SmartInsole in a sandal while strapping the control pack around the leg.

An experiment was conducted to evaluate the measuring of pressure force curves over time and how analysis of the sensed pressure and IMU data could be beneficial in detecting gait events and characteristics [28]. However, this study focused on temporal gait characteristics, and we used pressure sensors in the SmartInsole to detect time-related events to calculate these characteristics.

3.2. Reference System: Tekscan Strideway™

The Tekscan Strideway is a modular human gait analysis system used to analyze detailed spatiotemporal parameters [29]. The system is packed into a large case and weighs about 40 kg. It mainly consists of six tiles, four of which contain hundreds of embedded force sensors, a tile for gait initiation and a tile for gait inhibition. The assembled system covers an area of approximately 4 m^2 and is wired via a USB cable to a nearby computer containing the Strideway software. This 4-m^2 area is where the subject's gait data can be collected. Although the full Strideway system was only officially released in 2017, the technology/software used for this system was built based on the one-panel MatScan$^®$ pressure mat, which has produced reliable measures for human gait [30,31] and reliable and valid measures of postural stability [32,33].

This system is used widely in physiotherapy and rehabilitation applications in many health organizations. The provided software automatically reads from the physical sensors in the mat and performs calculations to derive different gait parameters such as step time, gait time, cadence, velocity and walked distance. It can also automatically detect which foot is right and which is left, which is useful in calculating toe-in/toe-out angles to compare to the subject's line of progression. During the tests, the software shows a visualization of the performed steps in the form of a heat-map. This display shows the locations of the performed steps on the mat and each step's pressure intensity. After the test, the Strideway provides detailed analysis in the form of graphs and tables showing calculated spatiotemporal data collected in the test.

3.3. Study Design and Analysis Parameters

Fifteen subjects were tested in this experiment, 8 females and 7 males, and their ages ranged between 20 and 45 years (average 31 years). The Tekscan Strideway mat was assembled in a spacious area and connected to a laptop that contained the Strideway software. Green tape was used to create a line that marks the start and the end of the actual reading area of the mat, and a video camera was used to record the lower body of test subjects. By referring to the camera footage, we used the green line to identify the first step and synchronize the steps acquired by the two systems. All subjects signed a consent for inclusion before they participated in the study. The study was conducted in accordance with the University of Ottawa Research Ethics Board, and was approved by the Office of Research Ethics and Integrity at the University of Ottawa (H10-17-08).

The goal of this experiment was to allow different subjects to walk at a normal pace, while acquiring their foot pressure data by both systems simultaneously. The outcome we aimed towards in this experiment was having comparable, ideally identical, time-related results for different gait parameters. Having this outcome supports the goal of validating the implemented CPS to be used as a reliable gait monitoring and measurement system.

We focussed on seven gait parameters in this study. Assuming the user was always walking forward, the initial contact of the person with the ground was normally at the heel. Therefore, one stride (gait cycle) began with heel contact (initial contact) of one foot with the floor and ended with the next heel contact of that same foot. Consequently, one complete gait cycle consisted of two steps, one of the right foot and one of the left foot [34]. Each gait cycle was divided into two phases: stance phase and swing phase. Stance phase began with the initial contact of one foot and ended with the toe-off of that same foot. Swing phase began with toe-off of one foot and ended with the subsequent heel contact of that same foot [35]. Stance phase usually made up about 60% of one gait cycle, and swing phase made up the remaining 40% of that gait cycle [21].

There were two periods during one gait cycle of normal walking where both feet were in contact with the ground; these were the initial and terminal double support periods. Double support time began with initial contact of one foot and ended with toe-off of the other [21]. Therefore, considering the right-foot to be the dominant foot, initial double support would start from the initial contact of the right foot and end at toe-off of the left foot. Consequently, terminal double support would start from initial contact of the left foot and end at toe-off of the right foot. For the purpose of this study, we added the average durations of the initial and terminal double support times and reported the average of total double support time for each trial.

The step time was the time duration from the initial contact of one foot to the initial contact of the subsequent step of the other foot. The gait time was the duration between the first contact of the first step and the first contact of the last step in each test. It started from the initial contact of the first step and ended with the toe-off of the last step, regardless of which foot the participant started or ended his/her gait. Cadence is calculated as the number of steps the user performed per minute. Figure 2 below shows different described gait phases and indicates each parameter's starting and ending point. In this study, the following components are collected from both systems:

- Stride time (gait cycle time)
- Stance time
- Swing time
- Double support time
- Step time
- Gait time
- Cadence

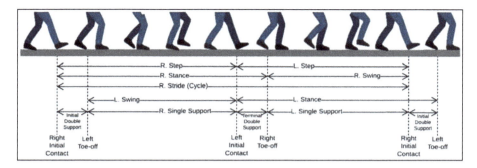

Figure 2. Description of start time and end time for different gait phases in a normal gait cycle.

3.4. Measurement Protocol

Multiple pairs of the SmartInsole were developed for different shoe sizes. Each insole was placed in a size-adjustable sandal, and subjects were asked to wear the pair with a size closest to their shoe size.

Before each subject performed a test, the experiment procedure and purpose were explained to them. They were, then, asked to sign a consent form that explained the purpose of the experiment again and indicated that the collected data would be used strictly for research purposes. Identifying information was not collected. Since the first plate in the Strideway did not contain sensors and could not collect data, we used it as the gait initiation stage. Therefore, at the beginning of each walk, subjects were asked to stand on one of the marked boxes (as seen in Figure 3), walk normally towards the other end of the mat and stop at the final box. After storing data and labeling them for post-experiment analysis, subjects were directed to stand on the starting box again for their next walk. As indicated earlier, each subject was directed to perform 10 rounds of walks.

Figure 3. Tekscan Strideway system showing marked start and stop boxes, as well as lines to indicate the start and end of the reading area (the 4 tiles with reading capability).

3.5. Analysis of Agreement

One of the main features of the Tekscan software is its ability to automatically produce spatiotemporal data details for tests performed on the Strideway mat. The results of each test are shown in the form of a video and information tables. The video shows a digital representation of the mat and the location and pressure intensity and distribution, in the form of a heat-map, of each step preformed during the test. In addition to the video, the software provides five tables for five different groups of data. These tables provide rich information on the step-stride times and forces applied, gait cycle times and the overall gait characteristics such as the distance, velocity, cadence, etc. In addition, two more tables are provided to show differential and symmetry characteristics by comparing data acquired from each foot.

The designed CPS, on the other hand, provides accurate force and time details for each of the 12 embedded pressure sensors from all of the connected SmartInsoles. These force values are used to extract timestamps for initial contact and toe-off of all steps that occurred during the operation of the system. After that, these timestamps were used to calculate all of the required gait parameters in this experiment.

Since the designed CPS reads all data coming from the SmartInsoles, some steps may not be read by the mat. Therefore, video footage was required to determine the number of first steps that occurred on the reading area of the Strideway. This process was needed to match/synchronize the correct step data acquired from each system.

Since it is almost impossible to get identical values acquired by two different systems, the amount of difference that was likely to occur between them was investigated, and an accuracy indicator was derived based on the results. The agreement accuracy was calculated for the results of this experiment using two methods. The first method, overall accuracy, looks at the overall values produced by both systems and derives the accuracy percentage based on the summations of values. The second method, average accuracy, looks at individual measures and calculates the accuracy for each pair of results from the two systems. Then, it is calculated as the average of all accuracy values derived from each pair of values (from the Strideway and the insole system). Overall accuracy and average accuracy were calculated using Equations (1) and (2), respectively.

$$Overall\ Accuracy = \left(\sum_{x=1}^{n} SW(x) - \left| \sum_{x=1}^{n} SW(x) - \sum_{x=1}^{n} IN(x) \right| \right) / \left(\sum_{x=1}^{n} SW(x) \right) \qquad (1)$$

$$Average\ Accuracy = \left(\sum_{x=1}^{n} \frac{SW(x) - |SW(x) - IN(x)|}{SW(x)} \right) / n \qquad (2)$$

where:

x	is the trial/test number
n	is the total number of trials/tests
$SW, , IN$	are the gait parameter values derived from the Strideway and the insole systems, respectively.

4. Results

Ten walks were performed by each of the 15 participants on the Strideway while wearing the smart insoles. Spatiotemporal data for over 450 unique steps were collected and recorded. Each step collected by the SmartInsoles was analyzed carefully and compared to its counterpart from the Strideway. In this section, we present the results of this experiment, where SW represents the results acquired by the Strideway system, and IN represents the results acquired by the implemented Insoles' CPS.

Each of the 12 FSR sensors embedded in the SmartInsoles produced its own force value between zero and 100 Newtons. The values acquired from all tests that were performed in this experiment were analyzed to retrieve each step's heel-contact and toe-off timestamps. These timestamps were then used to calculate the gait parameters as described in Figure 2.

The data used to plot the graphs in Figure 4 were the results produced after averaging left and right foot data for each of the seven analyzed gait parameters. This way, a single value was produced for each trial by each system. MATLAB (R2018) was used for all statistical analysis and to generate all graphs in Figure 4. In some cases, during the experiment, one of the systems could fail to deliver results for a specific test. Data from both systems were eliminated in such cases, and their results are not reported here. The final used sample, based on which all the results and graphs were derived, included 81 pairs of successful tests, which was 54% of all the performed tests.

Three types of graphs were generated for each gait parameter in this study: a scatterplot, a histogram and a Bland–Altman graph.

Scatterplots were used to find a correlation between two sets of data. In this case, we were comparing data from two systems: Strideway data (x-axis) and the insoles' CPS (y-axis). A trend line (or a line of best fit) on a scatterplot was used to represent the trend of the data and indicated the likelihood of results if other data were present. In each parameter's scatterplot shown in Figure 4, a trend line is shown as a continuous straight line. Since this was a comparison between the results of two systems measuring the same information, the trend line should ideally fall exactly on the 45-degree reference line ($y = x$), which is shown as a straight dashed line. This would mean that the data from both systems were identical. Therefore, a trend line that was close to the reference line indicated a trending agreement between the two systems' results.

Histograms show the number of occurrences of a value in a specific range. The values shown in the histograms in Figure 4 represent the time difference between the Strideway data and the insoles' data for each of the analyzed parameters. The width of each bar (bin) represents the range of error, and the y-axis shows how many times an error falls within this bin's range during our experiment. A straight line is also shown in all histograms and indicates the average difference between the values read by each system. The ideal case is when this line stands on the x-axis' zero mark. In these histograms, values should follow a bell-shaped normal distribution, and the peak y-axis value should be around the zero x-axis value.

A Bland–Altman graph is another way to analyze the agreement between datasets acquired by two systems. The y-axis represents the difference between the two values, while the x-axis represents the average of these two values. Furthermore, three horizontal lines can provide more information on the acquired data in a Bland–Altman graph. The solid straight line represents the average difference between the values read by each system (also called the bias line), which has the same value of the vertical line in histograms, and the two dashed lines are the Limits of Agreement (LoA). The upper and lower LoA lines were calculated as the average value ±1.96 standard deviations. If the differences were normally distributed, 95% of the values would be between these two limit lines [36].

Table 1 shows a numerical analysis and a summary of the data in Figure 4. The first column represents the analyzed parameters, and the mean difference is shown in the second column. The mean difference in this validation experiment is ideally aimed to be close to zero. As can be seen from this summary, the mean difference for time-related parameters (measured in seconds) ranged between −0.03 s and 0.02 s. This means that the average error between the acquisitions of both systems did not exceed 30 milliseconds. For cadence, however, the mean difference was measured at 1.01 steps per minute, which is also considered an insignificant error. The "Inside LoA%" shows the percentage of data that had a difference between the lower and upper LoA values. For example, data showed that 95.06% of the acquired cadence data had an error between −11.13 steps/min and 13.16 steps/min. The lower and upper LoA values in Bland–Altman graphs should wrap approximately 95% of the data, and a smaller range between the lower and upper LoA values meant higher agreement between the two sets of data.

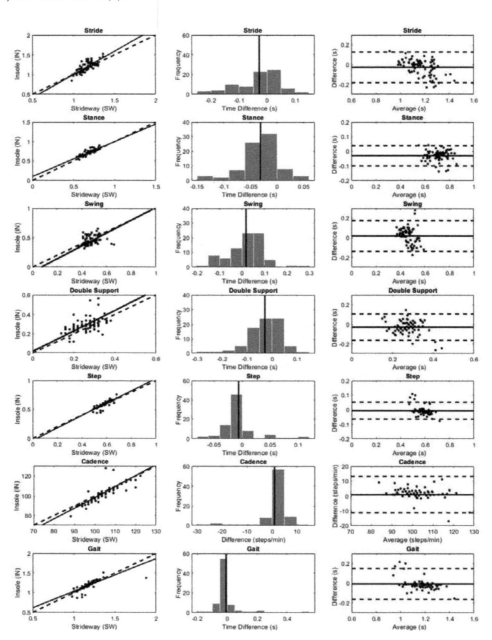

Figure 4. Scatterplots, histograms and Bland–Altman graphs that compare the data acquired by the Strideway (SW) and the SmartInsoles Cyber-Physical System (CPS) (IN).

Table 1. Analysis of agreement summary. Mean, median, standard deviation, range, lower and upper Limits of Agreement (LoA) values are all measured in seconds, while cadence is measured in steps/min. Range values represent the difference between the absolute minimum and maximum values.

Parameter	Mean	Median	St. Dev.	Range	Lower LoA	Upper LoA	Inside LoA%
Stride	−0.03	−0.01	0.08	0.37	−0.18	0.13	93.83%
Stance	−0.03	−0.03	0.04	0.18	−0.10	0.04	92.59%
Swing	0.02	0.03	0.08	0.46	−0.14	0.18	96.30%
Double Support	−0.03	−0.02	0.07	0.41	−0.16	0.11	93.83%
Step	−0.01	−0.01	0.03	0.19	−0.07	0.05	93.83%
Cadence	1.01	1.86	6.20	37.85	−11.13	13.16	95.06%
Gait	−0.01	−0.02	0.08	0.66	−0.17	0.15	95.06%

Table 2 shows the results of the five parameters analyzed in this study and compares the values acquired by both systems. The unit of measurement for all time-related parameters is seconds, and the unit for cadence values is steps per minute. Each row in Table 2 shows a calculated result that went through two stages. The first stage was averaging the left and right foot data for each parameter, and the second stage was averaging the first stage data for all 10 walks. Equations (3) and (4) below show how these values were calculated.

$$IN_{s,p} = \left(\sum_{x=1}^{10} \frac{IN_L(s,p,x) + IN_R(s,p,x)}{2} \right) / 10 \qquad (3)$$

$$SW_{s,p} = \left(\sum_{x=1}^{10} \frac{SW_L(s,p,x) + SW_R(s,p,x)}{2} \right) / 10 \qquad (4)$$

where:

s	represents the subject/participant
p	represents the gait parameter
x	is the trial number
IN_L, IN_R	are the left and right average values acquired by the SmartInsoles CPS
SW_L, SW_R	are the left and right average values acquired by the Strideway
$IN_{s,p}$	is the two-stage value for subject s parameter p acquired by the SmartInsoles CPS
$SW_{s,p}$	is the two-stage value for subject s parameter p acquired by the Strideway

This two-stage calculated value produces a single value for each subject and parameter, by each system, which makes them easily comparable. The last two rows in Table 2 show the overall accuracy and the average accuracy as described earlier using Equations (1) and (2).

Table 2. Average gait parameter values for each participant acquired by the Strideway (SW) and the Insole system (IN) after performing the 2-stage estimation (Equations (3) and (4)).

Participant	Stride Time (s)		Stance Time (s)		Swing Time (s)		Double Support Time (s)		Step Time (s)		Cadence (steps/min)		Gait Time (s)	
	SW	IN	SW	IN	SW	IN	SW	IN	SW	IN	SW	IN	SW	IN
1	1.15	1.22	0.71	0.76	0.44	0.48	0.29	0.37	0.57	0.57	104.83	106.23	1.23	1.22
2	1.05	1.04	0.61	0.65	0.46	0.39	0.18	0.25	0.52	0.54	114.72	112.70	1.05	1.07
3	1.05	1.09	0.62	0.64	0.43	0.45	0.20	0.21	0.52	0.54	114.85	111.53	1.05	1.08
4	1.22	1.23	0.70	0.78	0.53	0.45	0.27	0.30	0.61	0.64	98.07	93.53	1.43	1.29
5	1.21	1.28	0.75	0.75	0.49	0.55	0.31	0.25	0.61	0.63	99.69	95.22	1.21	1.26

Table 2. *Cont.*

Participant	Stride Time (s)		Stance Time (s)		Swing Time (s)		Double Support Time (s)		Step Time (s)		Cadence (steps/min)		Gait Time (s)	
	SW	IN	SW	IN	SW	IN	SW	IN	SW	IN	SW	IN	SW	IN
6	1.14	1.17	0.72	0.75	0.43	0.42	0.32	0.34	0.57	0.58	105.24	104.32	1.14	1.15
7	1.27	1.26	0.76	0.78	0.51	0.47	0.29	0.28	0.63	0.65	94.83	92.21	1.27	1.30
8	1.23	1.36	0.77	0.78	0.46	0.56	0.34	0.32	0.61	0.62	98.24	96.53	1.23	1.25
9	1.14	1.13	0.70	0.72	0.46	0.41	0.27	0.29	0.57	0.58	105.33	104.37	1.14	1.15
10	1.03	1.01	0.64	0.65	0.40	0.36	0.25	0.28	0.51	0.51	116.98	118.75	1.03	1.02
11	1.11	1.02	0.56	0.64	0.65	0.39	0.24	0.22	0.56	0.50	108.10	120.92	1.11	1.01
12	1.21	1.24	0.70	0.75	0.52	0.49	0.23	0.29	0.62	0.61	99.73	98.92	1.21	1.21
13	1.18	1.20	0.70	0.75	0.50	0.45	0.23	0.29	0.59	0.62	102.18	98.36	1.18	1.23
14	1.10	1.05	0.62	0.66	0.53	0.39	0.20	0.26	0.55	0.48	109.10	126.05	1.10	0.95
15	1.08	1.01	0.60	0.64	0.48	0.37	0.16	0.20	0.54	0.54	111.00	110.09	1.08	1.09
Overall Accuracy	99%		95%		91%		89%		100%		100%		99%	
Average Accuracy	96%		95%		86%		83%		97%		96%		96%	

5. Discussion

5.1. Comparison to Other Validation Studies

The current study is similar to Jagos et al. [21] in that the insoles were compared to a walkway pressure-sensitive system (Strideway by Tekscan). While it is certain that there will always be certain measurement differences due to the number of sensors in the insole versus the number of sensors in the gait mat, this study clearly demonstrates a high agreement between the Strideway and the insoles system. Jagos et al. revealed in their validation study that, for the healthy group, the average difference between the eSHOE and GAITRite acquisitions ranged between −0.029 and 0.029 s. The average difference in this study, as shown in Table 1, is between −0.03 and 0.02 s, which is very close to Jagos' results. However, it is worth mentioning that their subjects consisted of older adults (age 40.8 ± 9.1 years), while our sample's average age was 31 years, which makes it difficult to make a direct comparison.

In comparison to other validation studies [13,14,16], this study has the advantage of a large sample of steps (450 unique steps) with which to compare several gait parameters. In addition, based on previous research, the proposed SmartInsoles cyber-physical system was constructed to have the optimal number of sensors for sensitivity to gait parameters without unnecessarily increasing cost. Further, although many of the fabricated systems are wireless, this was one of the few systems that used WiFi for real-time viewing of data from multiple devices simultaneously rather than Bluetooth [15] or integrated internal storage [20,37].

As mentioned in the Background Section, the validation study conducted by the Italian National Institute of Health showcased different error margins for the five tested PMDs [8]. One of the main points of comparison in this study is the accuracy of the calculated Center of Pressure (CoP). In our implementation, however, CoP can be estimated using the average pressure in each insole and the locations of each sensor. This method estimates a relative location in-between the two feet, but cannot approximate a distance since the distance between the two feet is unknown (see Figure 5). In other words, CoP displacement for a wireless solution, such as our system, cannot be calculated on a compound basis, but rather as two separate measures where each insole calculates its own CoP (i.e., left foot CoP and right foot CoP).

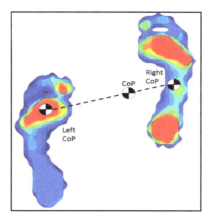

Figure 5. CoP estimation using the SmartInsole CPS showing how the Center of Pressure (CoP) could be estimated in reference to the left and right foot's CoP if the distance between the two feet is known.

5.2. Study Limitations

Previous work has examined the reliability of insole devices with different motor movements [37], as well as different populations that may have a more variable gait [13,14]. It would be important to follow up with this validation work with different movements, contexts and populations in order to ensure the greatest usability and generalizability of these insoles.

To test for the validity of the wearable SmartInsoles system, participants were required to wear sandals. This may have interfered with the results collected by the Strideway gait mat because it functions best when subjects are barefoot. We tried controlling this by ensuring that all participants wore the same type of sandal, allowing for standardized conditions and limited effects on the measured Strideway data. The gait mat has embedded pressure sensors and can measure footfalls even while using sandals. In gait acquisitions with the mat, participants typically wear their own footwear and do not walk barefoot across the mat. Although the mat may provide more information about pressure when a participant walks barefoot, this is not ecological, as people walk with shoes. In addition, the embedded pressure sensors provide accurate timestamps even with footwear, which leads to high-accuracy time-related parameters such as heel strike time and toe-off time, which are necessary measures to calculate several gait parameters (i.e., stride time). However, the limitation is related to the value/intensity of the pressure force, since the sandals add some padding and can weaken the measured pressure by the mat, not eliminate it. To overcome this limitation, our lab is experimenting with designing SmartSocks, which have the same sensors and circuitry as in the SmartInsole. This way, the padding problem can be minimized, and pressure force values can then be compared between the two systems.

Of the 15 participants included in our study, three participants (11, 14 and 15) performed a fewer number of steps on average due to their taller height. This affected the number of gait cycles they completed, with some having less than one. Data for these participants were still included, as they are still useful for validation purposes.

5.3. Future Work

One of the items that the Strideway calculates is the toe-in and toe-out angles in comparison to the subject's line of progression. These data provide information on how the subject's feet are tilted inwards or outwards, which has a direct effect on the subject's knee adduction according to [38]. For future work, we plan to calculate the toe-in and toe-off angles by using the information collected from the IMU sensor, which is already embedded in each SmartInsole.

The SmartInsoles can work by connecting them to a nearby smartphone device via Bluetooth. This opens the door for future experiments where people would wear these insoles and go on with their daily lives. The system would then be able to collect more realistic data that can be uploaded into a cloud database that physicians can access to monitor and analyze gait trends of their patients continuously without any location restrictions.

In our study, we evaluated young healthy subjects only. Future studies should include patients with conditions that can affect their gait such as diabetes [39], Parkinson's [40] or patients with Multiple Sclerosis (MS) disease [41]. Several studies have also confirmed a relationship between gait variability and age progression [42–44]. With this being a pilot study, our inclusion criteria consisted solely of young adults. For future studies, data from older individuals acquired with the wearable SmartInsoles and the Strideway gait mat should be evaluated, as there is typically more variability in collected data from older adults.

Therefore, collecting gait data for patients or long periods and away from the restrictions of a laboratory setting can provide rich information that can help physicians monitor the development of symptoms and the progression of disease for such cases.

6. Conclusions

Many studies in healthcare technologies and mHealth are moving towards facilitating remote patient monitoring [45–47], which can reduce costs and improve quality of care [48]. The objective of this study is to provide a reliable sensor network that provides the necessary information in a smart city where patients can live their normal lives and have their activities monitored by their caretakers and physicians. The developed system performs gait analysis by transmitting compressed and encoded sensory information wirelessly to a cloud server, which in turn, performs historical data collection, as well as the required analysis to extract gait parameters. This solution provides an alternative to the current high-cost and non-mobile solutions that have existed for decades. To validate the implemented system, a pilot study was performed in collaboration with the Interdisciplinary School of Health Sciences at the University of Ottawa. The performed experiment collected gait information of several subjects by using two systems simultaneously: the Tekscan Strideway gait mat and the SmartInsoles CPS. Comparison of the acquired data shows high agreement between the two datasets for the seven gait parameters analyzed in this study: stride time, stance, time, swing time, double support time, step time, cadence and gait time. At a fraction of the cost of the commonly-used gait measurement method in healthcare organizations, the in-house designed and implemented SmartInsoles CPS proves that it can reliably provide most of this information with high accuracy.

For the cost of the gait mat used in this study, at least 50 pairs of SmartInsoles, with different sizes, can be maintained. However, while the gait mat is not limited by shoe size, the main advantage of the SmartInsoles CPS is enabling continuous outdoor and home monitoring, away from a clinic or a lab setting. Therefore, the cost of having a custom insole for each shoe size, or each user, is tolerable considering the advantages it brings.

Author Contributions: All authors planned and designed the performed experiment. The ethical approval to perform the experiment was managed by A.A. and S.F. The SmartInsoles CPS was designed by F.A. The experiment was performed by F.A., C.H., and A.A. Results were analysed by F.A. and C.H., and revised by S.F. and A.E.S. All the authors wrote and revised the paper collaboratively.

Funding: This work was funded by an equipment grant from the University of Ottawa Brain and Mind Research Institute (uOBMRI) Stroke Research Consortium (Ottawa, ON, Canada). The funds supported the purchase of the Tekscan gait mat used in this study.

Conflicts of Interest: The authors declare no conflicts of interest.

References

1. Postolache, O.A.; Postolache, G.B. Development and selection of balance sensing devices. *IEEE Instrum. Meas. Mag.* **2017**, *20*, 38–48.
2. De Venuto, D.; Annese, V.F.; Ruta, M.; di Sciascio, E.; Vincentelli, A.L.S. Designing a cyber–physical system for fall prevention by cortico–muscular coupling detection. *IEEE Des. Test* **2016**, *33*, 66–76. [CrossRef]
3. Simon, S.R. Quantification of human motion: Gait analysis—Benefits and limitations to its application to clinical problems. *J. Biomech.* **2004**, *37*, 1869–1880. [CrossRef] [PubMed]
4. Bonato, P. Advances in wearable technology and applications in physical medicine and rehabilitation. *J. Neuroeng. Rehabil.* **2005**, *2*, 2–5. [CrossRef] [PubMed]
5. Muro-de-la-Herran, A.; García-Zapirain, B.; Méndez-Zorrilla, A. Gait analysis methods: An overview of wearable and non-wearable systems, highlighting clinical applications. *Sensors* **2014**, *14*, 3362–3394. [CrossRef] [PubMed]
6. Giacomozzi, C. Hardware performance assessment recommendations and tools for baropodometric sensor systems. *Ann. Ist. Super. Sanita* **2010**, *46*, 158–167. [PubMed]
7. Giacomozzi, C. Performance of plantar pressure measurement devices (PMDs): Update on consensus activities. *Ann. Ist. Super. Sanita* **2010**, *46*, 343–345. [PubMed]
8. Giacomozzi, C. Appropriateness of plantar pressure measurement devices: A comparative technical assessment. *Gait Posture* **2010**, *32*, 141–144. [CrossRef] [PubMed]
9. Hausdorff, J.M.; Ladin, Z.; Wei, J.Y. Footswitch system for measurement of the temporal parameters of gait. *J. Biomech.* **1995**, *28*, 347–351. [CrossRef]
10. Fraser, S.A.; Li, K.Z.; DeMont, R.G.; Penhune, V.B. Effects of balance status and age on muscle activation while walking under divided attention. *J. Gerontol. Ser. B* **2007**, *62*, P171–P178. [CrossRef]
11. Cutlip, R.G.; Mancinelli, C.; Huber, F.; DiPasquale, J. Evaluation of an instrumented walkway for measurement of the kinematic parameters of gait. *Gait Posture* **2000**, *12*, 134–138. [CrossRef]
12. Van Uden, C.J.; Besser, M.P. Test-retest reliability of temporal and spatial gait characteristics measured with an instrumented walkway system (GAITRite®). *BMC Musculoskelet. Disord.* **2004**, *5*, 13. [CrossRef] [PubMed]
13. Howell, A.M.; Kobayashi, T.; Hayes, H.A.; Foreman, K.B.; Bamberg, S.J.M. Kinetic gait analysis using a low-cost insole. *IEEE Trans. Biomed. Eng.* **2013**, *60*, 3284–3290. [CrossRef] [PubMed]
14. Howell, A.M. *Insole-Based Gait Analysis*; The University of Utah: Salt Lake City, UT, USA, 2012.
15. Tan, A.M.; Fuss, F.K.; Weizman, Y.; Woudstra, Y.; Troynikov, O. Design of low cost smart insole for real time measurement of plantar pressure. *Procedia Technol.* **2015**, *20*, 117–122. [CrossRef]
16. Tan, A.M.; Fuss, F.K.; Weizman, Y.; Azari, M.F. Centre of pressure detection and analysis with a high-resolution and low-cost smart insole. *Procedia Eng.* **2015**, *112*, 146–151. [CrossRef]
17. Motha, L.; Kim, J.; Kim, W.S. Instrumented rubber insole for plantar pressure sensing. *Org. Electron.* **2015**, *23*, 82–86. [CrossRef]
18. Kaya, T.; Shiari, B.; Petsch, K.; Yates, D. *Design of a MEMS Capacitive Comb-Drive Accelerometer*; Central Michigan University, University of Michigan: Mt Pleasant, MI, USA, 2011; p. 1953.
19. Crea, S.; Donati, M.; de Rossi, S.; Oddo, C.; Vitiello, N. A Wireless flexible sensorized insole for gait analysis. *Sensors* **2014**, *14*, 1073–1093. [CrossRef] [PubMed]
20. Braun, B.J.; Veith, N.T.; Hell, R.; Döbele, S.; Roland, M.; Rollmann, M.; Holstein, J.; Pohlemann, T. Validation and reliability testing of a new, fully integrated gait analysis insole. *J. Foot Ankle Res.* **2015**, *8*, 54. [CrossRef] [PubMed]
21. Jagos, H.; Pils, K.; Haller, M.; Wassermann, C.; Chhatwal, C.; Rafolt, D.; Rattay, F. Mobile gait analysis via eSHOEs instrumented shoe insoles: A pilot study for validation against the gold standard GAITRite®. *J. Med. Eng. Technol.* **2017**, *41*, 375–386. [CrossRef] [PubMed]
22. The GAITRite® Standard. Available online: https://www.gaitrite.com/ (accessed on 25 May 2018).
23. Hafidh, B.; al Osman, H.; el Saddik, A. SmartInsole: A foot-based activity and gait measurement device. In Proceedings of the 2013 IEEE International Conference on Multimedia and Expo Workshops (ICMEW), San Jose, CA, USA, 15–19 July 2013; pp. 1–4.
24. Interlink Electronics FSR Integration Guide. Available online: https://www.interlinkelectronics.com/request-integration-guides (accessed on 2 February 2018).

25. MPU-9250. Available online: https://www.invensense.com/products/motion-tracking/9-axis/mpu-9250/ (accessed on 2 February 2018).
26. ESP8266. Available online: https://www.espressif.com/en/products/hardware/esp8266ex/overview (accessed on 2 February 2018).
27. Adafruit Feather HUZZAH. Available online: https://www.adafruit.com/product/2821 (accessed on 2 February 2018).
28. Arafsha, F.; Laamarti, F.; el Saddik, A. Development of a wireless CPS for gait parameters measurement and analysis. In Proceedings of the 2018 IEEE International Instrumentation and Measurement Technology Conference (I2MTC), Houston, TX, USA, 14–17 May 2018; pp. 1–5.
29. Strideway System. Available online: https://www.tekscan.com/products-solutions/systems/strideway-system (accessed on 12 February 2018).
30. Coda, A.; Carline, T.; Santos, D. Repeatability and reproducibility of the Tekscan HR-Walkway system in healthy children. *Foot* **2014**, *24*, 49–55. [CrossRef] [PubMed]
31. Zammit, G.V.; Menz, H.B.; Munteanu, S.E. Reliability of the TekScan MatScan® system for the measurement of plantar forces and pressures during barefoot level walking in healthy adults. *J. Foot Ankle Res.* **2010**, *3*, 11. [CrossRef] [PubMed]
32. Brenton-Rule, A.; Mattock, J.; Carroll, M.; Dalbeth, N.; Bassett, S.; Menz, H.B.; Rome, K. Reliability of the TekScan MatScan® system for the measurement of postural stability in older people with rheumatoid arthritis. *J. Foot Ankle Res.* **2012**, *5*, 21. [CrossRef] [PubMed]
33. Goetschius, J.; Feger, M.A.; Hertel, J.; Hart, J.M. Validating center-of-pressure balance measurements using the MatScan® pressure mat. *J. Sport Rehabil.* **2018**, *27*. [CrossRef] [PubMed]
34. Zijlstra, W.; Hof, A.L. Assessment of spatio-temporal gait parameters from trunk accelerations during human walking. *Gait Posture* **2003**, *18*, 1–10. [CrossRef]
35. Titianova, E.B.; Mateev, P.S.; Tarkka, I.M. Footprint analysis of gait using a pressure sensor system. *J. Electromyogr. Kinesiol.* **2004**, *14*, 275–281. [CrossRef]
36. Myles, P.S.; Cui, J.I. Using the Bland–Altman method to measure agreement with repeated measures. *Br. J. Anaesth.* **2007**, *99*, 309–311. [CrossRef] [PubMed]
37. Stöggl, T.; Martiner, A. Validation of Moticon's OpenGo sensor insoles during gait, jumps, balance and cross-country skiing specific imitation movements. *J. Sports Sci.* **2017**, *35*, 196–206. [CrossRef] [PubMed]
38. Khan, S.S.; Khan, S.J.; Usman, J. Effects of toe-out and toe-in gait with varying walking speeds on knee joint mechanics and lower limb energetics. *Gait Posture* **2017**, *53*, 185–192. [CrossRef] [PubMed]
39. Cavanagh, P.R.; Derr, J.A.; Ulbrecht, J.S.; Maser, R.E.; Orchard, T.J. Problems with gait and posture in neuropathic patients with insulin-dependent diabetes mellitus. *Diabet. Med.* **1992**, *9*, 469–474. [CrossRef] [PubMed]
40. Schaafsma, J.D.; Giladi, N.; Balash, Y.; Bartels, A.L.; Gurevich, T.; Hausdorff, J.M. Gait dynamics in Parkinson's disease: Relationship to Parkinsonian features, falls and response to levodopa. *J. Neurol. Sci.* **2003**, *212*, 47–53. [CrossRef]
41. Martin, C.L.; Phillips, B.A.; Kilpatrick, T.J.; Butzkueven, H.; Tubridy, N.; McDonald, E.; Galea, M.P. Gait and balance impairment in early multiple sclerosis in the absence of clinical disability. *Mult. Scler. J.* **2006**, *12*, 620–628. [CrossRef] [PubMed]
42. Campbell, A.J.; Reinken, J.; Allan, B.C.; Martinez, G.S. Falls in old age: A study of frequency and related clinical factors. *Age Ageing* **1981**, *10*, 264–270. [CrossRef] [PubMed]
43. Gabell, A.; Nayak, U.S.L. The effect of age on variability in gait. *J. Gerontol.* **1984**, *39*, 662–666. [CrossRef] [PubMed]
44. Jahn, K.; Zwergal, A.; Schniepp, R. Gait disturbances in old age. *Dtsch. Aerzteblatt Online* **2010**, *107*, 306–316. [CrossRef] [PubMed]
45. Alemdar, H.; Ersoy, C. Wireless sensor networks for healthcare: A survey. *Comput. Netw.* **2010**, *54*, 2688–2710. [CrossRef]
46. Yuan, B.; Herbert, J. Web-based real-time remote monitoring for pervasive healthcare. In Proceedings of the 2011 IEEE International Conference on Pervasive Computing and Communications Workshops (PERCOM Workshops), Seattle, WA, USA, 21–25 March 2011; pp. 625–629.

47.   Latré, B.; Braem, B.; Moerman, I.; Blondia, C.; Demeester, P. A survey on wireless body area networks. *Wirel. Netw.* **2011**, *17*, 1–18. [CrossRef]

48.   Landolina, M.; Perego, G.B.; Lunati, M.; Curnis, A.; Guenzati, G.; Vicentini, A.; Parati, G.; Borghi, G.; Zanaboni, P.; Valsecchi, S.; et al. Remote monitoring reduces healthcare use and improves quality of care in heart failure patients with implantable defibrillators: The evolution of management strategies of heart failure patients with implantable defibrillators (EVOLVO) study. *Circulation* **2012**, *125*, 2985–2992. [CrossRef] [PubMed]

Article

Modeling and Optimisation of a Solar Energy Harvesting System for Wireless Sensor Network Nodes

Himanshu Sharma [1,*](#), Ahteshamul Haque [2] and Zainul Abdin Jaffery [2]

[1]   KIET Group of Institutions, APJ Abdul Kalam Technical University (AKTU), Ghaziabad-201206 U.P., India
[2]   Department of Electrical Engineering, Jamia Millia Islamia, New Delhi-110025, India;
     ahaque@jmi.ac.in (A.H.); zjaffery@jmi.ac.in (Z.A.J.)
*   Correspondence: himanshu.sharma@kiet.edu; Tel.: +91-1232-227-980

Received: 29 June 2018; Accepted: 3 September 2018; Published: 7 September 2018

Abstract: The Wireless Sensor Networks (WSN) are the basic building blocks of today's modern internet of Things (IoT) infrastructure in smart buildings, smart parking, and smart cities. The WSN nodes suffer from a major design constraint in that their battery energy is limited and can only work for a few days depending upon the duty cycle of operation. The main contribution of this research article is to propose an efficient solar energy harvesting solution to the limited battery energy problem of WSN nodes by utilizing ambient solar photovoltaic energy. Ideally, the Optimized Solar Energy Harvesting Wireless Sensor Network (SEH-WSN) nodes should operate for an infinite network lifetime (in years). In this paper, we propose a novel and efficient solar energy harvesting system with pulse width modulation (PWM) and maximum power point tracking (MPPT) for WSN nodes. The research focus is to increase the overall harvesting system efficiency, which further depends upon solar panel efficiency, PWM efficiency, and MPPT efficiency. Several models for solar energy harvester system have been designed and iterative simulations were performed in MATLAB/SIMULINK for solar powered DC-DC converters with PWM and MPPT to achieve optimum results. From the simulation results, it is shown that our designed solar energy harvesting system has 87% efficiency using PWM control and 96% efficiency (η_{sys}) by using the MPPT control technique. Finally, an experiment for PWM controlled SEH-WSN is performed using Scientech 2311 WSN trainer kit and a Generic LM2575 DC-DC buck converter based solar energy harvesting module for validation of simulation results.

Keywords: smart cities; solar energy harvesting; DC-DC Converters; maximum power point tracking (MPPT); battery charging; Wireless Sensor Nodes

1. Introduction

In the 21st century, the design of efficient renewable energy harvesting system is the most important technological challenge due to the increase in global warming and other environmental issues. Recently, in August 2016, the ZigBee Alliance, USA has announced the new standard for Energy harvesting wireless sensor networks (EHWSNs) which is known as ZigBee Green Power (*GP*) [1]. The amendments in the IEEE 802.15.4 communication standard protocol for low data rate wireless networks and the ZigBee Green Power (*GP*) standard for EHWSNs facilitate the use of the Green Power feature for ZigBee applications running on the low power wireless microcontroller platforms [2]. Nowadays, the commercial companies like Texas Instruments, ST Microelectronics, and Linear Technology, USA are proposing the renewable energy harvesting based power management solutions for wireless sensor networks (WSN). The design of an efficient solar energy harvesting systems is necessary for long network lifetime solar energy harvesting wireless sensor networks.

In SEH-WSN nodes, the harvester system takes the input from solar photovoltaic energy and converts it into electrical energy. Then, this electrical energy is used to charge the WSN node battery and provides the operating voltage to the sensor node. The advantage of using energy harvesting in WSN nodes is that it reduces the human efforts required to replace the battery of hundreds or thousands of sensor nodes by going out into remote areas for volcano monitoring, glacier monitoring, forest monitoring and battlefield monitoring applications. The energy harvesting enabled WSN nodes increases the overall sensor network operation lifetime. The SEH-WSN node is powered by ambient solar photovoltaic (PV) energy and can measure the temperature, light, humidity, and pressure simultaneously. Then, it sends the measured data to the remote WSN node wirelessly using Zigbee wireless communication protocol. The theoretical maximum distance limit in ZigBee (IEEE 802.15.4 standard) is up to 100 m with a maximum data rate of 250 kbps. The main contributions and innovations of this research article are as follows:

(1) A novel solar energy harvesting 3.6 volts battery charger using Pulse Width Modulation (PWM) control technique using MATLAB/Simulink.
(2) A novel solar energy harvesting 3.6 volts battery charger using Perturb & Observation (P&O) type Maximum Power Point Tracking (MPPT) control technique using MATLAB/Simulink.
(3) A novel hardware implementation of a solar battery charger using PWM control technique Solar Panel, DC-DC Buck Converter, and Scientech 2311 WSN trainer kit.
(4) The innovation claim entails the integration of a Commercial WSN trainer Kit (Scientech 2311) with a solar panel and a PWM controlled DC-DC converter, and showing the output on Digital Storage Oscilloscope (DSO).
(5) Another innovation claim made here involves the MATLAB/Simulink based implementation of solar energy harvester system to charge 3.6 volts battery using MATLAB/Simulink. This rechargeable battery is used to provide power to the WSN node.

In 2008, Ref. [3] proposed the modeling and optimization of a solar energy harvester system for self-powered wireless sensor networks. They proposed a Boost Converter model with MPPT. In this model, they considered variations in irradiance (W/m^2) and variations in Inductor (*L*) and capacitor (C) values to observe the effect on output efficiency. The maximum achieved efficiency is only 85% using theoretical simulation results. In 2009, Ref. [4] proposed the design of a solar-harvesting circuit for battery-less Embedded Systems. In this paper, the simulation results show that by using efficient solar energy harvester circuits, the sensor network lifetime can be increased from a few days to 20–30 years and higher. Section 1 provides an overview of a basic Solar Energy Harvesting System. Section 2 presents the operation of a SEH-WSN Node. Section 3 provides two types of solar energy harvester systems, i.e., pulse width modulation (PWM) controlled and P&O MPPT controlled. Section 4 presents the modeling of the solar cell and solar panels. Section 5 provides modeling of DC-DC Buck converters, and Section 6 provides modeling of maximum power point tracking techniques (MPPTs). The Section 7 provides simulation parameters and Section 8 provides simulation results. In Section 9, Energy harvester systems efficiency calculations are shown, and in Section 10, a hardware experiment is performed for SEH-WSN nodes. Finally, Section 11 provides the conclusion for simulation results and hardware experiment validation.

2. Operation of an SEH-WSN Node

The internal block diagram of an SEH-WSN node is shown in Figure 1. The solar energy-harvesting system provides a DC power supply (3.6 volts, Tektronix, Inc., Beaverton, OR, USA) to the WSN node. This voltage is harvested from the ambient sunlight by using the solar panels [5]. The solar panel converts light energy directly into the DC electrical energy. The DC-DC converter regulates this DC voltage to charge the battery. The rechargeable battery powers the WSN node. The WSN node measures the desired physical quantity (e.g., temp., light, humidity, and pressure) by using the sensor measurement unit. A microcontroller in computation unit processes this sensed data.

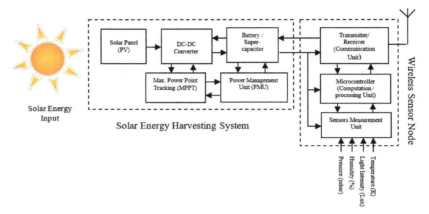

Figure 1. Block diagram of Solar Energy Harvesting Wireless Sensor Network Node (SEH-WSN).

The measured or sensed data is sent to the nearby network node wirelessly, in the form of data packets using the transmitter unit. The information is sent to the USB gateway node via cluster head nodes [6] from the end nodes. Finally, the user can remotely monitor & control the application process e.g., temperature monitoring, control of an industrial boiler plant, volcano monitoring, glacier monitoring, forest monitoring, battlefield monitoring applications, air conditioner cooling system control, traffic light management in a smart city.

3. Solar Energy Harvesting System

A basic solar energy harvesting system consists of a Solar Panel, DC-DC converter, rechargeable battery, a battery charge protection circuit called battery management system (BMS) and DC-DC converter control unit. Generally, there are two types of DC-DC converter control methods: (1) Pulse width modulation (PWM) control and (2) Maximum power point tracking (MPPT) control. The Figure 2a shows a block diagram of a pulse width modulation (PWM) controlled DC-DC buck converter. Similarly, the Figure 2b shows the block diagram of Perturb & Observation (P&O) maximum power point tracking (MPPT) controlled solar energy harvester (SEH) system. In Figure 2b, the SEH system consists of a solar panel, a DC-DC buck converter, a rechargeable battery, a maximum power point (MPPT) controller, and a WSN sensor node connected as a DC load. The ambient solar light energy is harvested using the solar panel and converted into the electrical energy. The DC-DC Buck converter steps down and regulates the magnitude of this harvested voltage, and supplied to the rechargeable battery. The MPPT controller tracks the voltage and current from the solar panel and adjusts the duty cycle accordingly for the MOSFET of DC-DC Buck converter [7]. Finally, the battery voltage is utilized to operate the wireless sensor node. The WSN performs the function of sensing, computation, and communication with other similar characteristics nodes. Thus, autonomous operation of monitoring and control of any physical phenomenon such as temperature, humidity, pressure or acceleration can be achieved using the SEH-WSN nodes. In this whole scenario, the efficiency of the solar energy harvester circuit plays a very important role. If the efficiency of the solar energy harvester system is poor, then the battery will not get recharged properly and hence the wireless sensor network lifetime will reduce.

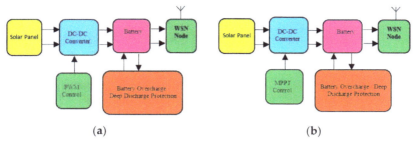

(**a**) (**b**)

Figure 2. Block diagram of solar energy harvesting system using PWM and MPPT control. (**a**) Using PWM control; (**b**) using MPPT control.

4. Modeling of a Solar PV Panel

A solar cell (also called photovoltaic cell) is a semiconductor device, which converts the light energy into electrical energy [8]. When a photon of light energy ($h\nu > E_g$) is incident over a solar cell the electron-hole pair (EHP) is generated. This newly generated EHP contributes to the electric current called a light generated current denoted by (I_L). The ideal theoretical current-voltage (I–V) equation of a solar cell is given as

$$Solar\ cell\ current\ (I) = I_L - I_o\left[exp\left(\frac{qV}{kT}\right) - 1\right] \tag{1}$$

where, I = total output current of solar cell, I_L = Light generated current by the solar cell, I_o = Reverse Saturation current due to recombination, q = charge of electron (1.6×10^{-19} C), V = open circuit voltage of solar cell, k = Boltzmann's constant (1.38×10^{-23} J/K), T = Temperature of Solar cell (300 K). The symbol of the solar cell is shown in Figure 3a. The solar cell equivalent circuit model can be represented as shown in Figure 3b. It consists of a light generated current source (I_L), a diode (D) modeled by Shockley equation, and two series and parallel resistances. A MATLAB Simulink model for a solar panel is shown in Figure 3c. In Figure 3b, Kirchhoff's current law (KCL) can give the characteristic current equation for this equivalent circuit:

$$Output\ Current\ of\ Equivalent\ Cell\ Model\ (I) = I_L - I_D - I_p \tag{2}$$

where, I_p = current in parallel resistance, I_L = Light generated current, and I_D = diode current.

$$Diode\ Current\ (I_D) = I_o\left[exp\left(\frac{V + IR_s}{nV_T}\right) - 1\right] \tag{3}$$

where, I_o = Reverse Saturation current due to recombination, V = open circuit voltage of solar cell, I = solar cell output current, R_s = series resistance, n = diode ideality factor, (1 for ideal, 2 for practical diode), V_T = Thermal voltage (kT/q), k = Boltzmann's constant (1.38×10^{-23} J/K), T = Temperature of Solar cell (300 K). q = charge of electron (1.6×10^{-19} C). The current in parallel resistance is given as:

$$Current\ in\ parallel\ resistance\left(I_p\right) = \frac{V + IR_s}{R_p} \tag{4}$$

Now, putting the value of I_D and I_p in current Equation (2), we get the complete IV equation of the equivalent circuit of a single solar Cell, for which related all parameters with output current and voltage are given as [9]:

$$Solar\ cell\ Current\ (I) = I_L - I_0\left[exp\left(\frac{q(V + IR_s)}{nkT}\right)\right] - \left(\frac{V + IR_s}{R_p}\right) \tag{5}$$

where, R_p = Parallel Resistance and remaining parameters I_L, I_o, q, V, I, R_s, n, k, T have been already defined in Equation (3). The efficiency (η) of the solar cell is given as:

$$Solar\ Cell\ Efficiency\ (\eta) = \frac{V_{oc} \cdot I_{sc} \cdot FF}{P_{in}} \tag{6}$$

where, V_{oc} is called Open Circuit Voltage, I_{sc} is Short Circuit Current, FF is Fill Factor and P_{in} = incident optical power. The Fill Factor (*FF*) of a solar cell is given as

$$Fill\ Factor\ (FF) = \frac{P_{max}}{P_{dc}} = \frac{I_m \cdot V_m}{I_{sc} \cdot V_{oc}} \tag{7}$$

where, I_m is called maximum current and V_m is the maximum voltage of the solar cell. Practically, there are many types of solar cells, such as monocrystalline silicon solar cell (c-Si), Amorphous Silicon solar cell (a-Si), Polycrystalline solar cell (multi-Si), Thin-film solar cell (TFSC) etc. However, the efficiency of a-Si solar cells is more than all others up to 18% efficiency [10].

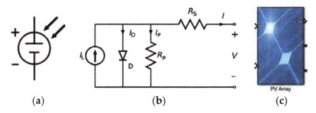

(a)   (b)   (c)

Figure 3. Modelling of Solar cell (**a**) Symbol; (**b**) Equivalent circuit of Solar Cell; (**c**) Solar Panel.

4.1. Effect of Solar Radiation (G)

The solar cell efficiency (η) is directly proportional to variations in solar radiations. If solar radiation increases, then the solar cell efficiency (η) also increases and vice versa. The Figure 4a shows Current-Voltage (I–V) characteristics of a commercial 10 watts solar panel (Dow Chemical DPS 10–1000) with varying irradiance levels. The 10 watts (Dow Chemical DPS 10–1000) Solar panel has a size of 546 mm × 232 mm with a module area of 0.13 m². From Figure 4a, it is observed that the current in solar panel increased with an increase in the irradiance level [11]. Here, the solar cell current is maximum (6.2 A) for solar irradiance of 1000 W/m². The Power-Voltage characteristics of a Solar Panel under different radiations levels is shown in Figure 4b. Here, the harvested power is the maximum (9.8 W) for the highest solar irradiance i.e., 1000 W/m².

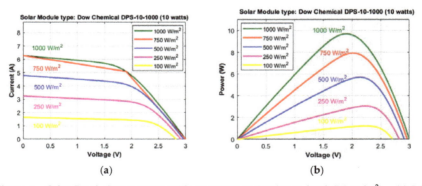

(a)   (b)

Figure 4. Solar Panel characteristics with variations in Irradiance level (Watts/m²). (**a**) I–V Characteristics; (**b**) P–V Characteristics.

4.2. *Effect of Temperature (T)*

As seen in Figure 5a, if the solar panel temperature is increased, then the output current decreases and vice versa. Thus, the output current is inversely proportional to temperature variations. Similarly, in Figure 5b if the temperature is increased, then output power decreases and vice versa. Thus, output power is also inversely proportional to variations in temperature.

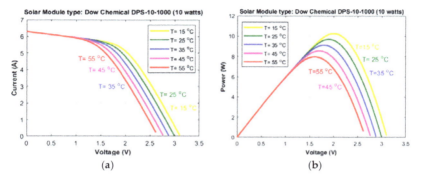

Figure 5. Solar Panel characteristics with variations in Temperature (°C). (**a**) I–V Characteristics; (**b**) P–V Characteristics.

The Figures 4 and 5 show I-V and P-V characteristics of a 10 watts solar module DPS-10-1000 of Dow Chemical Company (Midland, Michigan, United States) simulated in MATLAB/Simulink simulation software. In Ref. [12–14] some more simulation software are provided for energy harvesting wireless sensor networks.

5. Modeling of DC-DC Converter

There are generally three types of DC-DC converters [15] used in the design of a photovoltaic system: Buck Converter, Boost Converter, and Buck-Boost Converter. Here, we have used a DC-DC Buck converter because its efficiency is high as compared to Boost and Buck-Boost converters. A DC-DC buck converter is a power electronics converter in which the output voltage is always less than the input voltage. The Buck converter consists of a DC voltage source (V_{dc}), an inductor (L), a switch (MOSFET), a diode (D) and a capacitor (C) as shown in Figure 6. When MOSFET switch (S) is closed at time t_1, the input voltage V_s appears across the load resistor. If the MOSFET switch remains OFF for the time t_2, then the voltage across the load resistor is zero. The amplitude of output voltage (V_0) is less than the input voltage V_0. The Duty Cycle (D) can be varied from 0 to 1 by varying time period t_1. The duty cycle of the Buck converter is $D = V_0/V_{in}$. The average output voltage of the buck converter is given as:

$$V_0 = \frac{1}{T} \int_0^{t_1} v_o dt = \frac{t_1}{T} V_{in} = f \cdot t_1 \cdot V_{in} = V_{in} \cdot D \qquad (8)$$

where, V_0 is output voltage, V_{in} is input voltage, t_1 = MOSFET switch ON time duration, T = Total Time period, f is the frequency of operation, D is the duty cycle.

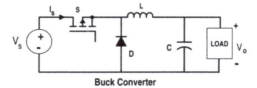

Buck Converter

Figure 6. Circuit Model of a DC-DC Buck Converter.

The average load current at output is given as:

$$I_0 = I_L = V_0 / R = D \cdot V_{in} / R \tag{9}$$

where, T = chopping period, $D = t_1/T$ is duty cycle, f = chopping frequency.

Power Losses in DC-DC Buck Converter

There are three main sections of power dissipation in DC-DC buck converter [16]: Inductor conduction losses, MOSFET conduction losses, and MOSFET switching losses.

In all types of DC-DC converters, the Inductor is the main sink for power consumption. The value of MOSFET switching loss and diode conduction losses are very small and as compared to inductor losses, can be neglected practically. The inductor power consumption loss is given as:

$$P_L = I_{L(rms)}^2 \times R_{L(dc)} \tag{10}$$

where, P_L = Power loss in Inductor (mW), $I_{L(rms)}$ = Inductor RMS current, $R_{L(dc)}$ = DC resistance of the Inductor.

6. Modeling of Maximum Power Point Tracking (MPPT) Technique

The MPPT techniques [17] are widely used in the design of photovoltaic (PV) solar systems to maximize power extraction from the Sun under varying solar irradiance conditions. It is an algorithm, which continuously measures the voltage (V_{pv}) and current (I_{pv}) from the solar panel and calculates the amount of duty cycle (D) to be fed to the MOSFET switch of the DC-DC buck converter. The following algorithms are generally used in photovoltaic applications as [18]:

- Perturbation and Observation (P&O) technique,
- Incremental Conductance (INC) technique and
- Fraction Open Circuit Voltage (OCV).

The P&O technique is mostly used in all types of solar energy harvester systems. A flow chart for the P&O algorithm is shown in Figure 7. The output of this algorithm is a varying duty cycle (ΔD) which depends on input solar irradiance (W/m^2). When solar irradiance changes then a change in duty cycle occurs and the solar panel voltage and current changes [19]. The MPPT algorithm senses these changes and adjusts the impedance of the solar panel to the maximum power point. Thus, maximum power (P) can still be extracted from the solar panel even if the irradiance changes. It generates a PWM waveform whose initial duty cycle (D) is 0.7 provided arbitrarily (in the range of 0 to 1) as a seed value during the simulation.

The P& O algorithm works on the principle of impedance matching between the load and the solar panel. For maximum power transfer, the impedance matching is necessary. This impedance matching is achieved by using a DC-DC converter. By using a DC-DC converter, the impedance is matched by changing the duty cycle (ΔD) of the MOSFET switch. The relation between the input voltage(V_{in}), the Output voltage (V_o) and duty cycle (D) is given as

$$V_o = V_{in} \cdot D \tag{11}$$

and,

$$R_{in} = R_L / D^2 \tag{12}$$

Therefore, if the duty cycle changes (ΔD), then the solar energy harvester output voltage (V_o) changes. If the duty cycle (D) is increased the output voltage (V_o) also increases and vice-versa. By changing the duty cycle (D), the impedance of the load resistance (R_L) can be matched with input solar panel impedance for maximum power transfer to the load for optimum performance.

The steps in the P&O algorithm are shown by a flowchart and MATLAB codes [17–19] are shown in Algorithm 1 respectively.

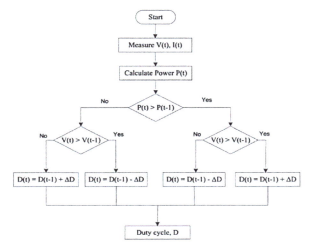

Figure 7. Flowchart of Perturb and Observation (P&O) Algorithm for MPPT.

Algorithm 1. P&O MPPT Algorithm.

```
function D = PandO(Vpv,Ipv)
persistent Dprev Pprev Vprev
if is empty (Dprev)
    Dprev = 0.7;
    Vprev = 190;
    Pprev = 2000;
end
deltaD = 0.0025;
Ppv = Vpv*Ipv;
if (Ppv-Pprev) ~= 0
    if (Ppv-Pprev) > 0
        if (Vpv-Vprev) > 0
            D = Dprev - deltaD;
        else
            D = Dprev + deltaD;
        end
    else
        if (Vpv-Vprev) > 0
            D = Dprev + deltaD;
        else
            D = Dprev - deltaD;
        end
    end
else
    D = Dprev;
end
Dprev = D;
Vprev = Vpv;
Pprev = Ppv;
```

---

7. Simulation Experiment Setup

The simulation parameters for a solar energy harvesting system are shown in Table 1. We used MATLAB Simulink 2017 for simulation of a solar-powered Boost converter with PWM control for battery charging of a WSN node as shown in Figure 8. The Figure 9 shows MATLAB Simulink model of solar energy harvester system using MPPT control. The solar irradiance of 1000 watts/cm^2 is incident on the solar panel with a constant temperature of 25-degree Celsius [20]. The Solar panel can extract only this solar energy into 15 mW/cm^2 with 15% efficiency [21]. For full irradiance on the simulated solar panel, the output voltage of the solar panel is 6 volts, 500 mA, and 3 watts. Now, this electrical energy from the solar cell is fed to the DC-DC boost converter, which increases the output voltage. The Boost converter output voltage is used to charge the rechargeable battery. The rechargeable battery is used to operate the WSN node. Here, the WSN load is modeled as output with a DC load resistance of 100 ohms. Table 1 shows various simulation parameters i.e. irradiance, temperature, DC-DC converter type, Solar panel current, voltage and power, battery type ad battery voltage, duty cycle, WN load model and power losses.

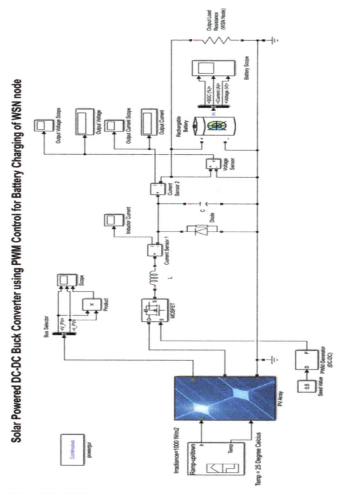

Figure 8. MATLAB/SIMULINK model for PWM controlled solar energy harvesting (SEH) system for WSN Node.

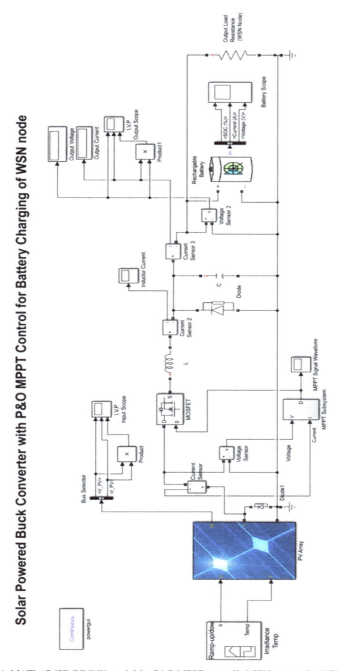

Figure 9. MATLAB/SIMULINK model for P&O MPPT controlled SEH system for WSN Node.

Table 1. Simulation Parameters.

Parameters	Value	Parameters	Value
Irradiance (W/m^2)	1000 Watts/m^2	Capacitor (C)	100 uF
Temperature (T)	25 degree Celsius	Inductor (L)	200 uH
DC-DC Converter	Boost Converter	MOSFET Switching Frequency (f)	5 KHz
Max. Solar Panel output voltage (V_m)	6 volts	Initial duty Cycle	0.5
Max. Solar Panel output current (I_m)	500 mA	MOSFET Switching Power Losses (P_{sw})	0.5 mW
Max. Power from Solar Cell (P_m)	3 watts	Switching Voltage Loss (V_{sw})	0.2 volts
Rechargeable Battery Type	NiCd	WSN Load Model	10-ohm resistor
Battery Voltage	3.6 volts	Inductor conduction Power Loss (P_L)	50 mW

8. Simulation Results

The simulation results with comparisons of Battery State of Charge (SoC), battery Current (I_B) and battery voltage (V_B) using PWM controlled and P&O MPPT controlled solar energy harvesting (SEH) system are shown in Figures 10–12.

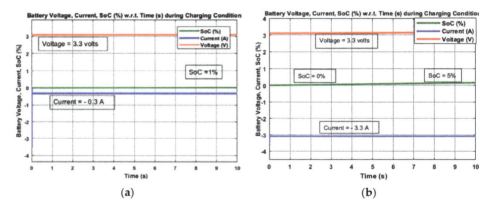

Figure 10. Simulation results of PWM controlled and P&O MPPT controlled solar energy harvesting (SEH) system for 10 s. (**a**) Battery SoC, Voltage and Current during Charging using PWM control; (**b**) Battery SoC, Voltage and Current during Charging using P&O MPPT control.

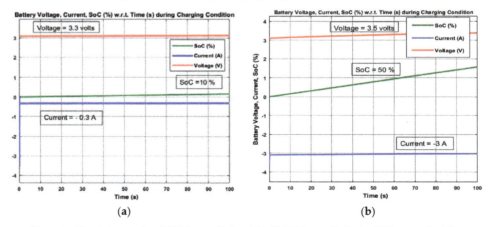

Figure 11. Simulation results of PWM controlled and P&O MPPT controlled solar SEH system for 100 s. (**a**) Battery SoC, Voltage and Current during Charging using PWM control; (**b**) Battery SoC, Voltage and Current during Charging using P&O MPPT control.

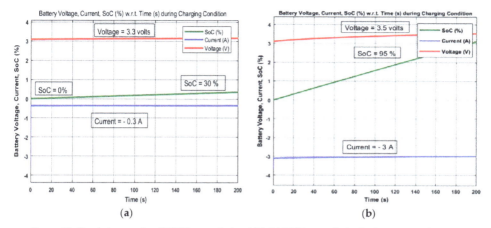

Figure 12. Simulation results of PWM controlled and P&O MPPT controlled solar SEH system for 200 s. (**a**) Battery SoC, Voltage and Current during Charging using PWM control; (**b**) Battery SoC, Voltage and Current during Charging using P&O MPPT control.

Comparison of Battery State of Charge (SoC), Voltage and Current during Charging Using PWM and MPPT Control Techniques

In Figure 10a, three parameters of the PWM controlled solar energy harvesting battery charger (i.e., Battery State of Charge (SoC), battery Current and Voltage) are shown for a simulation time of 10 s. The battery SoC reaches from zero to 1%. On the other hand, in Figure 10b, the MPPT controlled solar energy harvesting battery charger SoC, battery Current and Voltages are shown for a simulation time of 10 s. Here, the battery SoC reaches from 0 to 5%, which is greater as compared to PWM controlled results for 10 s (i.e., 1% only). In Figure 11a, for increased simulation time (T = 100 s), the battery SoC reaches 10% of its final value. However, in Figure 11b, the MPPT results for 100 s simulation time have battery SoC to 50% as compared to the results obtained in Figure 11a for PWM control (i.e., 10% only). The Battery current is negative while charging, which represents the oxidation process in the electrochemical cells of the battery. However, during discharging, the battery current is positive, which represents the reduction process in the electrochemical cell of the battery. Finally, in Figure 12a the battery SoC could reach only 30% in 200 s simulation time in the figure. But, in Figure 12b the battery SoC reaches 95% in just 200 s simulation time. Thus, the battery charging time is dynamically increased by using MPPT controlled solar energy harvesting systems for WSN nodes. The MPPT controlled SEH system shows better charging efficiency because it can extract the maximum solar power from the solar cells as compared to the ordinary PWM controlled system.

9. Energy Harvester Systems Efficiency (η_{sys}) Calculations

The energy harvester system efficiency is calculated for PWM control and MPPT control methods separately as:

9.1. PWM Efficiency

In our simulation, the solar panel was selected to have a maximum power of 3 watts. By using PWM control, the max. power available from that solar panel is only 2.5 watts. Therefore, the PWM efficiency is calculated as:

$$\text{PWM Efficiency } (\eta_{PWM}) = \frac{P_{PWM}}{P_m} \qquad (13)$$

The P_{PWM} is 2.5 watts but the rated max. power is 3 watts. Thus PWM efficiency is calculated as 2.5 w/3 w = 83.34%. Furthermore, the buck converter reduces (or regulates) this 2.5 watts power to 650 mW. The buck converter efficiency is defined as output power (P_0) divided by the power losses (P_{loss}). Mathematically,

$$DC - DC \text{ Buck Converter Efficiency } (\eta_{buck}) = \frac{P_0}{P_0 + P_{loss}} \quad (14)$$

where, P_{loss} is the sum of MOSFET switching loss (P_{sw}) and the Inductor conduction loss (P_L). From the simulation results table, the output power (P_0) is 650 mW and MOSFET switching losses are 5 mW and inductor power loss is 50 mW. Thus buck converter efficiency is calculated as 650 mW/(650 + 55 mW) = 92.19%. The overall harvester efficiency is the average of *PWM* efficiency and DC-DC buck converter efficiency. Thus

$$\text{Overall Energy Harvester Systems Efficiecny using PWM } (\eta_{sys}) = \frac{(\eta_{buck}) + (\eta_{PWM})}{2} \quad (15)$$

From the formula of Equation (15), the calculated overall energy harvester system efficiency using PWM (η_{sys}) is (92.19% + 83.34%)/2 = 87.76%. Thus, by using *PWM* controlled buck converter, the overall solar energy harvester efficiency (η_{sys}) is 87.76%.

9.2. P&O MPPT Efficiency

By using P&O MPPT the max. power available from the solar panel is 2.8 watts. Now the P&O MPPT efficiency is calculated as:

$$\text{MPPT Efficiency } (\eta_{MPP}) = \frac{P_{MPP}}{P_m} \quad (16)$$

From the simulation parameter table, the (P_{MPP}) is 2.8 watts and the maximum theoretical power (P_m) is 3 watts. Thus P&O MPPT efficiency is calculated as 2.8 w/3 w = 93.33%. Here, the P_{loss} also changes due to variations in P&O MPPT of DC-DC buck converter. The P_{loss} is the sum of MOSFET switching loss (P_{sw}) and Inductor conduction loss (P_L). From the simulation results table, the output power (P_o) is 1.8 W and MOSFET switching losses are 2 mW and inductor power loss is 20 mW. Thus buck converter efficiency is calculated as 1.8 W/1.8 W+ 22 mW = 98.79%. Finally, the overall energy harvester circuit efficiency (η_{sys}) is the average of Buck converter efficiency and P&O *MPPT* efficiency.

$$\text{Overall Energy Harvester Systems Efficiecny using MPPT } (\eta_{sys}) = \frac{(\eta_{buck}) + (\eta_{MPP})}{2} \quad (17)$$

From the formula of Equation (17), the calculated overall energy harvester system efficiency (η_{sys}) using P&O MPPT is (98.79% + 93.33%)/2 = 96.06%. Thus, the overall solar energy harvester efficiency (η_{sys}) using P&O MPPT is 96.06%.

The Table 2 shows the simulation results for PWM and MPPT controlled SEH systems. Here, the maximum solar power output power (P_m), average buck converter output voltage (V_m), average buck converter output current (I_m), buck converter output power, inductor loss, MOSFET switching loss, and harvester system efficiency (%) are shown. Clearly, from Table 2, the P&O MPPT controlled method gives better results as compared to PWM control in terms of output voltage, current, power, losses and efficiency.

In Figure 13, a comparision graph of PWM and P&O MPPT harvesting system efficiency $\left(\eta_{sys}\right)$ is shown. Here, the PWM efficiecny 87.76% and P&O MPPT efficiency is 96.06% which is better than PWM control method.

Table 2. Simulation Results for PWM and MPPT Controlled SEH systems.

Energy Harvester Parameters	PWM Control	P&O MPPT Control
Max. Solar Panel output Power (P_m)	2.5 watts	2.8 watts
Average Buck Converter Output Voltage (V_m)	3.3 volts	3.5 volts
Average Buck Converter Output Current (I_m)	260 mA	500 mA
Buck Converter Output Power	650 mW	1.8 watts
Inductor Loss	50 mW	20 mW
MOSFET Switching Loss	5 mW	2 mW
Harvester System Efficiency (%)	87.76%	96.06%

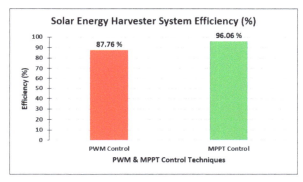

Figure 13. Comparison of PWM and P&O MPPT Harvesting System Efficiency $\left(\eta_{sys}\right)$.

10. Hardware Experiment

A hardware experiment for the SEH-WSN scenario is performed to monitor the room temperature wirelessly using a highly efficient of energy harvester system as shown in Figure 14. The complete SEH-WSN system is divided into two parts i.e., WSN system and an Energy harvesting system. The Scientech Technologies Private Limited, (New Delhi, India) made WSN trainer kit (Scientech 3211) is used for the WSN system and a commercial Buck converter (LM2575, Texas Instruments Inc., Dallas, TX, USA) with a solar panel is used for the solar energy harvesting system.

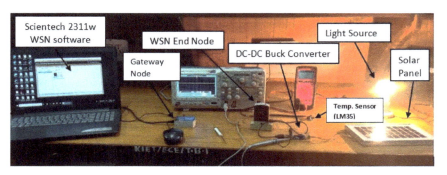

Figure 14. Hardware Experiment setup of SEH-WSN system.

10.1. Scientech 2311 WSN System

It consists of a temperature sensor (LM35, Texas Instruments Inc., Dallas, TX, USA), WSN end node, a WSN USB gateway node and a WSN monitoring software installed on a laptop PC. The temperature-sensing module (LM35) is connected to the Input-Output (I/O) port 1 of the end WSN node. The end WSN node measures the temperature and sends data wirelessly to the remote gateway. The measured data is sensed by the WSN node and sent to the remote gateway node. The gateway node is connected via USB cable to the computer system. At the computer system, a software Scientech-2311w is installed which can show the visual representation of the sensor nodes topology and measured temperature (in degrees Celsius) as shown in Figure 15. In our experimental setup, the maximum distance between the remote end WSN node and the gateway WSN node is less than 10 m. The maximum distance between the gateway node and the sensor node can be up to 100 m using ZigBee communication protocols.

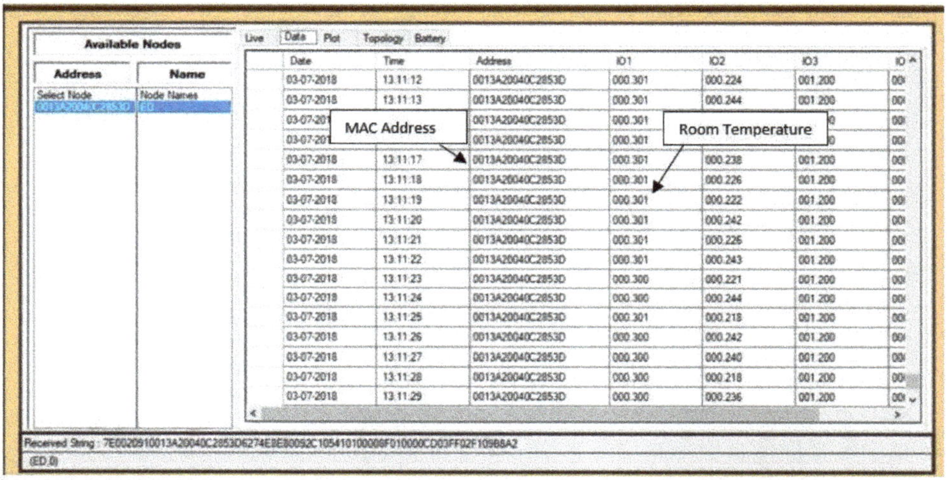

Figure 15. Temperature monitoring readings of the SEH-WSN node on a personal computer.

10.2. LM2575 Buck Converter Based Energy Harvesting System

A 5 watts solar panel and a commercial PWM controlled buck converter module is used as an energy harvesting system for the Scientech 2311W node. The output voltage from the solar panel is fed to buck converter, which removes ripples and regulates the output voltage. This ripple-free and purified dc voltage (3.3 v) is used to charge the rechargeable battery of the WSN node. The LM2575 MOSFET is used for switching action in the PWM controlled buck converter. It provides regulated dc output of 3.3 volts, 1 A to the WSN node. The maximum efficiency of the LM2575 buck converter using PWM control is only 80% as specified by manufacturer data sheets in [22]. Therefore, the actual hardware efficiency of a real-life PWM controlled LM2575 buck converter is less (i.e., 80%) as compared to theoretical simulation results (i.e., 87.76%). This validates our simulation results by comparing with a hardware experiment. Table 3 shows various hardware experiment parameters i.e. Scientech 2311w WSN system parameters, energy harvesting system parameters, and measuring instruments details.

Table 3. Hardware Experiment Parameters.

Hardware Experiment Parameters	Number of Components and Details
Scientech 2311w WSN system:	
WSN Gateway Node	1
WSN End node	1
Temperature Sensor Module (LM35)	1
Scientech 2311w WSN monitoring software installed on a Laptop PC	1
Energy Harvesting System:	
Solarcraft Solar Panel	5 w, 8 V, 0.65 A
Generic LM2576, 80% efficient, PWM controlled DC-DC Buck Converter	3.6 V–40 V, 2 A
Measuring Instruments:	
Tektronix 200MHz Digital Storage Oscilloscope (DSO)	1
Multimeter	1

The measured room temperature is $0.301 \times 100 = 30.1$ degree Celsius, as shown in the Scientech 2311 WSN monitoring software in Figure 15. The MAC address of the end WSN node is also shown with the actual date (3 July 2018) and time (13:11:12 p.m.) of the reporting of the WSN end node to the gateway node.

A comparison of various existing solar energy harvesting models for WSN nodes is shown in Table 4. Similarly, other researchers in Refs. [23,24] have proposed their solar energy harvesting models with various simulation parameters considered as shown in Table 4. Finally, our proposed solar energy-harvesting model has the highest efficiency of 96.06% as compared to the other simulation works reported by the various authors as presented in Table 4.

Table 4. Comparison of existing Solar Energy Harvesting models for WSN nodes.

Author & Year	Proposed Solar Energy Harvester Model	Irradiance (W/m²) Consider	Temperature (°C) Consider	Inductor and Capacitor Loss Consider	(PWM/MPPT) Consider	Super Capacitor/Battery Consider	Power Consumption of Harvester Circuit Consider	Maximum Efficiency	Model Validation Consider
Denis Dondi et al. [3], 2008	Boost Converter with MPPT	Yes (20–1000 W/m²)	No	Yes	MPPT only	Battery	No	85%	No
Davide Brunelli et al. [4], 2009	Boost Converter with MPPT	No	No	No	MPPT only	Both	Yes	80%	Yes
Andrea Castagnetti et al. [23], 2012	Boost Converter	No	No	No	Not Reported	Battery	Yes	Not Reported	yes
Alex S. Weddell et al. [24], 2012	Buck-Boost Converter with MPPT	Yes (200–5000 W/m²)	No	No	MPPT	Battery	Yes	Not reported	Yes
Our Proposed Model	Buck Converter with PWM & MPPT both	Yes	Yes	No	PWM & MPPT both	Both	Yes	96.06%	Yes

11. Conclusions

In this paper, Modeling, Simulation, Optimization and a hardware experiment are performed for SEH-WSN nodes. Two control techniques for solar energy harvester system i.e., PWM and MPPT have been analyzed and compared using the MATLAB simulation. The efficiency of the MPPT controlled buck converter is shown to be better than the PWM controlled counterpart. The battery SoC and Terminal voltage graphs have been shown. The overall energy harvester circuit efficiency (η_{sys}) is calculated by adding Buck converter efficiency and, PWM efficiency and MPPT efficiency. From the comparison of simulation results, as shown in Figure 14 that the MPPT based Solar Energy Harvester system efficiency (96.06%) is better than PWM controlled system efficiency (87.76%) in the MATLAB/SIMULINK simulation. The practical hardware experiment of the SEH-WSN node is used to monitor the room temperature wirelessly using a PWM controlled buck converter. The maximum efficiency of the practical LM2575 based PWM controlled buck converter is 80%, which is less than theoretical simulation results (i.e., 87.76%). In the future, the simulation and hardware experimental work presented in this paper for SEH-WSN systems can be extended to various advanced MPPT algorithms like neural networks, fuzzy logic, and machine learning algorithms.

Author Contributions: H.S. contributed to the most of the modelling, optimization, simulation and hardware experiments work. A.H. and Z.A.J. guided the overall work as supervisor and co-supervisors respectively.

Funding: This research received no external funding.

Acknowledgments: The authors are thankful for the Advanced Power Electronics Lab, Electrical Engineering Department, Jamia Millia Islamia, (a Central Government University), New Delhi, India. This lab is supported by the Ministry of New & Renewable Energy (MNRE), Government of India, New Delhi, India.

Conflicts of Interest: The authors declare no conflict of interest.

References

1. IEEE 802.15.4. *IEEE Standard for Low-Rate Wireless Networks, Amendment 2: Ultra-Low Power Physical Layer*; IEEE Standards Association: Piscataway, NJ, USA; IEEE Computer Society: Washington, DC, USA, 2016.
2. ZigBee Pro with Green Power User Guide. Revision 1.4. Available online: www.nxp.com/documents/user_manual/JN-UG-3095.pdf (accessed on 28 June 2018).
3. Dondi, D.; Bertacchini, A.; Brunelli, D. Modelling and optimization of a solar energy harvester system for self-powered wireless sensor networks. *IEEE Trans. Ind. Electron.* **2008**, *55*, 2759–2766. [CrossRef]
4. Brunelli, D.; Moser, C.; Thiele, L. Design of a solar-harvesting circuit for batteryless embedded systems. *IEEE Trans. Circuits Syst.* **2009**, *56*, 2519–2528. [CrossRef]
5. Mathews, I.; King, P.J.; Stafford, F.; Frizzell, R. Performance of III–V solar cells as indoor light energy harvesters. *IEEE J. Photovolt.* **2016**, *6*, 230–236. [CrossRef]
6. Liu, X.; Sánchez-Sinencio, E. A highly efficient ultralow photovoltaic power harvesting system with MPPT for internet of things smart nodes. *IEEE Trans. VLSI Syst.* **2015**, *23*, 3065–3075. [CrossRef]
7. Shiau, J.-K.; Ma, C.-W. Li-Ion battery charging with a buck-boost power converter for a solar powered battery management system. *Energies* **2013**, *6*, 1669–1699. [CrossRef]
8. Sivakumar, S.; Jagabar Sathik, M.; Manoj, P.S.; Sundararajan, G. An assessment on performance of DC-DC converters for renewable energy applications. *Renew. Sustain. Energy Rev.* **2016**, *58*, 1475–1485. [CrossRef]
9. Shin, M.; Joe, I. Energy management algorithm for solar-powered energy harvesting wireless sensor node for Internet of Things. *IET Commun.* **2016**, *10*, 1508–1521. [CrossRef]
10. Sharma, H.; Haque, A.; Jaffery, Z.A. Solar energy harvesting wireless sensor network nodes: A survey. *J. Renew. Sustain. Energy* **2018**, *10*, 023704. [CrossRef]
11. Sharma, H.; Haque, A.; Jaffery, Z.A. Design challenges in solar energy harvesting wireless sensor networks. In Proceedings of the 3rd IEEE International Conference on Nanotechnology for Instrumentation and Measurement (NANOFIM) Workshop, Greater Noida, India, 16–17 November 2017; pp. 442–448.

12. Didioui, A.; Bernier, C.; Morche, D.; Sentieys, O. HarvWSNet: A co-simulation framework for energy harvesting wireless sensor networks. In Proceedings of the IEEE International Conference on Computing, Networking and Communications, Wireless Ad Hoc and Sensor Networks Symposium, San Diego, CA, USA, 28–31 January 2013; pp. 808–812.

13. Yi, J.M.; Kang, M.J.; Noh, D.K. SolarCastalia: Solar energy harvesting wireless sensor network simulator. In Proceedings of the IEEE International Conference on Information and Communication Technology Convergence (ICTC), Busan, Korea, 22–24 October 2014.

14. Sanchez, A.; Blanc, S.; Climent, S.; Yuste, P.; Ors, R. SIVEH: Numerical computing simulation of wireless energy-harvesting sensor nodes. *Sensors* **2013**, *13*, 11750–11771. [CrossRef] [PubMed]

15. Texas Instruments Application Report on "Basic Calculation of a Boost Converter's Power Stage". Available online: www.ti.com (accessed on 28 June 2018).

16. Texas Instruments Application Report on "Calculating Efficiency of PMP-DC-DC Controllers". Available online: www.ti.com (accessed on 28 June 2018).

17. Haque, A. Maximum Power Point Tracking (MPPT) for Scheme for Solar Photovoltaic System. *J. Energy Policy Res.* **2014**, *1*, 115–122. [CrossRef]

18. Ibrahima, R.; Chung, T.D. Solar energy harvester for industrial wireless sensor nodes. In Proceedings of the IEEE International Symposium on Robotics and Intelligent Sensors, IRIS 2016, Tokyo, Japan, 17–20 December 2016; pp. 111–118.

19. Li, Y.; Shi, R. An intelligent solar energy-harvesting system for wireless sensor networks. *EURASIP J. Wirel. Commun. Netw.* **2015**, *179*. [CrossRef]

20. Praveen, K.; Pudipeddi, M.; Sivaramakrishna, M. Design, development and analysis of energy harvesting system for wireless pulsating sensors. In Proceedings of the IEEE Annual India Conference (INDICON), Bengaluru, India, 16–18 December 2016.

21. Win, K.K.; Wu, X.; Dasgupta, S.; Wen, W.J.; Kumar, R.; Panda, S.K. Efficient solar energy harvester for wireless sensor nodes. In Proceedings of the IEEE International Conference on Communication Systems, Singapore, 17–19 November 2010; pp. 289–294.

22. LM2575, 1 A, 3.3v-15v Adjustable Output Voltage, Step-Down Switching Regulator. ON Semiconductor Company Datasheets. 2009. Available online: http://onsemi.com (accessed on 28 June 2018).

23. Castagnetti, A.; Pegatoquet, A.; Auguin, M. A framework for modeling and simulating energy harvesting WSN nodes with efficient power management policies. *EURASIP J. Embed. Syst.* **2012**, *8*. [CrossRef]

24. Weddell, A.S.; Merrett, G.V.; Al-Hashimi, B.M. Ultra low-power photovoltaic MPPT technique for indoor and outdoor wireless sensor nodes. In Proceedings of the IEEE conference on Design, Automation & Test in Europe (DATE), Grenoble, France, 14–18 March 2011.

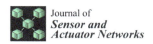

Article

Opportunistically Exploiting Internet of Things for Wireless Sensor Network Routing in Smart Cities

Shaza Hanif [1,*], Ahmed M. Khedr [1,2], Zaher Al Aghbari [1] and Dharma P. Agrawal [3]

[1] Department of Computer Science, University of Sharjah, Sharjah 27272, UAE;
akhedr@sharjah.ac.ae (A.M.K.); zaher@sharjah.ac.ae (Z.A.A.)
[2] Department of Mathematics, Zagazig University, Zagazig 44511, Egypt
[3] Department of Electrical Engineering and Computer Science, University of Cincinnati, Cincinnati, OH 45220, USA; dharmaagrawal@gmail.com
* Correspondence: shazahanif@gmail.com

Received: 8 July 2018; Accepted: 26 October 2018; Published: 30 October 2018

Abstract: With the emergence of Internet of Things (IoT), the research on Smart Cities with wireless sensor networks (WSNs) got leveraged due to similarities between objectives in both Smart City and IoT. Along with them, research in controlling WSN faces new challenges and opportunities for data aggregation and routing has received consistent focus from researchers. Yet new techniques are being proposed to address modern challenges in WSN and efficient resource utilization. Moreover, solutions are required to integrate existing deployed WSN with ever increasing numbers of IoT devices in Smart Cities, that benefit both. In this work, we present an approach for routing in a WSN, in which IoT is used opportunistically to reduce the communication overhead of the sensors. In our approach, WSN deployed in a Smart City interacts with the IoT devices to route the data to the sink. We build a prototype Integration Platform for the WSN that allows interaction with IoT devices and utilizes them opportunistically that results in an energy efficient routing of data. Simulation results show that the direction is quite promising and our approach offers to utilize IoT to gain unique advantages.

Keywords: data collection; Internet of Things; wireless sensor networks; Smart Cities; Middleware; routing protocols

---

1. Introduction

In this era, there are billions of sensor-enabled intelligent devices on the Internet that collectively form a huge entity known as Internet of Things (IoTs) [1]. According to Cisco [2], by 2020 fifty billion devices will be connected to the Internet, thus depicting the potential and complexity of using such an inter-connectivity. An underlying simple concept of "Anything connected at anytime" [3] in an IoT opens new ways of interdisciplinary research. From bare hardware sensing platforms to upper most application layer, IoTs has created new horizons for researchers. IoT devices are spread city wide, perform their functions and share information for the betterment of quality of citizens' lives. It is important to notice similarities in the aims and objectives of both Smart City and IoTs [1].

IoTs encapsulate Wireless Sensor Networks (WSN) as an important component. WSN emerged as a dominant technology, much before the emergence of IoT, addressing a wide spectrum of application domains [4,5]. With successful deployment of IoT infrastructure and Smart City test-beds in real cities, i.e., Padova [6] and Santander [7], more and more government municipalities and corporations are interested to leverage the strengths of Smart City. The aim is to make better use of public resources, increasing the quality of life of the citizens, while minimizing the operational costs.

For monitoring and surveillance of a Smart City application, sensors are deployed in a large area, city wide. Typical examples include traffic management systems [8], structural health management systems [9], traffic signal monitoring [8], electronic toll collection systems [10], highway data collection [8], and automatic number plate recognition systems [11].

Routing is essentially a service required in a WSN wherein sensors sense data using individual inexpensive sensor nodes and routes the data towards the sink for drawing meaningful conclusions. Since the advent of WSN in 1960's [12], there is a plethora of techniques and protocols proposed for routing and data aggregation in WSN [13–15]. Though sensors are becoming smarter, cheaper, and smaller in size, they are always energy constrained [4]. Therefore, there is an unparalleled need for developing innovative energy efficient routing approaches. In the applications mentioned above, often data has to traverse through a long series of intermediate sensors before it reaches the sink. Thus, much of the WSN energy is consumed in multi-hop routing.

Practically, Smart City and IoTs in our cities are currently in infancy. There are very few fully functional IoTs serving the objective of a Smart City. The majority of research works are related to IoT frameworks, ideas, prototypes, and use cases, which is quite common for an emerging technology. The ultimate aim of a deployed IoT in the context of Smart City is that every IoT device can be connected and can share data with other devices for the public betterment. Recent developments in Low Power Long Range (LPLR) network protocols [16] e.g., LoRa, SigFox, offer low power alternative for sensors. Yet, they also have shortcomings and cannot be used in each and every application where sensors are required [16,17]. Moreover, with trends towards Heterogeneous ad hoc networks [18], a wide community still uses and will keep using traditional mutltihop WSN as a part of their solution [19], and may use LPLR as well. Thus, our approach can be easily integrated in such scenarios.

In practice, there is a transitional phase where existing deployed WSNs are working, functioning, serving, and administered separately, while other smart devices are around them, achieving basic goals of a Smart City and being administered by public sector or a private organization. In our work, we aim to exploit the IoT devices opportunistically in routing data of separately administered WSN.

Sensors essentially use their energy resources in (i) sensing, (ii) local computation, (iii) communication of its own data, and (iv) communication of other sensors data. This paper presents an opportunistic use of IoT for better resource utilization of a WSN by building Integration Platform (IT Platform). In our work, we reduce resource utilization by allowing sensors to route few data packets of other sensors to the Sink. Thus, instead of utilizing traditional WSN routing protocols, we opportunistically use IoT devices in the surrounding environment for routing. This enables the Sensor in deployed area to conserve energy [20].

To better understand the problem scenario, let us consider a series of sensors deployed at road side of a Smart City, and there are intelligent cars (as IoT devices) using the road. Figure 1 shows an example scenario in Dubai City where monitoring sensors are deployed at the highway bridge. Our main idea is that instead of sensors routing data to the sink located at the end of the road, IT Platform can be used to let a passing smart car collect the data (on sensor's behalf) and deliver it to the sink. In case a smart car starts moving away from the sink, it will inform a sensor of WSN, which in turn may use another IoT device or may use WSN routing. Usually, IoT devices that are near WSN, are more likely to get re-charged by their own sources. In contrast, the WSN, once deployed, is hardly re-charged. Thus, it is natural to use communication resources of these IoT devices and save energy of sensors in WSN. Since the IoT device owners enable resource sharing and allow IT Platform to be installed, they should receive some reward. Although detailed discussion of this reward is out of scope of this paper, we do state a couple of examples. The reward could be in the form of points, redeemed at a car parking or public charging space. It could also be in the form of giving access to a specific public information portal.

Figure 1. A motivational scenario of road infrastructure in Dubai city. The blue star in the middle is the Sink location. Different roads have red, gray, blue, pink color where sensors are deployed.

We want to emphasize that using our IT Platform, we are making explicit use of IoT devices, considering them as a part of the environment [20] in which WSN is deployed. This is contrary to the traditional research conducted for routing in WSN for IoT, where in most cases an existing protocol is adapted and reused for routing in WSN for IoT applications. Thus, IoT devices are not an integral part of our WSN, rather they are the Smart devices passing by the area where a separately administered WSN is deployed. This makes our approach a novel data collection and routing scheme.

The main contribution of this paper is (1) a novel idea with a prototype that uses IoT devices in a pragmatic scenario for conserving energy in a WSN, (2) IT Platform connects an existing WSN with IoT devices that are in the surrounding environment, and (3) evaluation of the prototype from multiple aspects. We describe our problem scenario and illustrate by extensive simulations that demonstrate and evaluate the IT Platform. It is observed that by using IT Platform that opportunistically uses IoT devices, not only WSN energy is conserved but packet reception rate is also improved.

The rest of the paper is organized as follows. Section 2 summarizes other research efforts related to our work. In Section 3, problem scenario and requirements are defined. IT Platform is detailed in Section 4. The Castalia simulator, experiment details, and evaluation are discussed in Section 5. Finally, Section 6 concludes the paper.

2. Related Work

Our work is related to routing and data aggregation in the context of IoTs and Smart City. Right from the beginning of WSN in 1970's, routing in WSN has always been one of the main concern. There are a large number of techniques proposed for energy efficient routing and data aggregation. These include routing with heterogeneous sensor nodes, cross network protocols and platforms, and routing with mobile sinks. A few recent surveys by Pantazis et al. [21], Sheng Yu et al. [22], and Sara et al. [13], can be referred for details. An interesting research related to our work, is to use few high power long range devices in a network of short ranged sensor nodes. For instance, Yarvis et al. [23], demonstrates that the network life time and delivery ratio can be increased by using few long range sensors.

With the advent of IoT and Smart City, the routing protocols are revisited. Most of the routing and data aggregation schemes in IoT can be categorized in to two kinds. One is related to the IoT applications only, where the research discusses IoT application requirements and suggests adjustments or compatibility of a protocol in the new application domain. For instance, Machado et al. [24] present an improvement of AODV (Ad hoc On-demand Distance Vector) routing protocol [25] for the IoT applications that considers QoS (Quality of Service), reliability, and energy efficiency. Park et al. [26] also enhances AODV protocol using a probabilistic approach for increasing the network lifetime and reducing consumed energy. There are works that focus on specific WSN types, such as wireless mulimedia sensor networks [27].

In contrast, the second kind of research, which is more related to our work, uses multiple types of machines with heterogeneous capabilities to communicate and aggregate data. This requires substantial support by middle-ware frameworks and platforms to cope with heterogeneity of devices. For instance, Sancheze et al. [7] illustrate the design of a large scale IoT test bed and discuss the use of hierarchical architecture for routing data. Similarly, Zanella et al. [6], present technologies, protocols, and architecture for Smart Cities and suggest guidelines adapted in Padova Smart City project.

A rather different approach is used by Al-fagin et al. [28], wherein a priced public sensing framework is proposed for public data delivery gathered from cloud and heterogeneous resources. The work is data centric, focused on supply and demand chain of public data from mobile phones. Orsino et al. [29] introduce data collection in cellular devices using device to device communications in an IoT and Smart City setting. This results in more efficient resource utilization and minimizes energy consumption. They use one device that aggregates data from several surrounding devices and then sends the data to cellular station, instead of each device sending data individually. Very recently, an overview of using traditional WSN protocols for achieving device to device communication in IoT has been presented by Bello et al. [30].

Our work is different from existing works since it considers a static WSN, deployed in a Smart City. Mobile IoT devices owned by public or private owners are external to this deployed WSN. This is a typical scenario for technological evolution in a city, where every device may get connected yet some internal systems may remain individually working. Thus, as explained later, we exploit the presence of these IoT devices. They are used by our platform for the benefit of both WSN and IoT devices. In our IT Platform, we can use any routing protocol that is suitable to the domain of WSN applications. We use AODV routing protocol [25], which is a well accepted and a well studied protocol for WSN [21].

Emerging technologies of low power long range sensors [16] mostly use ISM band and keep power consumption low at the cost of increased delay and low data rate. These technologies, typically LoRa and SigFox, use star topology to connect to the base station while we are interested in improving a generic WSN that uses multihop routing.

To the best of our knowledge, the work close to our research of using environment opportunistically is by Cardone et al. [31] and Jayaraman et al. [32]. In the former, the authors construct MANETs (Mobile Ad hoc NETworks) of a machinery in a mine to route urgent data. While in the latter, the authors use context-aware mobile phones to act as data collectors from sensors. Our work is different from both as sensors work in multiple activity modes and search for IoT devices in vicinity while their basic idea is to use context based architecture or MANETS by smart devices. Moreover, our sensors are in sleep mode when not communicating to save energy. Khalil et al. [33] integrate an existing WSN of a Smart building to an IoT environment using gateways and main server to deliver the data to the mobile user. However, their work is not related to exploiting IoT devices, rather they connect WSN with Internet and hence the mobile user.

3. Problem Details

In this section, we describe the scenario and the details of the problem we address.

3.1. Problem Scenario

Typically, each sensor node consumes energy in three major ways of, sensing, local computation, and communication. The communication is related not only for its own data, but also for multi hop routing of other sensor's data to the sink. In the context of Smart City, we want to exploit the presence of IoT devices near our WSN. Consider a typical case in a city where sensors are deployed city wide. Sensor nodes are equipped with short range communications. The data is gathered at the sink, located in the middle of the city. In a normal scenario, the data is aggregated at the sink by using multi hop routing in WSN. IoT devices, are moving on the road where sensors are deployed along its sides. Figure 2 shows example of a typical scenario of city center of Sharjah, UAE.

Figure 2. Sharjah city center, a typical scenario in which 100 sensors (red dots) are being placed at random location in a 200 by 200 m region.

3.2. Requirements

Considering the above scenario, our IT Platform should be able to satisfy the following requirements:

1. **Interaction with the IoT devices:** The IT Platform should enable WSN to interact with IoT devices when they are available.
2. **Independent routing:** The platform must allow WSN to continue delivering data to the sink using their normal routing protocol, if there is no IoT devices in the vicinity. This is important since WSN should not be fully dependent on IoT devices, as IoT devices are not a part of their network. Rather they are exploited opportunistically.
3. **Energy efficiency:** By exploiting IoT devices, energy consumption in WSN is conserved.
4. **Network lifetime:** The energy of WSN should be consumed in such a way that a few sensor nodes shouldn't be drained quicker than rest of the network, rather all sensor nodes should be used in a balanced way. This means that along with energy conservation the time duration between first dieing node and the most dieing nodes (making network non-functional) shouldn't be long.
5. **Data delivery:** Typically when IoT devices are exploited, the amount of received packets should either be the same or should be increased as compared to routed only using WSN. Thus, packet loss could be minimized.

Following, assumptions are made that simplify the problem scenario and provide better understanding:

- IoT devices are Vehicles/cars/passengers;
- WSN is surrounded by IoT devices, but can function without them; and
- WSN nodes send their data to a single sink.

4. The Integration Platform

Before discussing IT Platform, we first clarify our envisioned IoT. Although there are many alternative definitions of IoTs, we particularly want to state the one by Versman et al. [3] as "*Internet of Things could allow people and things to be connected Anytime, Anyplace, with Anything and Anyone, ideally using Any path/network and Any service*". We adopt this definition since we believe that it encompasses a broader vision of IoT.

In our IT Platform, we used a two layered approach for routing data, WSN layer and IoT layer. As shown in Figure 3, the IoT layer is independent of WSN, and is not a part of WSN. IoT devices are moving in the vicinity of the WSN nodes, while their communication capabilities for data transfer in WSN is being exploited. To route the data packets to the sink. WSN layer can use any routing protocol, according to the requirements of its application. We use AODV (Adhoc On-demand Distance Vector) routing protocol [25] which is a well known routing protocol for WSNs.

Figure 4 shows the role of the IT Platform in internal architecture of both a sensor node and an IoT device. IT Platform is responsible for routing the data packets either using WSN routing or an IoT device. When an IoT device is in the vicinity, it is discovered and data is sent to it. When IoT device moves away from sink, IT Platform fetches data back to WSN layer by selecting a suitable sensor. If there are enough IoT devices around, the sensors remain in the sleep state and avoid multihop routing. The work-flow is briefed in the following subsections.

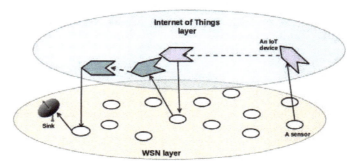

Figure 3. The two layers used by our platform.

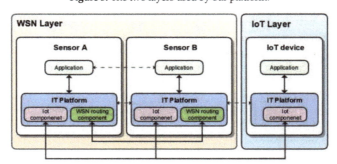

Figure 4. The internal architecture of a Sensor and an Internet of Things (IoT) device.

4.1. IoT Discovery and Negotiation in IT Platform

When a sensor has data, it first tries to send it via IoT layer. A hello message is broadcasted to find any IoT device in vicinity. If an IoT receives such message and its direction is towards Sink, it replies to the sensor. The reply message contains IoT's distance from the Sink, and the speed. When multiple IoTs reply, on discovering them the sensor will select one based on RSSI value, distance and speed of

IoT using Algorithm 1. In lines 7 and 8, while calculating the score of an IoT device, the RSSI value is given increased importance as compared to distance and speed. *bestValue* is the score of so far best IoT device. The sensor sends a confirmation message and on receiving the acknowledgement of that message, the data is sent to the selected IoT device. The IoT acknowledges the data reception.

Algorithm 1 getBestIoT

---

iots[] = //*array of IoT objects*
iot.rssi = //*received signal strength indicator value*
iot.distance = //*Maximum distance between two points* **minus** *distance of IoT from Sink*
iot.speed = //*Maximum allowed speed in which communication is possible* **minus** *speed of IoT*

1:   **procedure** GETBESTIOT(IOTS[])
2:     **for each** $p \in iots$ **do** //*remove iot replies with less than threshold RSSI.*
3:       **if** $p.rssi < threshholdRssi$ **then**
4:         iots.remove (p)
5:       **end if**
6:     **end for**
7:     best = iots[1]
8:     **for each** $p \in iots$ **do**
9:       bestValue = 2 * best.rssi + best.speed + best.distance
10:       pValue = 2 * p.rssi + p.speed + p.distance
11:       **if** $pValue > bestValue$ **then**
12:         best = p
13:       **end if**
14:     **end for**
      return best
15: **end procedure**

When a sensor doesn't get any reply from IoT, it uses its WSN routing protocol and sends the data to the next hope accordingly. If the next hope is in IoT mode (modes discussed in next sub-section), the sensor knows the next hope (neighbor's) time slot and sends data accordingly. When next hop is in Normal mode, its Rx will be ON all the time and can receive data from the sender sensor at any time.

4.2. Sensor Activity Modes in WSN Layer

There are two activity modes for Sensors; (1) Normal mode, (2) IoT mode. The sensors select between the communication modes using a gossiping protocol [34]. The main idea is that by default a sensor remains in Normal mode which uses maximum energy. When there are ample IoT's in the environment to take the communication load from sensors, sensors switch to IoT mode that uses lesser energy. The algorithm for switching between the two modes is discussed in Section 4.5. When appropriate, IoT mode is turned On for some time.

The time is divided into frames of 500 ms, and each frame is subdivided into slots as shown in Figure 5. In each frame, there is an initial listening slot (ILS), in which all sensors keep their receivers on regardless of which mode they are in. When in IoT mode, there are 10 equal slots for communication so that (1) Radio remains On only in relevant time; (2) minimal signal interference from neighbors while message passing; and (3) the neighbors do not face contention. The slots are assigned among sensors using a simple method, node id modulo number of slots in a frame.

$$ReceiveSlotNo = SNId/noOfSlotsInFrame \qquad (1)$$

In this way each node is aware of its own communication slot and its neighbors communication slots.

In normal mode, the radio Rx is On for the whole time. When there is any data to send then it goes to Tx mode and after transfer switch back to Rx mode. It is ensured that Rx is on at ILS in the beginning of each frame. In IoT mode, the Rx turns On only at ILS and if any data is expected, it keeps Rx ON in the sensors own communication slot. The Tx is turned ON according to the Rx slot of the next hop.

For IoT discovery and negotiation the sensor's own communication slot is used. For the rest of the frame sensors the radio is in the sleep mode for saving energy.

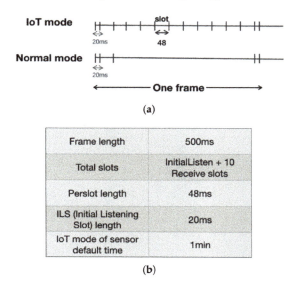

(a)

Frame length	500ms
Total slots	InitialListen + 10 Receive slots
Perslot length	48ms
ILS (Initial Listening Slot) length	20ms
IoT mode of sensor default time	1min

(b)

Figure 5. Sensor communication frames. (**a**) Frame structure for sensors in the two activity modes. (**b**) Frame and slot length information.

4.3. Sensor Selection By IoT

When an IoT changes its direction and goes away from the Sink, it has to drop data back to the WSN layer. To avoid sending data to sensors while they are sleeping, IoT device is given the time synchronization information about when sensors are awake and ready to listen to data. When data is sent to IoT (Section 4.1), frame start times are also shared. This makes IoT aware of the ILS at WSN layer. Therefore, it broadcasts a dropHello message to WSN layer sensors considering this ILS's time. Sensors reply IoT with in a dropReply message with their location, Rx slot and energy level. Based on RSSI value, energy level and distance from Sink, IoT selects a best sensor using Algorithm 2. In lines 2 to 4, the replies of Sensor nodes with lower than threshold value of RSSI are discarded, which ensures quality in communication. Lines 6 to 10 finds the Sensor node with best score. The IoT then informs the sensor to send the data in the sensor's Rx slot.

4.4. Traversing of Data Packets

In a nutshell, data packets are sent towards the sink using two layered approach. Figure 6 depicts basic sequence of communication between Sensor nodes and an IoT devices. After discovery and negotiation with IoT, Sensor sends the packet to the IoT device. IoT acknowledges the receipt of packet to the sensor so that sensor does not have to forward the packet using default routing protocol. When the IoT device changes the direction, it sends the information (data packet) back to the WSN layer, where the receiving sensor repeats the process.

Algorithm 2 getBestSN

SN[] = //*array of SN objects*
SN.rssi = //*received signal strength indicator value*
SN.distance = //*Maximum distance between two points **minus** IoT's distance from Sink*
SN.energyLevel = //*Remaining Energy of Sensor*

1: **procedure** GETBESTSN(SN[])
2:     **for each** $p \in SN$ **do** //*remove SN replies with less than threshold RSSI.*
3:         **if** $SN[i].rssi < threshholdRssi$ **then**
4:             SN.remove (p)
5:         **end if**
6:     **end for**
7:     best = SN[1]
8:     **for each** $p \in SN$ **do**
9:         bestValue = 2 * best.rssi + best.energyLevel + best.distance
10:        pValue = 2 * p.rssi + p.energyLevel + p.distance
11:       **if** $pValue > bestValue$ **then**
12:          best = p
13:       **end if**
14:     **end for**

    return best
15: **end procedure**

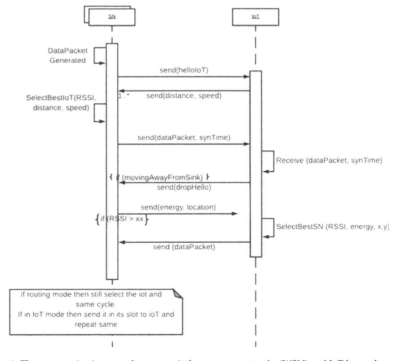

Figure 6. The communication steps between wireless sensor networks (WSN) and IoT layer elements.

In case the IT Platform component in the Sensor is unable to find any IoT device that is moving towards the Sink, the sensor continues the multi hop routing using its default routing protocol in the WSN layer. When the IoT device changes its direction, IT Platform enables IoT to send data packet back to WSN layer. Algorithm 3 shows the IsDirectionToSink algorithm in the platform for the IoT device. The algorithm is used to decide if it is moving towards or away from the sink based on euclidean distance as shown in lines 2 to 3. Table 1, shows the list of messages used in communication during traversing of Data Packets.

Algorithm 3 IsDirectionToSink
---
previousX = //previous X position of IoT device
previousY = //previous Y position of IoT device
currentX = //current X position of IoT device
currentY = //current X position of IoT device
sinkX = // X position of Sink
sinkY = // Y position of Sink
getDistance(x1,y1, x2,y2) // returns euclidean distance between two points

1: **procedure** IsDirectionToSink(DATA)
2:     currentDistance = getDistance(currentX, currentY, sinkX, sinkY)
3:     previousDistance = getDistance(previousX, previousY, sinkX, sinkY)
4:     **if** *currentDistance > previousDistance* **then**
5:         returnValue = True
6:     **else**
7:         returnValue = False
8:     **end if**

    return returnValue
9: **end procedure**

Table 1. List of messages exchanged by elements of integration platform (IT) Platform.

Message	From	To	Description
send (helloIoT)	SN	IoT	Message to search IoT in vicinity
send (distance, speed)	IoT	SN	IoT reply message to SN
send (selectedOK)	SN	IoT	SN confirms IoT as selected candidate
send (OK)	IoT	SN	IoT reply OK to selection as approval to send data and waits for dataPacket.
send (dataPacket, synchTime)	SN	IoT	SN sends dataPacket along with synchTime of WSN
send (dataAck)	IoT	SN	Acknowledge message for data reception
send (dropHello)	IoT	SN	Hello message to find SN to drop dataPacket to WSN layer.
send (energy, RxSlot, location)	SN	IoT	Reply to dropHello message with SN's energy level and location
send (selectedOK)	IoT	SN	IoT confirms SN as selected SN for sending data
send (OK)	SN	IoT	Reply OK to selection as approval to send dataPacket
send (dataPacket)	IoT	SN	IoT drops datapacket to selected SN
send (dataAck)	SN	IoT	Acknowledge message for data reception

4.5. Gossip Protocol

By default the sensor remains in the Normal mode. Based on two factors, (1) number of replies from IoT devices and (2) number of received messages (IoTExists messages) from neighbors, IoT mode is turned On for 1 min. IoT exists messages are sent using gossip algorithm inspired from

SIR gossip protocols [34]. The Gossip protocol algorithm is shown Algorithm 4. The push method is used by a Sensor node when it is discovering IoT devices. In line 6, on receiving ample replies from IoT devices, it changes its state to IOT and pushes this information to other sensor nodes using pushIoTExistMessage(m) method at line 12.

Algorithm 4 GossipAlgorithm

---

sendIoTExistMessageTo (P,m) = *//sends message m to neighbor P*
isIoTRepliesEnough() = *//returns True if no. of IoT replies is >= 3, else returns False*
state = *//represents the current state of node*

1: **procedure** GOSSIPALGORITHM() //Push method
2:     **while** true **do**
3:         wait Δ
4:         **if** *isIoTRepliesEnough()* **then**
5:             m.age = -1
6:             pushIoTExistMessage(m)
7:         **end if**
8:
9:     **end while**
10: **end procedure**
11: **procedure** ONIOTEXISTRECEIVE(M) //Push Receiver method
12:     **if** *m.age* < 2 **then**
13:         pushIoTExistMessage(m)
14:
15:     **end if**
16: **end procedure**
17: **procedure** PUSHIOTEXISTMESSAGE(M)
18:     P = //random neighbor
19:     **if** *state* == *NORMAL* **then**
20:         state = IOT
21:     **end if**
22:     IoTTimerSet(1min)
23:     m.age ++
24:     sendIoTExistMessageTo (P,m)
25: **end procedure**

Once a sensor decides to turn On IoT mode, it is for 1 minute. It broadcasts IoTExist (age = 1) messages to other sensors. Each receiving sensor that receives using procedure at line 8, re-broadcasts message after incrementing age unless age of the received message is two. Thus such messages stop after two hops.

If a Sensor node does not receive such messages, and only one IoT reply, then it keeps itself in the Normal mode. The sensor can still communicate with IoTs. However its energy consumption can not be avoided.

4.6. Advantages of IT Platform

We used a layered approach which is not hierarchical. We claim that there are several advantages of this approach. For example:

- Using IT Platform and IoT devices, there is no notable overhead on a sensor due to communication between the two layers.
- When the network gets disconnected due to nodes with depleted energy or any other reason, then packets can still reach the the Sink via IoT devices.

- Overall WSN communication load is reduced by exploiting the IoT devices. This is because the inter communication between the sensor nodes for multi-hop routing to the Sink is reduced.
- By allowing sensors nodes to sleep more, the idle listening is reduced and less energy is consumed.
- The platform does not require any extra computations, thus no additional computational overhead on sensors.
- There is no additional sensing load on the sensors of WSN.

5. Simulation Details and Results

To evaluate the proposed approach, we used a well known network simulator Omnet++ (version 4.6). For simulating WSN particularly, we used Castalia framework [35] on top of Omnet++. Castalia is a specialized simulator that mimics the real world sensors. It is commonly used by developers for prototype testing of naive ideas and protocols [36].

5.1. Evaluation Metrics

WSN performance can be evaluated by a variety of metrics. Corresponding to our requirements discussed in Section 3.2, and considering those used by most of the researchers, we used the following metrics:

1. Energy consumed: Average energy consumed by all sensors is depicted using this metric. The simulator measures energy consumption by considering the amount of time sensor radio has been in receive or transfer mode [37]. It is independent of data transfer or receive activity in a mode rather depends on duration the sensor is in specific mode. Table 2 displays the energy consumption of CC2420 Radio we simulated, in different modes [38].

Table 2. Power consumption in CC2420 Radio.

Parameter	Power
Radio Off	0.04 mW
Radio Sleep	1.4 mW
Radio Receiver	62 mW
Radio Transmitter (0 dBm)	57.42 mW
Radio Transmitter (−5 dBm)	46.2 mW

2. Network lifetime: This metric also depicts energy consumed, but shows the lifetime of the whole network. Using a conservative approach, the network is considered non-functional whenever the first node dies.
3. Nodes Alive: Shows the percentage of sensor nodes alive at specific simulation time.
4. Packet reception rate: This metric shows the rate of number of packets received by the sink as compared to the number of packets sent by each of the sensors. Any duplicate packet is discarded by the sink. The packet loss is there because, in all kinds of wireless communication, as we are using realistic simulation models (Section 5.2), it is common that there is some packet loss.

5.2. Simulation Environment

In our simulator, we visualize our approach with realistic wireless channel conditions and radio models. Interference is handled using received signal strength. Due to this realistic channel modeling, there is some packet loss caused by interference or poor value of received signal strength. The wireless channel is defined as a map of path loss and not simply by connection between sensor nodes. Moreover, at radio level, probability of reception depends on SINR (Signal to Interference and Noise Ratio). Multiple TX power levels of Radio can be configured for individual sensor nodes.

5.3. Simulation Setup

A two dimensional coordinate plane is used with 10 to 100 m, with multiple network configurations of 20 to 90 nodes, spread uniformly. There is one sink in the middle of the network. Mobile IoT devices randomly move in the region in straight lines. The radio power of each Sensor nodes and IoT device is −5 dBm and 1 dBm, respectively. The simulation time of each run of the experiment is set to 915 s, and each experiment is repeated 20 times with random seeds. Considering the data rate guidance by Zanella et al. [6], Sensor nodes generates 20 bytes of data every 2 s. This data rate is specifically suitable for monitoring applications wherein data rate is consistent but not very high. As discussed by Zanella et al. [6], many application domains of WSN have similar data rates with most of the sensors generating data at a consistent frequency.

5.4. Simulation Results

In this section, we discuss the evaluation results of our simulations using the three metrics discussed earlier.

To restate, IoT devices are not a part of WSN, rather they are external to the WSN, and WSN opportunistically uses them to route its data. Figure 7 shows our main result that with our prototype implementation Sensor nodes energy consumption is reduced almost four folds. WSNOnly means no IoT's are involved in routing data to Sink. With-IoTs means there are IoTs available that move around in WSN environment and the IT Platform uses them opportunistically.

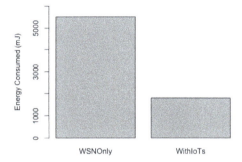

Figure 7. The energy consumption of WSN when integration platform (IT) Platform is used.

A more detailed view of energy consumption is depicted in Figure 8. As shown in Figure 8a, with increase in network size when only WSN routing is used, energy consumption is increased in a linear fashion. While with the IT Platform, the energy consumption is increasing much slowly. With bigger networks the gain of using IT Platform is three times larger.

We designed an experiment to understand the effect of using IoT devices. In this simulation, we kept the network fixed and added IoT devices in the environment. The results are shown in Figure 8b, where less energy is consumed with more IoT devices. This is because using IT Platform, the sensors are able to sleep more and their routing load is lowered. When the number of IoT devices is 30, there is a three times gain in energy conservation. In Figure 8c, it is found that as a result of lower energy consumption, the network lifetime is increased. The WithioTs line shows that the gain is almost three to four times consistently as network size is increased.

In Figure 9, we showed results of analyzing the energy usage of sensors over the simulation time. The gradual depletion of energy in sensor nodes can be clearly seen in Figure 9a. Figure 9b shows the sudden death of the whole network in three seconds, while a slow death of network in 20 s is seen in case IoT devices are used. Thus, it gives more margin of action to take appropriate measures. Furthermore, due to the use of IoT devices, the sensors are still able to send data to the Sink when their multihop routing is no longer working due to dead sensor nodes.

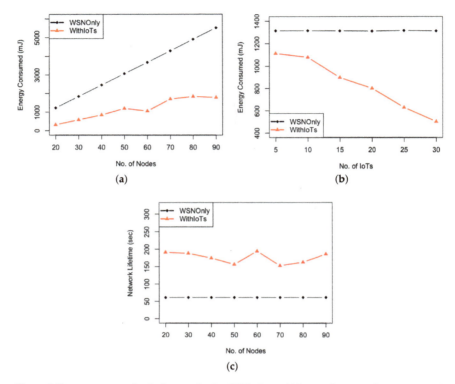

Figure 8. Energy consumption is decreased using IT Platform. (**a**) Larger the network, more energy is saved; (**b**) With increase in no. of IoTs, Sensor nodes consume less energy; (**c**) Consistent increase in Network lifetime with increase in network size.

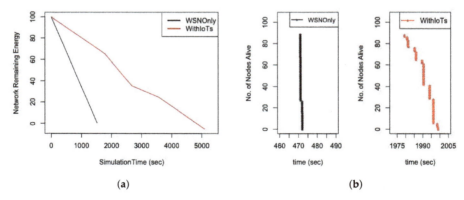

Figure 9. (**a**) Network lasts four times longer by using IT Platform that uses IoT devices. (**b**) [Left] All nodes die instantly, [Right] Nodes die in slow fashion using IT Platform.

From the perspective of Reception rate, as depicted by Figure 10, it is slightly increased and more stable by the use of IT Platform. We think that it is due to our careful selection of IoTdevices and sensor nodes using RSSI values. Moreover, due to the use of frames and slots for communication, there is less chance of interference while communicating. This packet loss is due to near realistic modeling of Radio and wireless channel of Castalia.

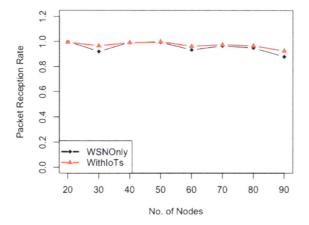

Figure 10. Improvement in Reception rate of WSN when IT Platform is used.

6. Conclusions

Our society is continually adapting and embracing the new paradigms of IoTs and Smart City as they come along with not only new requirements and challenges, but have new opportunities to embrace and exploit as well. Moreover, there is a need to integrate existing systems with new paradigms that utilize new platforms and frameworks.

In this paper, we have introduced and detailed an IT Platform that exploits IoT devices to bypass existing traditional multihop routing in WSN. This leads to an overall improvement in the performance of WSN with respect to energy consumption, network lifetime, and reception rate without creating any significant load on the sensors. The IT Platform enables WSN to save its communication cost and use its energy mainly in sensing, while giving reward opportunities to the IoT device owners. Currently, our cities have Smart devices, but are not fully integrated with each other and do not exploit the full potential of IoTs and Smart Cities. Thus, IT Platform can be used in such scenarios to improve the efficiency of a deployed WSN using the ever growing number of IoT devices in the city.

In the future, we plan to use our framework alongside other energy saving recent MAC protocols like TMAC. We will evaluate the effect of using IoT devices if TMAC protocol is used while overcoming the synchronization challenges for mobile IoT. Moreover, we can also extend our work by improving the algorithms for specific application domains and by evaluating our approach with multiple routing protocols. Additional efforts are required to fine tune the frame size and slot size according to the network density and network traffic, which can yield more energy savings.

Author Contributions: All authors contributed together to realize this work and its hard to specify. Conceptualization and methodology by S.H., Z.A.A. and A.M.K. Software and original draft preparation by S.H. Validation, writing, reviewing, editing, supervision, by D.P.A., Z.A.A. and A.M.K.

Funding: This research work is funded by University of Sharjah, Big Data Minning & Multimedia Research Group.

Acknowledgments: The authors are thankful to the University of Sharjah for its support. Special thanks to Nayyab Zia Naqvi and Shahab Ud Din for their valuable discussion and comments.

Conflicts of Interest: The authors declare no conflict of interest.

J. Sens. Actuator Netw. **2018**, *7*, 46

Abbreviations

The following abbreviations are used in this manuscript:

IoT	Internet of Things
WSN	Wireless Sensor Networks
IT Platform	Integration Platform
SN	Sensor Node
QoS	Quality of Service
MANETS	Mobile Adhoc NETworks
AODV	Ad hoc On-demand Distance Vector
LPLR	Low Power Long Range

References

1. Friess, P. *Internet of Things: Converging Technologies for Smart Environments and Integrated Ecosystems*; River Publishers: Aalborg, Denmark, 2013.
2. Evans, D. The Internet of things: How the next evolution of the Internet is changing everything. *CISCO White Paper* **2011**, *1*, 1–11.
3. Vermesan, O.; Friess, P.; Guillemin, P.; Gusmeroli, S.; Sundmaeker, H.; Bassi, A.; Jubert, I.S.; Mazura, M.; Harrison, M.; Eisenhauer, M.; et al. Internet of things strategic research roadmap. *Internet Things-Glob. Technol. Soc. Trends* **2011**, *1*, 9–52.
4. Rawat, P.; Singh, K.D.; Chaouchi, H.; Bonnin, J.M. Wireless sensor networks: A survey on recent developments and potential synergies. *J. Supercomput.* **2014**, *68*, 1–48. [CrossRef]
5. Yick, J.; Mukherjee, B.; Ghosal, D. Wireless sensor network survey. *Comput. Netw.* **2008**, *52*, 2292–2330. [CrossRef]
6. Zanella, A.; Bui, N.; Castellani, A.; Vangelista, L.; Zorzi, M. Internet of things for smart cities. *IEEE Internet Things J.* **2014**, *1*, 22–32. [CrossRef]
7. Sanchez, L.; Muñoz, L.; Galache, J.A.; Sotres, P.; Santana, J.R.; Gutierrez, V.; Ramdhany, R.; Gluhak, A.; Krco, S.; Theodoridis, E.; Pfisterer, D. SmartSantander: IoT experimentation over a Smart City testbed. *Comput. Netw.* **2014**, *61*, 217–238. [CrossRef]
8. Qureshi, K.N.; Abdullah, A.H. A survey on intelligent transportation systems. *Middle-East J. Sci. Res.* **2013**, *15*, 629–642.
9. Hu, X.; Wang, B.; Ji, H. Wireless sensor network-based structural health monitoring system for highway bridges. *Comput.-Aided Civ. Infrastruct. Eng.* **2013**, *28*, 193–209. [CrossRef]
10. Li, H.Z.; Yang, T.; Xin, C.L. Electronic Toll Collection System Based on ZigBee_MCU. *Adv. Mater. Res.* **2013**, *756*, 2255–2259. [CrossRef]
11. Patel, C.; Shah, D.; Patel, A. Automatic number plate recognition system (anpr): A survey. *Int. J. Comput. Appl.* **2013**, *69*, 2013. [CrossRef]
12. Chong, C.Y.; Kumar, S.P. Sensor networks: evolution, opportunities, and challenges. *Proc. IEEE* **2003**, *91*, 1247–1256. [CrossRef]
13. Sara, G.S.; Sridharan, D. Routing in mobile wireless sensor network: A survey. *Telecommun. Syst.* **2014**, *57*, 51–79. [CrossRef]
14. Banerjee, T.; Chowdhury, K.; Agrawal, D.P. Tree based data aggregation in sensor networks using polynomial regression. In Proceedings of the 8th International Conference on Information Fusion, Philadelphia, PA, USA, 25–28 July 2005; Volume 2, p. 8.
15. Di Francesco, M.; Das, S.K.; Anastasi, G. Data collection in wireless sensor networks with mobile elements: A survey. *ACM Trans. Sens. Netw. (TOSN)* **2011**, *8*, 7. [CrossRef]
16. Raza, U.; Kulkarni, K.P.; Sooriyabandara, M. Low power wide area networks: An overview. *IEEE Commun. Surv. Tutor.* **2017**, *19*, 855–873. [CrossRef]
17. Konstantin, M.; Petaejaejaervi, J.; Haenninen, T. Analysis of capacity and scalability of the LoRa low power wide area network technology. In Proceedings of the 22th European Wireless Conference, European Wireless, Oulu, Finland, 18–20 May 2016.

18. Daji, Q.; Qiu, T.; Kim, H. Self-organizing and smart protocols for heterogeneous ad hoc networks in the Internet of Things. *Ad Hoc Netw. Elsevier* **2017**, *55*.
19. Tie, Q.; Chen, N.; Li, K.; Qiao, D.; Fu, Z. Heterogeneous ad hoc networks: Architectures, advances and challenges. *Ad Hoc Netw. Elsevier* **2017**, *55*, 143–152.
20. Weyns, D.; Schumacher, M.; Ricci, A.; Viroli, M.; Holvoet, T. Environments in multiagent systems. *Knowl. Eng. Rev.* **2005**, *20*, 127–141. [CrossRef]
21. Pantazis, N.; Nikolidakis, S.A.; Vergados, D.D. Energy-efficient routing protocols in wireless sensor networks: A survey. *IEEE Chic. Commun. Surv. Tutor.* **2013**, *15*, 551–591. [CrossRef]
22. Yu, S.; Zhang, B.; Li, C.; Mouftah, H. Routing protocols for wireless sensor networks with mobile sinks: A survey. *IEEE Commun. Mag.* **2014**, *52*, 150–157. [CrossRef]
23. Yarvis, M.; Kushalnagar, N.; Singh, H.; Rangarajan, A.; Liu, Y.; Singh, S. Exploiting heterogeneity in sensor networks. In Proceedings of the IEEE INFOCOM 2005. 24th Annual Joint Conference of the IEEE Computer and Communications Societies, Miami, FL, USA, 13–17 March 2005; Volume 2, pp. 878–890.
24. Machado, K.; Rosário, D.; Cerqueira, E.; Loureiro, A.A.; Neto, A.; de Souza, J.N. Routing protocol based on energy and link quality for Internet of things applications. *Sensors* **2013**, *13*, 1942–1964. [CrossRef] [PubMed]
25. Perkins, C.; Belding-Royer, E.; Das, S. *Ad Hoc on-Demand Distance Vector (AODV) Routing*; No. RFC 3561; The Internet Society: Reston, VA, USA, 2003.
26. Park, S.H.; Cho, S.; Lee, J.R. Energy-efficient probabilistic routing algorithm for Internet of things. *J. Appl. Math.* **2014**, *2014*, 213106. [CrossRef]
27. Ehsan, S.; Hamdaoui, B. A survey on energy-efficient routing techniques with QoS assurances for wireless multimedia sensor networks. *IEEE Commun. Surv. Tutor.* **2012**, *14*, 265–278. [CrossRef]
28. Al-Fagih, A.E.; Al-Turjman, F.M.; Alsalih, W.M.; Hassanein, H.S. A priced public sensing framework for heterogeneous IoT architectures. *IEEE Trans. Emerg. Top. Comput.* **2013**, *1*, 133–147. [CrossRef]
29. Orsino, A.; Araniti, G.; Militano, L.; Alonso-Zarate, J.; Molinaro, A.; Iera, A. Energy efficient iot data collection in smart cities exploiting D2D communications. *Sensors* **2016**, *16*, 836. [CrossRef] [PubMed]
30. Bello, O.; Zeadally, S. Intelligent device-to-device communication in the Internet of things. *IEEE Syst. J.* **2016**, *10*, 1172–1182. [CrossRef]
31. Cardone, G.; Corradi, A.; Foschini, L. Cross-network opportunistic collection of urgent data in wireless sensor networks. *Comput. J.* **2011**, *54*, 1949–1962. [CrossRef]
32. Jayaraman, P.P.; Zaslavsky, A.; Delsing, J. Sensor data collection using heterogeneous mobile devices. In Proceedings of the IEEE International Conference on Pervasive Services, Istanbul, Turkey, 15–20 July 2007; pp. 161–164.
33. Khalil, N.; Abid, M.R.; Benhaddou, D.; Gerndt, M. Wireless sensors networks for Internet of Things. In Proceedings of the 2014 IEEE Ninth International Conference on Intelligent Sensors, Sensor Networks and Information Processing (ISSNIP), Singapore, 21–24 April 2014; pp. 1–6.
34. Jelasity, M. Gossip-based Protocols for Large-Scale Distributed Systems. Ph.D. Thesis, University of Szeged, Szeged, Hungary, 2013.
35. Castalia Manual. Available online: https://castalia.forge.nicta.com.au/index.php/en/documentation.html (accessed on 1 March 2018).
36. Pediaditakis, D.; Tselishchev, Y.; Boulis, A. Performance and scalability evaluation of the Castalia wireless sensor network simulator. In Proceedings of the 3rd International ICST Conference on Simulation Tools and Techniques, ICST (Institute for Computer Sciences, Social-Informatics and Telecommunications Engineering), Torremolinos, Malaga, Spain, 15–19 March 2010; p. 53.
37. Wan, D.; Mieyeville, F.; Navarro, D. Modeling energy consumption of wireless sensor networks by systemc. In Proceedings of the 2010 Fifth International Conference on Systems and Networks Communications, Nice, France, 22–27 August 2010.
38. CC2420 Datasheet. Available online: http://focus.ti.com/lit/ds/symlink/cc2420.pdf (accessed on 5 August 2018).

158

MDPI

St. Alban-Anlage 66

4052 Basel

Switzerland

Tel. +41 61 683 77 34

Fax +41 61 302 89 18

www.mdpi.com

Journal of Sensor and Actuator Networks Editorial Office

E-mail: jsan@mdpi.com

www.mdpi.com/journal/jsan

MDPI
St. Alban-Anlage 66
4052 Basel
Switzerland

Tel: +41 61 683 77 34
Fax: +41 61 302 89 18

www.mdpi.com

ISBN 978-3-03897-424-6